THE CREOLIZING SUBJECT

just ideas

transformative ideals of justice in ethical and politcal thought

series editors

Drucilla Cornell

Roger Berkowitz

Kenneth Michael Panfilio

THE CREOLIZING SUBJECT

RACE, REASON, AND THE POLITICS OF PURITY

Michael J. Monahan

FORDHAM UNIVERSITY PRESS

NEW YORK   2011

Library of Congress Cataloging-in-Publication Data

Monahan, Michael J.
    The creolizing subject : race, reason, and the politics of purity /
Michael J. Monahan.—1st ed.
        p.   cm.—(Just ideas)
    Includes bibliographical references and index.
    ISBN 978-0-8232-3449-3 (cloth : alk. paper)—
    ISBN 978-0-8232-3450-9 (pbk. : alk. paper)
    1. Race—Philosophy.   2. Race relations—Philosophy.   3. Racism.   I. Title.

    HT1523.M63   2011
    305.8001—dc22

                                                                2011005357
Printed in the United States of America

13 12 11   5 4 3 2 1

First edition

Contents

Acknowledgments

I take a particular (and perhaps peculiar) pleasure in reading the acknowledgments sections of academic books. Learning about the social circles and connections that shaped the genesis of a project can often shed a great deal of light on the result. The book you now hold in your hands is, I would guess, no different, insofar as my thinking has been shaped by a variety of institutions and individuals to whom I am tremendously indebted. I will try to give them credit for their good work and thanks for their support while distancing them from my shortcomings and errors.

The presence of Lewis Gordon, both as a thinker and as a human being, is felt throughout this book. He has been my teacher, mentor, colleague, and friend since I was an undergraduate at Purdue University in one of his first courses as a newly minted assistant professor more than fifteen years ago. Though I did not study with him formally as a graduate student, he nevertheless generously gave me his time and attention, for which I cannot thank him enough. He and Jane Gordon have been tremendously supportive and generous, yet rigorous and critical, interlocutors, having both provided careful critical comments on an earlier draft of this manuscript. I am very grateful indeed for their support of my work.

This project was born, so to speak, at the first meeting of the Caribbean Philosophical Association, which itself has ties to the Phenomenology Roundtable. The mark on this project of both of these institutions and their membership is readily apparent to anyone familiar with them. The Phenomenology Roundtable taught me a great deal about philosophical method in my thinking and writing, to be sure, but it also modeled a method of intellectual dialogue and collegiality that I seek to emulate as much and as well as I am able. Particular thanks go to Doug Ficek, Erik Garret, Paget Henry, Joan Jasak, Kenneth Knies, Michael Michau, Marilyn Nissim-Sabat, Neil Rosen, and my philosophical siblings, Carolyn Cusick and David Fryer. The Caribbean Philosophical Association likewise broadened my philosophical horizons in ways that have been tremendously helpful. I am especially grateful to Patrick Goodin and Clevis Headley (whom I must thank for having taught me a great deal not only about philosophy but also about the finer points of rum appreciation), Marina Banchetti, Charles Mills (whose support and encouragement I have enjoyed since approaching him as a young graduate student at a conference in Chicago), and Nelson Maldonado-Torres. The California Roundtable on Philosophy and Race is another institution that provided a rich environment for the development of the ideas in this book. I want to acknowledge specifically Ron Sundstrom, Falguni Sheth, and Gregory Velazco y Trianosky. While all of the individuals named here have been instrumental in shaping whatever virtues this book might manifest, the beautiful thing about good *groups* like these is that they are in so many ways more than the sum of their parts (however impressive those parts may be).

Another such group has been the Feminist Philosophy Reading Group at Marquette University. Our intense and fruitful discussions over the past six years have been a highlight of my time in Milwaukee, and one of the most intellectually stimulating environments I have ever encountered. Thanks go to Sheena Carey, Colin Hahn, Celeste Harvey, Kyle McNeel, Melissa Mosko, Mike Norton, Julie Ragatz, Trevor Smith, and Margaret Steele. I am especially grateful for the support and friendship of my colleague and coconspirator Theresa Tobin. Many of the ideas in this book were shaped and tested out both in this group and in my seminar on the Philosophy of Race, and so I would like additionally to thank Daniel Esposito, David McPherson, Fuad Rahmat, and Michael Ystad.

Elements of this book were presented at several forums and benefited greatly from the critical attention of the audiences at the Cave Hill Philosophy Symposium, the Central Division of the American Philosophical Association, and the North American Society for Social Philosophy. I have also been fortunate to benefit from the support and critical attention of Bernard Boxill, Allison Jaggar, and Howard McGary. Linda Alcoff, in particular, has been an invaluable interlocutor at numerous stages in the development of this project.

My colleagues at Marquette have been a particular help to me both in my work on this book and as I have tried to negotiate life as a professional philosopher. Their friendship and mentorship (both formal and informal) have been invaluable to me. Timothy Crockett, Susanne Foster, Kevin Gibson, Anthony Perressini, Eric Sanday, Nancy Snow, and Franco Trivigno have all helped to make Marquette's Philosophy Department more intellectually and socially stimulating. Particular thanks go to my department chair (and dear friend), James South, whose advice and support helped me to navigate the unpredictable path to tenure. I also thank my McNair Scholars, Erika Charleston, Vincent Stevenson, and Desiree Valentine, for being such excellent interlocutors and inspiring pupils.

This project was furthered in addition by financial support from the Institute for the Study of Race and Social Thought at Temple University, and a Summer Faculty Fellowship from Marquette University. The Department of Philosophy and History at the University of the West Indies Cave Hill Campus in Barbados was also very welcoming and supportive of my research during my visit there. I want especially to acknowledge Ed Brandon, Marcia Burrowes, Roxanne Burton, Richard Clarke, Richard Goodridge, Frederick O'Chieng O'Dhiambo, and Karl Watson. I was also helped tremendously by my research assistant at Marquette, Celeste Harvey.

Of course, a task like this cannot come to fruition without the support and help of so many friends and family. In Barbados, we were fortunate to know Harry Husbands and Charmaine Napoleon-Ramsay. My parents, Mike and Elizabeth, have never wavered in their support for my efforts; and my siblings, Arya, Brian, and Erin, have always been close no matter how many miles may separate us.

Most important, I thank Camille, who made this book possible in more ways than I can count.

THE CREOLIZING SUBJECT

Introduction

In the spring of 2008 I went to Barbados for a few months to conduct research for and begin the writing of this book. During my stay I rented a house in the Parish of Christchurch, in the southern part of the island. One afternoon, my landlord—I'll call him Terrence—was giving me a tour of the apartment building next door, which he also owned. We stood on the balcony at the back of the building in the top-floor apartment, looking inland over a small gully at the main road connecting the nearby airport (to the east) with the capitol city of Bridgetown (to the west). Beyond the highway rose a hill dotted with the rooftops of large houses obscured by coconut and breadfruit trees. It was a picturesque scene by any standard, though I, having just left behind a Wisconsin January, found it particularly compelling.

Terrence was a retiree whose Barbadian parents had taken him to England as a child. Twenty-some years later, around 1980, he and his English wife returned to Barbados. Terrence—through hard work, business acumen, and a bit of luck—had managed to make a significant amount of money in real estate. His real estate empire was still quite small, however, and it was with a great deal of pride and even affection that he led me through his apartments. We lingered on the balcony, and as I soaked up the trade winds that swept in from the Atlantic, I thought of my colleagues at my home department in Milwaukee, who were even then trudging through knee-deep snow and leaning into the bitterly cold winds off Lake Michigan that scour the campus in winter. I must confess that I felt more than a little *schadenfreude* at that moment. Terrence, in the course of our tour, asked me what I was researching during my visit, and I rattled off the standard brief explanation I tended to provide to nonphilosophers. I told him I work in the philosophy of race and racism, and that I was in Barbados to research the racial climate during the early colonial period.

No   "You know," he said after a moment of reflection, "there really isn't any racism here at all. Sometimes people from outside will come and stir up trouble, but *Bajans* [the colloquial term for Barbadians] aren't racist." I was rather surprised and puzzled at this claim. To be sure, the racial climate on Barbados was quite different from the United States, but the idea that a nation built upon chattel slavery that had only gained its independence from a European colonial power roughly forty-five years before could be free of racism struck me as implausible. Indeed, my partner, who had joined me in Barbados, and was on a fellowship conducting research into the gender dynamics of leading businesses in the British West Indies, had shown me picture after picture of boards of directors of Barbadian companies who were not only overwhelmingly male but also overwhelmingly pale skinned. Why would Terrence say that, and what could he mean?

My puzzlement only grew as he elaborated on the racial dynamics of the island, especially on the way in which light skin conferred status and privilege. He kept apologizing for using racial terminology at all, explaining that people use terms such as *black* and *white* but "don't mean anything by them." "For instance," he said, gesturing toward my sunscreen-slathered skin still pale from an autumn on the shore of Lake Michigan, "as a white guy, Bajans will treat you with more respect than me." He waved his hands over his exposed arms, which were quite dark. "Even among Bajans themselves, lighter-skinned people get more respect," he turned toward me, "I find myself doing it—I defer to the lighter Bajans . . . you know . . . I find myself showing them more respect automatically."

I said that one of the topics of my research was the way that racial categories were constituted in the Caribbean, and that my sense was that the kind of phenomena he described was common not only in other parts of the Caribbean but also to the United States. He smiled, "Do you know the difference between a White Bajan and a Bajan White?" I confessed my ignorance, and he explained that a White Bajan is a white person who is from

Barbados, while the Bajan White is a Barbadian who might seem to be white at first but, as Terrence put it, "is really black, and once you look closely, you can tell." We talked a bit about the different racial terms one might find in Barbados, or Jamaica, or Cuba, as opposed to the United States or Britain. He mentioned as well that his own daughters, children of a black Barbadian father and a white English mother, were referred to as the "white girls" in Barbados but were taken to be very clearly black now that they were back in England attending university. "It's all nonsense," he said, "people use all these terms but they don't really mean anything."

"Of course," he went on, "it is all about history. You see, the first slaves on the island were whites from England, Scotland, and Ireland." Once again, Terrence had managed to bring up the very subject of my research, though I expressed my discomfort with referring to white indentured servants as "slaves," suggesting that there are important differences between indentured servitude and chattel slavery. Terrence, however, was not persuaded of the significance of my distinction. "Well, sure," he said in response, "they call them 'indentured servants,' but they worked without pay, so they were slaves." Having settled the matter to his satisfaction, he continued his history lesson: "The white slaves didn't do too well in the heat, so the English started bringing in Africans, and eventually didn't use white slaves any more. That house right up there," he pointed toward a rather large roof jutting from the greenery on the hillside in front of us, "was the plantation house for the Walker[1] family, and it was their land we're on right now."

Terrence explained, as I looked up at the big house, that the present matriarch was planning to sell her estate to developers intent on turning it into a golf course, but for the time being the land remains in the hands of the Walker family (though their demesne is quite reduced from its colonial grandeur). Terrence had managed, through his invocation of the history of the island, to strike once again to the heart of my reasons for coming there in the first place. Then I looked to my left, at the house I was renting for the next three months, and saw yet another reference to that history. Terrence and his family had built and improved that house lovingly over the course of fifteen years, before they moved into a larger home. He had, as is common on the island, given a name to his home, which is posted clearly in blue letters by the front door: "Walker Towers." A man descended from slaves, and born while Barbados was still a British colony, had named his house after the plantation owning family who had once driven slaves on this very land. Terrence seemed to think that this was further evidence of the way in which Barbados, or at least Terrence, had moved beyond all of that "nonsense." Perhaps he was right, and I am a pessimist, but it seemed to me that it was indicative of precisely the opposite interpretation.

OPAQUE DISCOURSES—RACE, RACISM, AND HISTORY

W. E. B. Du Bois famously said more than a century ago, in 1903, that "the problem of the twentieth century is the problem of the color-line" (1994, 12). As the twenty-first century gets well and truly under way, we find that globalization, the Internet, advances in neuroscience, and the Human Genome Project have perhaps changed some of the contours and shading of the color line but done little to erase it altogether. To be sure, the racial climate of the United States in 1903 was quite different from that of 2003, and while I would not wish to deny the real progress toward racial justice that has been achieved in the last hundred years, including the election of a president of African descent in the United States, it is clear that there remains much room for improvement. Indeed, getting clear about exactly what that progress has amounted to is one of the goals of the present work. As to the future, unless one holds a stridently teleological view of human history, any improvement will not simply happen on its own. If the line between the global North and South, between that 2 percent of the world's population that own half of its wealth and the half of the world's population that own 1 percent of its wealth,[2] also happens to map rather neatly onto the global color line, then there clearly remains important work to be done. This book takes as its starting point the belief that at least some of that work is philosophical, and despite its preoccupation with certain historical moments, it is ultimately directed toward the future.

Serious engagement with the future, however, demands a serious engagement with the lessons of the past. Indeed, one of the central arguments I will be advancing here is that, to a significant extent, our misunderstandings of the past are in part responsible for the failures of racial justice in the present, and will continue to thwart future efforts toward change.

I have opened with this cursory sketch of my conversation with Terrence as a way to illustrate some of the central themes, and central sites of confusion, in contemporary discourse on race and racism. The apparent contradiction between Terrence's opening claim that there is no racism in Barbados on the one hand, and his subsequent musings on the *de facto* racial hierarchy and the informal rules of racial deference on the other, is paradigmatic of the deep-seated confusion, vagueness, and inconsistency that is the hallmark of standard racial discourse. Even as we were engaged in that conversation on the balcony, Barack Obama's victory in the Iowa Democratic Caucuses was rousing the mainstream news media in North America from its dogmatic slumber to do something it hates to do, and does quite poorly: talk about race.[3] Can we elect a black president? Is Obama even *really* black? Does his win demonstrate, as a conservative pundit opined, that race is irrelevant (Will 2008)? Academic discourse fares, thankfully, somewhat better than the mass media but is certainly not without its own blind spots and sources of confusion. This book stands as an effort to sort out some of this fundamental confusion at a very basic, conceptual level.

What, for example, could Terrence have meant in his claim that there was no racism in Barbados? Perhaps he was not uttering a contradiction, he was only employing a very strict and narrow definition of what racism could mean. If *racism* refers only to what we might in the United States refer to as a hate crime, then there is no contradiction in what he was saying. Violence in general is quite rare in Barbados (certainly by U.S. standards), and violence explicitly motivated by race is virtually unheard of. If racism could only refer to overt acts of violence, then the kinds of subtle, informal racialized ways of interacting that he was describing simply would not count as racism for him. But is this the best definition of racism? If we were to make such a definition explicit, it would strike many people, most likely including Terrence, as too narrow.

Of course, in order to understand and appraise his definition of racism, something will have to be said about the meaning of *race* itself. Our conversation neatly illustrated the variations in racial schema from place to place. The "racial landscape," so to speak, in the Unites States differs from that in Barbados, or Jamaica, or England, let alone Cuba, Puerto Rico, Martinique, or Haiti. If *racism*, as its name suggests, must have some reference to *race*, then it becomes imperative, if we are to define the former, to also define the latter. This is in large part why questions about the ontology of race have received such a preponderance of attention in academic circles recently, and philosophers especially (including me) have devoted a great deal of time and ink to debates regarding the reality, or lack thereof, of race as a category of being. This is not entirely misguided. Indeed, one of the central themes of

Theme

this book will be the *interrelatedness* of race and racism. Very often the relation between these concepts is ignored, or at best given a cursory acknowledgment. However, our attempts to explore one always lead to the other, and a thorough answer to the question of what racism is will need to include a theory of race, and, I will argue, vice versa. The concepts are, in effect, inextricably related, and attempts to logically separate them only succeed in doing damage to the concepts themselves.

Finally, as my conversation with Terrence also demonstrated, discussions of the contemporary racial *milieu* lead rather quickly to discussions of history. Another crucial theme of this book will be the role of history in our efforts to grapple with these abstract questions concerning the nature of race and racism. Pure conceptual analysis, to use a favorite term in philosophical circles, is inadequate in these cases. This is not to say that the rigorous scrutiny and critique of our use of concepts such as race and racism is unimportant—quite the contrary. My claim is in part that a rigorous analysis of *these* particular concepts (and others that are like them in relevant ways) is not susceptible to *pure* conceptual analysis at all. The history of the concepts themselves, and also of the reality and phenomena they are attempting to describe, cannot be separated from each other. Most importantly, the relationship between deeply socially significant concepts like race/racism and history is reciprocal. As I will argue, not only does history condition the meaning and use of these concepts in unavoidable ways but the concepts in turn condition the way we understand and make meaning out of history.

can't have pure conceptual analysis history

THE USES AND ABUSES OF WHITENESS STUDIES

The specific historical focus of this project will be the Caribbean island of Barbados during the latter half of the seventeenth century. I have chosen this time and this place for several reasons. First, the situation of Irish indentured laborers on the island during this time is analogous in significant ways to that of Irish immigrants to the United States during the nineteenth century, a topic that has both received a great deal of attention in the literature on immigration history in the United States, and that is at the forefront of a theoretical and political movement known as the *new abolitionism*. Since I see this movement as indicative of many of the important failures in our understandings of race and racism, I have chosen to use this historical moment in Barbados in order to make those failures clear. Second, the Caribbean during the seventeenth and eighteenth centuries was a principle crucible in which the proto-racial elements of language, culture, biology, ideology, and religion were rendered into the modern concepts of race and racism as we have come to know them. I will argue throughout this book that this developed into (and out of) what I will call a *politics of purity*—a normative principle (offered primarily as a kind of political and moral imperative) directed toward processes of purification. The politics of purity compels the purification of racial categories such that specific individuals are of one and only one category, all of which is in turn directed toward the purification of a normative conception of the human as manifesting a purified notion of rationality. By understanding the ontology of race and the practice of racism as moments within the larger schema of the politics of purity, I will argue, we will have an account of racial reality with more explanatory and prescriptive power.

My focus on the Irish during this historical period in the Caribbean is used to illustrate an important historical manifestation of the politics of purity, and in turn naturally places the question of whiteness at the forefront of my investigation. What does whiteness mean? When did it emerge as a salient racial category? What is its political and moral significance? One central question in this regard has to do with the relation between whiteness and antiracism. If racism is principally a manifestation of white supremacy, then must antiracism also be antiwhite? The very idea of being *pro-white* seems to entail racism necessarily, so surely there is no way to be antiracist without in some strong sense distancing oneself from whiteness. This is not to say that it demands that one hate or otherwise undertake a project of oppression directed toward white people, but rather that one identifies racism with whiteness, and so identifies antiracism with the rejection or abolition of whiteness. Whether this is an accurate view or not will be a recurring and significant issue throughout this book.

Thus, while my intention in pursuing this project is to contribute to the philosophy of race and racism, given my methodology and historical focus, this book also turns out to be a contribution to the growing body of literature that can be referred to as *critical whiteness studies*. This literature has involved scholars from history and philosophy, as well as cultural studies, psychology, sociology, and political science (among others). I confess that I tend in general to be critical of the bulk of this literature, for reasons that will become clear through the course of this book. Nevertheless, despite it's limitations, the critical investigation of the meaning and significance of whiteness as a racial category is an important task for critical race theory, and we ignore it (warts and all) at our peril. That being said, there are numerous pitfalls and dangers that accompany this type of endeavor that need to be spelled out and addressed, not the least of which is the very terminology it employs. For one thing, if part of the purpose is to call into question the very meaning of racial categories, then one has to be careful in the employment of those categories and terms in the course of one's critical endeavor. Thus, it may become necessary to refer to "races" or "racial categories" even as one is calling into question their reality and meaning. One common way to do this is by setting the terms apart through the use of quotation marks, but I have decided to eschew this practice as much as possible. In a work of this nature, it would be overly burdensome for the reader, and so I will begin by asking that we take my use of the term *race* and its cognates as simply appealing to the received opinion and dominant usage, allowing (and even suspecting) that such opinion and usage may be grievously mistaken. As this study develops, I will begin to make clear exactly how I understand such terminology, but since we must begin somewhere, let it be with the confused, sometimes contradictory, and often naïve understanding of race that dominates popular discourse.

Another troublesome terminological point has to do with the terms used as a contrast for white and whiteness. If the task is to place the concept of whiteness under critical scrutiny, it becomes necessary to raise the question of what it is that whiteness is distinct *from*. In one sense, whites and whiteness are distinguished from other particular racial groups (again, understood in the common sense, allowing that such alleged racial groups could be ultimately illusory). There are whites, and then there are blacks, Asians, Latinas/Latinos, Amerindians, Aborigines, and so on. Of course, enumerating a complete list of racial groups that are not white would not only be rather cumbersome in terms of textual accessibility but would require me to take some position from the outset regarding exactly how many such groups there are. This is something I am unwilling to do. One obvious solution is to simply use the term *nonwhite* to pick out such racial groups, however many they may be. Of course, this term, as well, suffers from the danger of maintaining whiteness as the normative center of the universe—there are whites, and then all other groups are negatively defined in terms of their *lack* of whiteness. As David Roediger points out: "To refer to people of color as nonwhites almost perfectly exemplifies the tendency to place whites at the normative center of everything and to marginalize everyone else" (2002, 17). At the same time, the term *people of color* suffers from a similar problem, insofar as it places whites in the position of being those *without* color and without particularity (thus, as *universal*).

Roediger's own solution to this problem is to conceive of nonwhiteness in purely political terms, having to do with "the humanist potential of setting forth the goal of creating space for nonwhiteness" (17). This offers some important advantages but nevertheless continues to suffer from a normative *centering* of whiteness, insofar as it persists, by equating the struggle against "institutional racism" with the "abolition of whiteness," in reducing all racial categories and membership to some relation to whiteness (17). In other words, whiteness remains the keystone or lynchpin holding systems of racial oppression together, and social justice must lead to a "nonwhite" society. Make the "nation," in Roediger's terms, "other than white," and you make it more just (17). As we shall see, one of the assumptions I will call into question within critical whiteness studies is the reduction of racial categories to political categories, and thus of whiteness (racial category) to white supremacy (political project).

There is, in the end, no easy solution to this terminological problem, and so again I have decided to make do with an imperfect term, and ask that the reader bear its very real and significant limitations in mind. I have decided to contrast white with "nonwhite." In part, I do this in order to leave some ontological elbow room for racial categories that do not simply reduce to political categories, as Roediger's solution does. Furthermore, while I ultimately would like to resist the normative centering of whiteness, it cannot be denied that it has occupied this central position for quite some time and in fact has shaped our understanding of all racial categories and their respective interrelations. It is in no way my intention to deny the particularity and specificity of nonwhite groups. Indeed, such denial is part of the pernicious modus operandi of white supremacy as a political project of racial oppression, and must be whole-heartedly resisted.[4] At the same time, however, the historical success of white supremacy, as a political project of racial oppression, has made it the case that one significant commonality among all groups that can be understood as racially nonwhite is precisely their shared relation to that oppressive history. They have all been displaced from the normative center, they have all been marginalized, if to different degrees and in particular ways, and in that sense their shared nonwhiteness has become a salient feature. So, I will use *nonwhite* as a term throughout this study, knowing that it is flawed, and can be misleading. Sadly, it is the best term I have been able to come up with, and provided that the reader bears in mind its limitations, I trust it will be adequate.

Richard Dyer's excellent contribution to the study of whiteness offers a careful and insightful enumeration of some of the traps to be avoided in the critical study of whiteness (1997, 10–11), and they are worth rehearsing here. One of these, which Dyer refers to as the "green light problem" (10), is the idea that critical whiteness studies offers a venue in which white people are given permission to talk about themselves, without being "compelled" to spend our time fretting over nonwhite issues. Much of the backlash against the real—though one hopes still merely beginning—inroads being made in the academy and the larger mainstream culture by those raising issues of racial justice is directed toward the idea that people in general, but whites in particular, are somehow being *forced* to ingest nonwhite history, ideas, and culture.[5] Advocates of this view see themselves as under siege by the nefarious forces of multiculturalism, which not only engage in the closing of the American mind (to allude to the title of Alan Bloom's 1987 bestseller) but force otherwise normal academics to waste their time studying African-American history, or Latina literature. Any effort, no matter how well intentioned, that lends credence to this view can be a very real and present danger.

Such danger can be mitigated, however, if not avoided altogether. We must bear in mind W. E. B. DuBois's insight that the so-called "Negro Problem" is actually a *white* problem. As Dyer points out, there is a sense in which the study of whiteness and of white people has been going on for a very long time indeed. "In fact for most of the time white people speak about nothing but white people, it's just that we couch it in terms of 'people' in general" (1997, 3). The *critical* study of whiteness, however, aims to displace this focus on whiteness as the universal norm, and as DuBois's own work illustrates, nonwhites have been engaged in this effort for quite some time, and what is allegedly new about much of the recent literature is the extent to which white people are themselves taking up this critical project. Thus, what motivates the worry on the part of cultural conservatives is not that *people* are studying nonwhite subjects but rather that *white* academics are engaging in such studies, and *white* students are attending such lectures and reading such texts. The worry, in this way, is itself a manifestation of the normative centering of whiteness. In his excellent discussion of the state of "whiteness studies," Mason Stokes compares examining whiteness to looking at the sun, noting that "the only way to see it is to refract our vision" (2001, 191). The *critical* study of whiteness, consequently, is not about creating a "safe" space for whites to ignore nonwhite subjects and issues but rather is directed toward understanding and elaborating the ways in which the study of whiteness, when it *refracts* in this critical way, is an important contribution to and continuation of the struggles against racial oppression by both whites and nonwhites alike that have been going on for far longer than the so-called culture wars.

A related danger is described by Dyer as "me-too-ism" (1997, 10), which involves the misconception that white people are being somehow left out of all the fun when it comes to cultural and ethnic studies. When oppressed and marginalized groups begin to make progress, it is typically viewed by those in power as a kind of unfair advantage. In the twentieth-century United States, (some) white males suddenly found themselves under assault by feminists and civil rights activists. The effort to decentralize whiteness was understood by them as an attempt to gain "unfair" advantage in what had, up until recently, been an open and fair marketplace not only of labor but of ideas and culture. Me-too-ism is a way to wield whiteness studies *un-critically* as a kind of backlash tool for marginalizing nonwhite voices and perspectives. It can manifest itself as an effort to maintain the intellectual spotlight, so to speak, on white people and their history, literature, philosophy, and so forth. Or it can take the form of an effort to show that whiteness is really not such an advantage, including the effort to portray whites (especially males) as a victim group. The critical study of whiteness, clearly, needs to avoid these dangers. What makes me-too-ism so pernicious is in part the way in which it makes use of some of the efforts to undermine the status of whiteness as a universal norm, at least on the surface. Me-too-ism allows that whites are just one particular group among others, but in denying the reality of systematic oppression, it holds that whites just happen to have been the most successful group historically within a free and competitive marketplace. Now that progressive forces have begun to "cheat"—to rig the game unfairly to the advantage of not only of nonwhites but also white homosexuals, white women, and so on—white heterosexual males themselves have become the marginalized victims of the culture wars. This is, of course, a recurring theme within popular conservative discourse in the United

States, and to the extent that whiteness studies supports this point of view, it is failing to be properly critical, insofar as the implicit assumption of whiteness as the universal norm remains intact.

A final important trap to be avoided, according to Dyer, is that of guilt. There can be a tendency for white people, in undertaking a serious study of the history of whiteness and white peoples, to get bogged down in guilt. Dyer rightly observes that this can take the form of a kind of moral narcissism. "We may lacerate ourselves with admission of our guilt," Dyer points out, "but that bears witness to the fineness of a moral spirit that can feel such guilt" (1997, 11). Whiteness studies as an exercise in guilt continues to emphasize whites as the principal actors on the stage of history by dwelling on our role in violence and oppression, thereby leaving nonwhites cast in the role of victims—extras (or perhaps even merely backdrop) in the moral drama of white guilt and (ultimately) redemption. At the same time, by focusing on white guilt, whites remain the focus of present attention as well. Public pronouncements of feelings of guilt are calls to bear witness to that guilt. Such calls are ultimately demands for recognition of *my* suffering ("Look how bad I feel!"), and validation of *my* moral worth ("I *must* be a good person in order to feel so awful"). In this way it is a completely self-absorbed activity. What is more, by focusing on guilt, little effort, if any, is spent on actually trying to redress continuing injustice and oppression. Guilt is ultimately, in other words, *depoliticizing*—rather than taking responsibility for my position within a deeply oppressive social context by acting to change it, I direct my own attention, and that of others, inward to my experience of suffering. To be sure, a genuinely *critical* study of whiteness must be unflinching in its exploration of the past and present of racial injustice. By no means am I suggesting that we should avoid white guilt by ignoring that past, or selling short the present manifestations of racial injustice. But the point of such study is ultimately to inform and guide our struggles *against* racial oppression, and not simply moral or psychological autopsy for its own sake. Guilt may be a motivator for positive change (though I am hardly certain of this), but at the moment it becomes an end it itself, it can only be described as pathological.

Thus, insofar as it is a contribution to the critical study of whiteness (though I intend it to be more than that), this book will work both to understand the ways and means of whiteness as the historical (and continuing) norm, while ultimately working to undermine that very normativity. My focus on the Irish, therefore, is not intended as an attempt to claim nonwhite status for the Irish. While the racial history of the Irish both in Ireland and the diaspora is characterized by an ambiguity that can be very instructive, their present white status is rarely, if ever, seriously contested. Nor is it my intention to gain some sort of moral currency by exploring the reality of Irish oppression historically. The fact of Irish oppression in no way threatens their present white status, nor does it undermine the significance of their historical complicity with, and direct participation in, political projects of white supremacy. There are those who have claimed that past Irish oppression makes them nonwhite in the present, and such claims are meant to indicate some essential solidarity with nonwhite groups, or to deny the fact that the Irish enjoy fully the privileges of white status. Such claims are, I submit, self-deceptive evasion and rationalization at best, and opportunistic racism at worst. To the extent that I give the impression of making any such claim, I have failed to take my critical task seriously enough, or at least to communicate it clearly enough.

Of course, even as this book stands as a critique of naïve and overly abstract appeals to a universal raceless humanity, there is also a sense in which it is meant for everyone. Indeed, my account of the creolizing subject is meant to offer a normative account of antiracist *praxis* that has very broad application indeed. That is, what motivates my discussion of whiteness is the firm belief that such discussion is a necessary part (but surely only a part) of the pursuit of racial justice, a fact, as I have already mentioned, made clear historically by figures like DuBois and Ellison. This book is by no means solely about racial whiteness, and certainly not solely for or about white people.

Firstly, I strive to understand and incorporate the crucial roles of nonwhite agents in the shaping and development of racial categories, including whiteness. The negotiation of the racial status of the Irish in the colonial Caribbean, for example, did not take place simply between Irish indentured servants and the English plantation elite. It most decidedly *mattered* what the enslaved West African population thought and said about the Irish, and how they interacted with the white indentured servant classes. Secondly, the meaning and power of whiteness both as a political force, and as an organizing principle of identity, is in symbiosis with nonwhiteness. Part of what it means to be white is to *not* be nonwhite, and so any serious engagement with whiteness must take up questions of nonwhiteness, just as thinkers such as DuBois and Frantz Fanon have taken up questions of the meaning of whiteness in their efforts to understand blackness. This is not to say that they collapse into each other, or that one is reducible to the other, or that one is simply the negation of the other. It is rather to say that the *meanings* of whiteness and nonwhiteness are deeply and inextricably intertwined. Finally, the claims I will advance here regarding racial ontology and racial liberation will be relevant for and applicable to all races, though perhaps in different ways and to different degrees. That is, even though I will be focusing rhetorically on the ontology of whiteness, much of what I say will be about racial ontology generally, and not restricted solely to whiteness. Thus, this book remains first and foremost a critical inquiry directed toward the articulation and realization of racial justice in general, and I hope that it will be read as such.

Before moving on, it would be disingenuous of me not to acknowledge my own struggle with the meaning and significance of my whiteness as a motivation for this project. If one of the ways in which whiteness has articulated its position as the norm is by positing itself as the universal theoretical voice, the perspective from nowhere, then one important component of redress is to make clear my own authorial specificity. And so I offer this brief biographical account in the spirit of taking seriously the way in which efforts to theorize in a *disembodied* voice are ultimately misleading and undermine the kind of self-critical work necessary in order to theorize rigorously.[6] My point is not to establish that I am somehow special or "tapped in" to these issues in some sort of natural way. What my biography points toward are the *kinds* of things that need to happen in order for whiteness to even *recognize* itself as such. That is, given the place of whiteness as normative, a *critical* awareness of oneself as white is unlikely to happen by inertia alone, so to speak.

Until I was eleven, my family lived in small towns in Southern Indiana, at which time my father entered the U.S. Navy, and we lived on several different military bases from San Diego to Chicago to Spain. The beginning of my childhood was thus spent in the deeply segregated rural Midwest of the United States, while the latter half was spent in one of the most racially diverse institutions in the country. In base housing on Camp Pendleton in Southern California, my family could share a duplex with a black family, something that would simply never have happened in rural Cloverdale, Indiana. One of the functions of white normativity is that it generates an "epistemology of ignorance" (Sullivan and Tuana 2007), and that ignorance was significantly undermined by this shift. By the time I got to high school, and a politically progressive English teacher (thank you, Mr. Donahue!) introduced me to Richard Wright, Ralph Ellison, and Zora Neale Hurston, I had become "interested in race relations," as it was frequently put. My academic interests throughout my post-secondary education developed as a result of positive encouragement (I was fortunate enough to attend a University where I could take a course in African-American Philosophy) but also more negative experiences (one of my first graduate seminar papers on Hegel and Race was dismissed as "a hot-button social issue" rather than as proper philosophy), into a focus on the philosophy of race and racism.

One of the things that happen quite often when one is a white person focusing on race in philosophy is that we are asked (almost always by other white philosophers—I don't recall a nonwhite philosopher ever asking such a question) about what led us to our interest in this topic, as if it somehow makes obvious sense to be interested in modal logic or the metaphysics of identity, but being interested in race demands some kind of explanation. While the more mischievous (and frustrated) part of me wants to respond that it is *obvious* that my interest in race, paired with the murkiness of my ancestry, must indicate that I am not *really* white, what I actually do is relay a story similar to the one I just told. What this phenomenon illustrates, in any event, is another of the ways in which whiteness functions within academia. Because of my race, I am called to account for my interest in race precisely because my racial position is supposed to be above and beyond such worldly topics.[7] While this can certainly be personally annoying, and is indicative of a host of problems both individual and institutional, it has also given me ample opportunity to reflect upon, and try to articulate, what it is that I take myself to be doing and why. And while it is problematic that *I* am called to account for my interest while others are not, given the way in which this sort of background information can indeed be relevant and illuminating, the failure is ultimately in *not* asking the logician to explain his[8] interest rather than in asking me to explain mine.

THE QUESTION OF METHOD

There is, to be sure, a growing body of literature from a variety of disciplines taking up issues of race and racism. While there is a strong sense in which, given the enduring presence of racial injustice, there is always more to be said about such issues, there is a further sense in which yet another text on these topics requires some justification. What is striking about much of the existing literature is the presumption by each text that the methods employed within it are both sufficient and complete. They take for granted that biology is the final arbiter of the meaning and reality of race, or that history can offer a complete explanation of racialized political phenomena, or even that pure philosophical conceptual analysis is able to provide all of the answers.[9] One of my principal motivations for this project is to raise the question of the *method* of inquiry into racial reality itself. By striving to avoid a commitment *a priori* to any particular method of questioning the nature and reality of race, I hope to place the question of its *meaning* at the forefront of my investigation. That is, the presumption of the methodology of genetics, for example, assumes that the meaning of race must have to do with the parsing out of categories of biological organisms (in particular, the existence of human subspecies). The "problem" of race then becomes one of describing the appropriate taxonomic categories along with the necessary and sufficient conditions for membership in those categories. The presumption of historical methodology, likewise, takes race to be significant primarily as a means for sorting out and comprehending historical events. Both of these approaches, therefore, take for granted a particular understanding of the meaning of race, and then argue for its suitability or even reality (or lack thereof), given that particular purpose. Thus, it has been argued that race cannot fulfill the functions it purports to fill biologically, and therefore it is not real at all. We may, at the end of the day, find that one of these approaches does indeed better understand what race is and how it functions, but the prior assumption of such an approach must be avoided.

In this way, I take my methodology to be informed by the Husserlian phenomenological tradition, which calls upon us to submit to critical inquiry all of our underlying assumptions, including especially those regarding not only the methodology of inquiry but the criteria for success of that inquiry as well. The failure to raise such fundamental questions, the "naturalism" (Husserl 1965, 79–81) underlying much of the literature on race, prevents it from being truly and radically rigorous—it cannot go to the root of the problem. To be rigorous in this Husserlian sense, one must raise the question of why and how, for example, one might take biology to be determinate of racial membership, and what that implies about our sense of the meaning and significance of race. What am I assuming about race, in other words, such that I turn immediately to biology (or to history, or to conceptual analysis) when I want to interrogate the concept? None of this is to argue that biology, philosophy, or history are irrelevant to our understanding of race, which would surely be a difficult position to make sense of, let alone defend. Rather, the point is to raise the question of *how* and *why* biology and history matter to our understanding of race—it is to open to critical scrutiny not merely the question of the *meaning* of race but also to raise questions about the criteria by which we evaluate the success of our potential answers to that question. We must ask, in other words, not only whether races are real but also how we understand the meaning and significance of *that* question, and what would count as a good answer to it.

It is in this Husserlian spirit that this text will operate.[10] In chapter 1 I begin with an analysis of historical approaches to the question of race not because I take the issue to be a fundamentally or exclusively historical one but rather because I must begin *somewhere*, and there are certain advantages to this approach. Provided one does not fall into the trap of taking history to be the only valid methodology, a close critical look at the history of race leads one inexorably to questions of biology, not to mention psychology, sociology, and a whole host of (to echo Husserl's own concern) "human sciences." While I cannot be exhaustive in my exploration of all of these different approaches to race, my hope is to show both how they can all be relevant to the inquiry in significant ways, how none are complete in themselves, and how the boundaries between them (like the boundaries between races) are not nearly as clear, distinct, and rigid as they often purport to be. Beginning with history, in other words, leads inevitably to questions of biology, quickly pushing the enquiry beyond the disciplinary boundaries of historical methodology, though not to such an extent that they are abandoned or repudiated completely.

My choice to begin the present work with an investigation of history, therefore, is not at all *necessary* in the strictest sense—I could just as well have started with biology, or sociology, or anthropology, or even linguistics. It is mainly a matter of my own interests and proficiencies that I begin where I do (yet another way in which biography is relevant). After undertaking this exploration of historical treatments of race (in chapters 1 and 2), I will go on to offer a general account of the ontological status of race (in chapters 3 and 4) consistent with the broadly phenomenological approach I sketched above. Race is fundamentally a question of human meaning, and as such it cannot be adequately accounted for by any single methodology. The more common approach is to begin with a description of what race *is*, and from there proceed to offer an account of what it can mean. Thus, we might find an argument that race is nothing more than a myth or illusion (because it has no biological reality, for example), and thus its meaning is inseparable from the fundamentally oppressive mythos that generated it. Contrary to this approach, I am beginning with the question of the meaning of race. What has it meant in the past, what does it mean today, what can it mean in the future? By taking these questions seriously as my starting point, it then becomes possible to articulate an ontology of race (to describe what race is) that avoids what I will argue are the significant pitfalls of the traditional approach (not the least of which is its naturalism).

In placing the question of the meaning of race at the center of my articulation of its ontology, I will be pointing toward the link between race as a category of being and racism as a social phenomenon. Thus it will be necessary to devote time to exploring the meaning and significance of racism (in chapter 5) given the particular ontological account that will be advanced in the fourth chapter. Finally (in chapter 6), I will point toward possible strategies for realizing a more racially just future given the accounts of race and racism that emerge within this text. These last three chapters collectively will be organized around what I am calling the *politics of purity*, which is my way of conceptualizing the manifestations of naturalism that inform much of our thinking about race and racism. By understanding the workings of the politics of purity, and attempting to articulate an alternative to that politics, I hope to further the cause of a more racially just world.

1

Contingency, History, and Ontology:
On Abolishing Whiteness

ontology
counts

One of the truths that emerge rather quickly when one is attempting to theorize race and racism, and which I emphasize explicitly in my classroom, is that ontological questions about the reality of race, or lack thereof, lead quickly to more ethical and political questions about the nature of racism as a social phenomenon and vice-versa. That is, if I want to offer a definition of racism as a form of oppression or injustice, something must be said about what race itself might be—what makes the oppression or injustice specifically *racial*. At the same time, our understanding of race as a category of being will be impoverished if it is not informed by a sense of how it functions socially. Even if one is an eliminativist about race—if one holds it to be non-existent, mythological, or otherwise illusory—the assertion of that position has social and political ramifications that cannot be ignored.

In beginning my own theoretical grappling with the question of racial ontology, I will be bearing this point very much in mind. Getting clear about what race is or is not will invite answers not merely to questions about biology and human variation but also about history, political and social relations of power, the nature of individual and social identity, and the constitution of meaning within a social world. Given this interpretive circularity, there is a way in which any particular starting point is both arbitrary, in the sense that one could just as well start elsewhere, and incomplete, in the sense that one is likely to return to that starting point as the investigation continues with new and more sophisticated insights. It is in this spirit that I will begin with the virtually axiomatic assertion that race has no biological foundation. I begin here in part because it is such a commonly held and understood position, and because it so well lends itself to much deeper questions concerning the nature and limitations of *reality* itself. If race is not biological, does it follow that it cannot be real? If it can be real, what kind of reality does it have?

Rather than beginning with a strictly philosophical articulation of this position, however, I will open with its more interdisciplinary cousin—the new abolitionist movement within immigration and ethnic history. It is my hope that beginning with this approach will offer new insights into a debate that has already received significant philosophical attention. What is more, this will better enable me to advance the more historically sensitive argument regarding racial ontology that is my ultimate goal.

RADICAL CONTINGENCY AND THE NEW ABOLITIONISM

If, as the American Anthropological Association tells us, race "evolved as a worldview, a body of prejudices that distorts our ideas about human differences and group behavior," (1998), then questions emerge as to how this worldview came into being, how it developed over time, and how it has come to exert so much power in the shaping of human society. Historically, this is a question of identifying some time or moment at which the "myth" of race began to exist and to acquire cultural and political salience. This need not be some very specific time but could instead be a gradual process, taking place over decades or even centuries. Nor need it be understood as a global phenomenon, but can be seen rather as having taken place at, and over, different times in different places. It is simply the claim that for a given place that presently has and employs racial concepts, there was some prior stretch of time at which no such concepts were known and used, and that this is not because they had yet to be "discovered" but rather is a matter of their not yet being *invented*.

Recent works discussing the history of race in North America have undertaken exactly this task of exploring the process whereby race comes into being. These works have grappled with the question of whiteness in particular, asking both how whiteness itself came to be a salient social category, and how particular immigrant groups in the United States came to have white status. Throughout this body of literature, the various authors make an appeal to some process or moment whereby either whiteness itself comes into being, or some particular group comes to be white. Thus, Noel Ignatiev built the notion of "becoming" white into the title of his important work, *How the Irish Became White* (1995). Theodore Allen titled his monumental two-volume study of race in North America (with a significant prelude in Ireland) *The Invention of the White Race* (1994; 1997). Matthew Frye Jacobson's *Whiteness of a Different Color* (1998) includes a reference to the "alchemy" of race in the subtitle, and opens with a discussion of the "fabrication" of race. David Roediger, one of the more prominent and prolific historians working on this set of problems, as well, appeals to the notion of "becoming white" in *The Wages of Whiteness* (1991), and includes a reference to becoming in the subtitle of his most recent book, *Working Toward Whiteness: How America's Immigrants Became White* (2005).

All of these figures have produced challenging and important texts that have made significant contributions to the understanding of the racial landscape of North America historically, which in turn, of course, enhances our understanding of the present. These are all indeed valuable texts, and though I am ultimately critical of some of the positions they describe, I have learned a great deal from them, and much of my own work would have been impossible without them. All of these writers, as well, deal significantly with Irish immigrants to the United States, a fact that will become particularly important in the next chapter. My purpose in the present chapter, however, will be to explore the larger themes of their work as indicative of certain positions regarding racial ontology.

It is both an assumption and an implication of the work of these historians that race as a category of being is historically contingent. They embark upon their studies from a position that rejects any biologically essential notion of racial membership, and through the course of their work demonstrate the historical fluidity and contingency both of racial categories themselves, and the place of particular populations within them. Race, they aver, has no underlying biological reality we are bound to respect. There is, therefore, no necessary, mind-independent, ahistorical ground to which our concept of race can appeal (or correspond). What we have instead is, again in the words of the American Anthropological Association, "a social mechanism invented during the eighteenth century to refer to those populations brought together in colonial America" (1998). The "white race," therefore, "consists of those who partake of the privileges of the white skin in this society" (Ignatiev 1995, 1). Race is, in other words, a social construct, with no underlying bio-logical foundation. Just as Simone De Beauvoir argued in the middle of the twentieth century that "One is not born, but rather becomes, a woman" (1952, 281), fifty years later Matthew Frye Jacobson will tell us that "Cau-casians are made and not born" (1998, 4).

In short, at some point in the past, there was no such thing as race. Pop-ulations may have been divided by language or religion, among other possible classifications, but never by race. Later, however, race was invented, for decidedly pernicious motives directed toward the oppression and ex-ploitation of certain raced others by those who proclaimed themselves white. What is important is that prior to this point, there were no white people, nor were there people of any other race, as race itself simply did not exist. As the processes of oppression and exploitation that generated racial categories developed over time, certain populations (such as Irish and Italian immigrants to North America, among many others) that had originally been excluded from the powers and privileges of racial whiteness, gradually gained access to those powers and privileges, thereby becoming white. In this way the "alchemy of race" took place, and continues to take place, as understandings of who is or is not a legitimate member of a particular racial group are con-tinually contested, renegotiated, and altered over time.

Indeed, the contemporary political salience of this body of work lies in this character of racial alchemy as an ongoing process. None of these books are *strictly* works of history (if this is even possible), but are also deeply, if sometimes only implicitly, engaged with the racial challenges of the present. By emphasizing the radical contingency of race—that the racial landscape is far from set in stone, and not only could have been but still can be otherwise than it is—the authors hope to emphasize the mutability of race. Race is a myth, an invention, a fabrication, or a social construction. We may think that we are members of one or another race, but at a different time or in a different place we would not be, or at least our claims to such membership would be contentious. Since this is so, they suggest, we need not accept the present racial status quo. Jacobson, for example, closes his book with the following:

> It is my hope that in recognizing the historical fabrication, the change-ability, and the contingencies of whiteness, we might begin to look in a new way upon race, the power relations it generates, and the social

racial landscape not set in stone

havoc it wreaks. Only then might we find our way to that political realm beyond racism that W. E. B. Du Bois significantly called *transcaucasia.* (1998, 280)

Roediger,[1] however, and in particular Ignatiev, go even further, advocating the abolition of whiteness as a key step in overcoming the enduring harms of racism. Once we understand the contingency of race, and the way in which racial whiteness in particular has always marked a position of power and privilege vis-à-vis those left outside of that category, then it becomes clear, they argue, that the continued existence of racial whiteness is incompatible with antiracism. We must, they argue, turn the alchemy of race on its head by de-inventing race in general, and whiteness in particular. If race is a social construct, the sole function of which is oppression, then we will all be better off once this construct has been torn down.

By accepting a racial ontology that describes racial categories as ultimately fictive inventions directed toward oppression and exploitation, racism comes in part to be understood as the use of or appeal to such inventions to secure and legitimate political power. Within this line of argumentation, racism is neither more nor less than the use of this invention for exploitative and oppressive ends. Furthermore, even if one attempts to use race for more positive purposes, in appealing to this mythical category, one is adding legitimacy to it, and thereby inadvertently furthering its oppressive ends. Racial liberation therefore means, effectively, liberation from race itself, since racial categories are inextricably linked to the oppressive political machinations in which they are employed. Since whiteness, as a racial category, is the bastion of privilege and power within this historically contingent racial hierarchy, according to advocates of this view the overcoming or transcending of racial oppression demands the abolition of whiteness.

We see the connection here between a particular racial ontology and a corresponding view of racism and racial liberation. Given the radical contingency of race and the pernicious purposes to which it has been put, it is clear that racism must be understood as the application of these pernicious concepts, and a liberated society is one devoid of those concepts. Once this ontological position is accepted, the rest follows quite naturally, while at the same time, accepting the abolitionist prescription seems to necessitate an acceptance of the ontology on pain of incoherence. It only makes sense to call for the elimination or abolition of race if it is both unreal and can only serve (or at least is largely conducive to) nefarious ends. Since it is a kind of tool that can only be put to evil purpose, such that even the most well-intentioned user will only end up doing more harm than good, the only rational response is to take the tool away.

The argument for and debate surrounding the abolition of whiteness is therefore situated in a rejection of realism about race. Races, to the extent that they exist at all (and I shall be returning to the question of how to understand this existence later), are reduced to a particular relation to an ongoing political project of racial oppression and domination. For Roediger and Ignatiev, this is the project of establishing and enforcing the domination of whites over and against nonwhites (white supremacy). In this instance, the use of the term *nonwhite* is quite deliberate, since, for the abolitionist, whiteness is the center of gravity around which all racial terms revolve. The whole point of generating racial categories such as black or Asian is to distinguish them from white, which in turn functions as the normative center of the racial universe. The important distinction, therefore, is between the *normal* white race, and those who deviate form this norm—nonwhites.[2]

All of this means that races only came into being, according to this view, because of the particular way in which the European colonial encounter with Africa, Asia, and the so-called New World took shape. What meaning and significance race happens to possess, therefore, it has only by virtue of the political project of white supremacy (the establishment of a racialized social hierarchy with whites at the pinnacle of this hierarchy), and outside of that project (or before its inception) it has no meaning and no existence. This being the case, there is no way to preserve any meaningful notion of racial whiteness without at least implicitly endorsing or preserving white supremacy. *Whiteness* means quite simply occupation of the top position within a vertical racialized social hierarchy.[3] Thus, the only viable way to end white supremacy is to end or abolish the white race. Whiteness is only accidentally associated with skin color; its real meaning has to do with the exercise of power, and so claims to racial whiteness are always already claims to power—for whiteness just *is* the presumption of that power. Any assertion of white identity, therefore, is the same thing as an assertion of superiority vis-à-vis nonwhites because that superiority, or at least the presumption thereof, is what makes whiteness have any meaning at all. In a world devoid of white supremacy there would be no white people, understood as people exercising political and social superiority over others on the basis of alleged

Whiteness

racial distinctions. What is more, if one rejects that exercise of superiority, one is *by definition* rejecting whiteness (a move especially significant for those with relatively pale flesh).

All of the new abolitionist texts mentioned above work within this basic framework to explore the experiences of European immigrants to the Unites States in the nineteenth and early twentieth centuries. Each makes a case that certain immigrant groups were understood by the dominant U.S. society, which was composed principally of English, French, Dutch, German, Scottish, and Welsh immigrants and their descendants, to be in some important sense nonwhite. The texts focus upon Irish, Italian, Greek, Jewish (largely Ashkenazim), and Eastern European (mainly Hungarian and Serbian) immigrant populations. All of these groups at different times experienced some forms of discrimination in labor and housing, were seen to a greater or lesser extent as threats to the purity of the Anglo or Nordic character of the republic, and were portrayed as degenerate and racially inferior to the Western European and English inheritors of the American experiment. They were not white upon their immigration, according to the accounts offered by Roediger and Ignatiev, or at least, not *fully* white. Over time, however, this condition altered such that these immigrants came to be accepted as fully racially white, with all (or at least most) of the privileges pertaining thereto.[4] Thus we come to see how racial whiteness is historically contingent, and that the understanding of what whiteness means, and who counts as white, has changed dramatically over time.

Noel Ignatiev's *How the Irish Became White* offers the most explicit practice of this methodology. While opening with a brief discussion of racial politics in early nineteenth-century Ireland—and especially the views of the leader of the movement for Catholic Emancipation there, Daniel O'Connell (1995, 6–31)—Ignatiev moves quickly to the United States, and attempts to establish the nonwhite status of Irish Immigrants at that time. While immigration from Ireland to North America was nothing new, "the majority of Irish immigrants to America in the eighteenth century and for the first third of the nineteenth were Presbyterians, descendants of Scots who had been settled in Ireland beginning with Cromwell and carrying on through William and Mary" (39). These earlier Irish immigrants, who came to be known in North America as the Scotch-Irish, were in important ways different from those Irish-Catholic immigrants that flooded into the United States in the wake of the famine and political unrest of mid–nineteenth-century Ireland, a difference those who came to refer to themselves as Scotch-Irish were eager to point out.[5] These later, largely Irish-Gaelic–speaking and Roman Catholic immigrants were viewed as a unique racial group, distinct not only from the largely English, Scottish, Welsh, Dutch, and French white population at the time but also from the earlier Scotch-Irish immigrants. Ignatiev makes much both of this racial distinction and of the early association between these Irish immigrants and Northern free blacks and Southern enslaved blacks. "On their arrival in America," Ignatiev tells us, "the Irish were thrown together with black people on jobs and in neighborhoods," resulting in "mixed matings" between blacks and Irish as well as less physically intimate social interaction (40–41). The association between the two groups was sufficient to enter into common parlance, evidenced by the fact that "in the early years Irish were frequently referred to as 'niggers turned inside out'; the Negroes, for their part, were sometimes called 'smoked Irish'" (41).

Ignatiev's point is by no means to make a case for the existence of an idyllic nineteenth-century utopia of racial solidarity. Indeed, he goes on immediately to point out that "the more Irish and Afro-Americans were lumped together, the greater the hostility between them" (42). His point, rather, is twofold. First, he wishes to establish that the Irish immigrants of this period were most decidedly *not* white, and second, that the *potential* for significant solidarity between Irish and black existed, even if it was only ever sporadically and incompletely realized. At the close of this stage-setting chapter, Ignatiev states that "I have tried to suggest that, while the white skin made the Irish eligible for membership in the white race, it did not guarantee their admission; they had to earn it" (59). This statement makes clear that, for Ignatiev, there is a difference between "white skin" and "membership in the white race." As he goes on to describe the process whereby the Irish "earned" their membership in the white race, the nature of this distinction becomes ever more clear.

The means whereby the Irish became members of the white race, for Ignatiev, was a matter both of distancing themselves from blacks in terms of labor and housing, and aligning themselves with proslavery political organizations. Ignatiev details patterns of Irish exclusion of blacks from their workplaces and social organizations,[6] violence against blacks in the form of alarmingly frequent "race riots" (124–44), and support of political organizations dedicated to maintaining slavery. The most notable among the latter was the Democratic Party, who supported extending the franchise to include the (largely unpropertied) Irish but was vehemently opposed to abolitionism. According to Ignatiev, the Irish became a significant, if informal, political force against the abolitionist movement, manifesting their opposition largely through riot, arson, and intimidation (132–38). Of course, since they were denied formal political voice through the vote, their recourse to such tactics are understandable from a purely practical perspective (which in no way excuses them morally). Ignatiev thus builds a case for the nonwhite status of Irish immigrants in the middle of the nineteenth century, and then describes a process of their becoming white through open hostility and violence toward blacks, and political allegiance with white supremacy in the form of support for the institution of slavery.

In this way we can begin to understand the distinction Ignatiev has drawn between white skin and white racial membership. The former may be a necessary condition for the latter, but it is hardly sufficient. Membership in the white race, it seems, is "earned" through explicit and sustained support of the political projects of white supremacy. One must labor for the support of white interests over and against nonwhite interests. In this way, someone who possesses pale skin (though, presumably, not those who lack it) may over time become a fully fledged member of the white race. Racial whiteness, in short, has as much to do with one's position within a racialized social hierarchy as it does with melanin content (or the lack thereof). Membership in the white race according to Ignatiev, in other words, is about politics more than pigment.

While some of his historical methodology has been called into question (Mulderink 1996; Yacavone 1996), Ignatiev makes it clear that, "like a paleontologist who builds a dinosaur from a tooth, I have been forced to reconstruct from fragments, and to infer" (Ignatiev 1995, 179). It seems, in other words, that he is mainly concerned with the overall picture he develops of the shift from being outside of the white race to being inside. Ignatiev's target is the "New Labor History" of the 1970s and 80s (180), and his goal is to bring race to the foreground of our understanding of the history of labor in the United States. He states:

> For my part, my insistence on addressing problems of race as central to the formation (or nonformation) of an American working class stems from my view that there have been (and continue to be) moments when an anticapitalist course is a real possibility, and that the adherence of some workers to an alliance with capital on the basis of a shared "whiteness"

has been and is the greatest obstacle to the realization of those possibilities. (183–84)

This "shared whiteness" cannot have been white skin, since that has, at least in the populations with which Ignatiev and the New Labor Historians are concerned, been there all along. Rather, the shared whiteness to which Ignatiev refers is this distinctly *political* aspect. It is precisely this identification with white supremacist political interests, which often coincides with the interests of capital, that confers white racial status upon these initially racially ambiguous immigrant groups, such as the nineteenth-century Irish. Given these goals, debates about methodological shortcomings do not necessarily undermine his ultimate aim, unless it can further be shown that some overlooked or misinterpreted data demonstrates either that the Irish were white (in Ignatiev's sense) all along, or that they *never* became white. None of the critiques of Ignatiev's work make such a case, and so they stand as arguments for incompleteness, but they are hardly refutations. While I am critical of the account of "becoming white" that Ignatiev describes, he does show quite clearly the ambiguity of the Irish racial position within the larger opinion of both white and nonwhite populations within the United States at the time, and points toward the shifting political allegiances that lead to the end (or at least the marked reduction) of that ambiguity.

Another very important figure in the new abolitionist literature is David Roediger, whose earlier work, *The Wages of Whiteness* (1991), explores the ways and means whereby immigrant groups coming to the United States in the early nineteenth century gradually came to assume white status and be accepted as white by their contemporary "Native" neighbors.[7] He is particularly focused upon the role of race in labor history, and the way in which the racial politics of the early labor movement in North America shaped the national racial landscape (and vice-versa). The title is an allusion to W. E. B. Du Bois's notion, expressed in *Black Reconstruction in America* (2007, 573–74), that for the impoverished white worker, whiteness itself offered "wages" that were worth fighting for, even at the expense of interracial working-class solidarity. These early European immigrants from Ireland, the Mediterranean, and Eastern Europe would arrive as racial inferiors from the point of view of the Anglo-Saxon and "Nordic" elites who owned and controlled the factories, farms, and mines in which they worked. But the ladder of racial hierarchy has many rungs, and even if these immigrants were not white enough to occupy the top, they were not so unfortunate as to occupy the very bottom. And so the *psychological* value of racial superiority became an inducement to weaken labor by largely excluding black, Asian, Amerindian, and Latin American workers. The psychological "wages" of whiteness were thus suffi-cient to justify accepting lower monetary wages for one's labor and sacrificing class solidarity. Over time, these immigrant workers, who Roediger refers to in his more recent work as racially "inbetween" (Roediger 2002, 138–68; Roediger 2005, 12), came eventually to occupy fully white status, largely through a demonstration of their willingness to affirm and struggle for white supremacist political projects.

In this way, as with Ignatiev's account, one "became" white only upon the fulfillment of two conditions. First, one had to possess some provisional, though perhaps only marginal, status as "white" in the first place. Indeed, it is for this reason that Roediger, in his later work, appeals to the notion of racial "inbetweenness," since it emphasizes how such groups were "'[i]nbe-tween' hard racism and full inclusion—neither securely white nor nonwhite" (2005, 12). It is that modicum of whiteness that made it possible for these immigrant groups to enter the United States at all, since at the time immi-gration was restricted to "free white persons." But of course, such juridical assignations of racial membership are only a part (though surely a very sig-nificant part)[8] of the picture, and these "free white persons" were widely viewed as a threat to American cultural and racial purity (2005, 59–72), were deemed "inconclusively white" in the legal adjudication of antimiscegenation laws (48), and were victimized in race riots and even lynchings (45). Thus, while this kind of provisional whiteness was a necessary condition for full and equal participation in U.S. civil, political, and economic life, it was hardly sufficient (like Ignatiev's distinction between having white skin and being racially white). Roediger's work thus provides an account not only of Irish but also Italian, Greek, and Hungarian (among others) immigrant groups arriving on North American shores in a position of racial ambiguity (inbetweenness), but gradually coming to assume "fully white" racial status.

The second condition for becoming white in Roediger's account, like Ig-natiev's, requires that a group demonstrate its commitment to the political project of white supremacy. That is, one must show a willingness to advance the political and economic interests of (fully) white elites. This could be ac-complished by practicing racially exclusionary policies within political and social organizations (such as churches, social clubs, and labor unions), and by identifying one's own political interests with those of the ruling, fully white elites. Thus, signs of solidarity with blacks, for example, would threaten the path to racial whiteness, while excluding or distancing oneself from blacks would hasten progress toward racial whiteness. Failure to meet this condition is construed as evidence not merely of a political inclination but ultimately of the underlying impurity of one's racial character. That is, one's political actions and inclinations were understood as indicative of one's underlying biological attributes. To show solidarity with or empathy for blacks constituted evidence of one's "impure blood," since one must surely ultimately be (at least somewhat) black oneself in order to so identify with *them* as opposed to *us* (whites).

If, as Roediger points out, the received opinion of the day held that "Europe 'ends at Naples' and 'all the rest belongs to Africa,'" then a Sicilian immigrant who wished to be seen as white and (fully) European needed to distance herself from Africa, and this was often best achieved by distancing herself from African-Americans (2005, 112). A true and genuine white person, secure in her own superiority to and racial distance from blacks, would, according to this logic, never deign to work side by side with them, or allow them into political or labor organizations. If an immigrant from one of these "inbetween" groups does work or live with blacks, or form political coalitions with them, then it must be because he is in some deep and significant way *similar* to them. Purity of blood, it was understood, will in this way "prove-out" in the end as a manifestation of white supremacy, and if that manifestation never occurs, then it demonstrates the corruption (nonwhiteness) of that blood. Thus, while Roediger and Ignatiev are arguing for the strictly social and political meaning of racial whiteness, in the popular imaginary of the era they are describing, at least, politics and biology (blood) were inseparable.

Likewise, demonstrating a resistance to the political goals of the dominant groups also called into question one's whiteness by demonstrating a political *irrationality*. This is because conceptions of racial whiteness have always been tied directly to fitness for citizenship and, above all, rationality (a point to be revisited at length in chapter 5. This is made most clear philosophically in the work of Kant (Eze 1997), and Hegel (Gordon 1997, 28), both of whom explicitly linked rationality with racial whiteness, while at the same time understanding rationality as a necessary condition for autonomous self-government and citizenship. In other words, to be a full citizen is to be rational, and to be rational is to be white, and *that* is why full citizenship must be restricted to whites and why, all other things being equal, evidence of rational citizenship (understood in part as support for capitalism and white supremacy) was simultaneously evidence of whiteness. Conversely, if one's whiteness is in question or otherwise "inconclusive," evidence of political irrationality constitutes evidence of one's *non*whiteness. Nothing, from this perspective, could be more irrational than resisting the agenda of power and privilege. Thus, the racial *bona fides* of political radicals and socialists among the "inbetween" immigrant groups were always made explicitly suspect (Roediger 2005, 88), and the U.S. government went so far as to offer a breakdown of the "propensity toward unionism" of the different immigrant groups using explicitly racial terminology (73).

This is not to suggest that the ethos of white supremacy was limited *exclusively* to identification with the interests of dominant elite. Again, using trade unionism as an example, while factory owners and government officials may have seen unionism as racially suspect, the union movement itself in the United States was notoriously racially exclusive, and at various times excluded many of these inbetween immigrant groups in addition to the unambiguously nonwhite groups. Roediger, in fact, suggests that "the union bureaucracy enjoyed its greatest pre–World War I legitimation by the state precisely by questioning the rights of immigrants" (2005, 89). This expression of a white supremacist unionism, however, is the exception that proves the rule—what legitimacy unions were able to secure from the point of view of those in power came in large part by advancing exclusionary practices that functioned to secure white power and privilege. Gradually, the understanding of "white labor" came to include immigrant groups that had once been excluded, but this coincided both with a continued exclusion of African, Asian, American Indian, and Latina/o labor, along with a retreat from political radicality within the U.S. labor movement (Roediger 1991, 6–15). Identification with whiteness in this way assumed pride of place among white laborers in the United States, and thus it serves as an excellent example of this second condition of "becoming white," according to the new abolitionist literature: one must demonstrate a willingness both to exclude nonwhites, and to advance the interests of the unambiguously white.

I shall return to these texts, as well as those of Matthew Frye Jacobson and Theodore Allen, below. At this point, however, the basic argument for the new abolitionism can be spelled out. As I have argued, both Ignatiev and

Roediger begin with a rejection of biological accounts of race, affirming instead an understanding of race as socially and politically constructed. Thus, following Ignatiev, white skin may be biological but that is not really what race is or how it functions. The white race, and membership therein, is a matter of political relations—whiteness is a position of superiority within a racially demarcated and hierarchically structured distribution of power. White skin may be a necessary condition for occupying those superior positions that constitute membership in the white race, but racial membership itself is nothing more nor less than the occupation of those positions and the relations of oppression, power, and privilege they engender. Racial whiteness, in other words, is wholly constituted by political projects of white supremacy. Differences in the relative darkness or lightness of skin would of course exist in any event, but *racial* differences require white supremacy and its formal and informal institutions that work to make race a salient social category in the first place. The negotiation of a particular group's racial membership, therefore, is a matter of assuming a particular position within the white supremacist hierarchy. Of course, differences between groups, as between individuals, are manifold, and occupying a dominant or superior *racial* position does not mean that one is dominant or superior absolutely. Differences in gender, class, ability, and so on remain salient. The point is only that *racial* membership is reducible to one's place within a distinctly *racial* social hierarchy in which whiteness, by definition, means a place at the top of that hierarchy. This racial hierarchy will, of course, be simultaneously intersected by hierarchies described by class, gender, ability, sexuality, and so on.

Since whiteness is effectively reducible to white supremacy, becoming white necessarily entails an affirmation of and participation (direct or indirect) in white supremacy. In the historical cases offered by Roediger and Ignatiev, this is clear. One becomes white both by keeping nonwhite, and those who are at least less white than oneself, in positions of inferiority, while helping to protect the dominant positions of those who have already assumed full whiteness. Thus, as Roediger points out, the descendants of those Irish immigrants discussed by Ignatiev could, by the early twentieth century, demonstrate their own whiteness in part by asserting the nonwhiteness of Italians and Hungarians, which, within the economic realm, meant serving as foremen in mining and other industrial operations who organized their laborers along racial lines, reserving the most onerous and dangerous jobs for the least white workers. If one fails to engage in these acts of domination, one will be denied white status, or at least remain racially ambiguous in ways that will, within a white supremacist political structure, offer significant disadvantage. In short, to work against white supremacy is to be nonwhite in some significant sense, and becoming white necessitates an affirmation of white supremacy. This points toward an ontology of racial whiteness in which being white means nothing more nor less than affirming and assuming a dominant position within a white supremacist racial hierarchy.

This being the case, both Ignatiev and Roediger have called explicitly for the abolition of whiteness. Those of us with white skin, they tell us, ought to engage in acts of what Ignatiev refers to as *racial treason*, for "[t]reason to whiteness is loyalty to humanity" (Ignatiev and Garvey 1996, 10). If white people only exist *qua* white people by virtue of white supremacy, then the elimination of white supremacy and the abolition of whiteness (the elimination of *racially* white people) are one and the same. If one is truly committed to ending white supremacy and racial injustice, then whiteness must be abolished, since it is whiteness and the promise of its "wages" that has so long undermined efforts to bring about a more just society. Ignatiev's distinction between white skin and membership in the white race is crucial here. Clearly, the new abolitionists are not endorsing the elimination of white skin or white-skinned people. Rather, they are calling for an end to *racial* whiteness, a category that only has meaning and significance by virtue of its creation by and legitimation of political projects of white supremacy. The abolition of racial whiteness demands the destruction of racial categories of superiority and inferiority, and the social structures that exploit those categories in order to benefit some (whites) at the expense of others (nonwhites).

Given the radical contingency of racial categories, and their reduction to oppressive social relations and institutions (white supremacy), liberation demands the abolition of all such categories. Thus, ultimately, even though the new abolitionists focus upon the abolition of whiteness, their argument necessitates the abolition of all races (*qua* races). Their rhetorical and analytical focus upon whiteness is therefore motivated, it seems, by the fact that whiteness is the lynchpin holding the racial hierarchy together. If all political institutions and structures come about in order to serve certain sets of interests, racialized structures and institutions are clearly designed to serve white interests. Of course, in order to do this, white people, as a *racial* category, had not only to be *created* but also to be depoliticized. It had, in other words, to be made to appear natural and inevitable, so that its genesis and continued function as a *political* category remained invisible and thus beyond critique and revision. Even at the height of chattel slavery and colonialism, the rhetoric and justification surrounding those practices had to do with *natural* endowments and *divine* rights, not with straightforward political struggle and exploitation. The new abolitionists must focus upon the abolition of the white race, therefore, for at least two related reasons. First, if whiteness is the category of power and domination, any shifts in power relations will come at the expense of that power and domination. Indeed, ending racial oppression necessitates stripping whiteness of that capacity to dominate, and since whiteness *is* nothing more than that capacity, it requires the end of whiteness.

Second, one of the ways in which racial whiteness functions in the contemporary context is as an invisible yet omnipresent universal human norm. That is, it is invisible as a particular category or perspective—whiteness tends not to think of itself in racial terms—precisely because everywhere at all times within a white supremacist context the human, as such, is presumed to be white. Thus, not only do white individuals tend not to think of ourselves in racial terms, we likewise tend not to think about the white business community, or white music, even though we frequently hear about the Latina/o business community, or black music. Given this rhetorical invisibility of whiteness, calling for the abolition of the white race has particular potency. It at once summons forth and renders whiteness visible both historically and in the contemporary context, it denaturalizes and politicizes whiteness. Furthermore, in doing all of this, it demands taking *responsibility* for whiteness. If I am made aware of my own whiteness, for example, and I am brought to realize that it is not an inevitable natural fact but rather a contingent, and inherently oppressive, historical contingency, then I am immediately brought into an *ethical* confrontation with my whiteness. If it is contingent in this way, and it is necessarily oppressive, then to allow it to continue to exist is to implicitly affirm that oppression. Accepting the basic premises of the abolitionist position at face value, the argument is a powerful and compelling one.

Furthermore, it follows from this that the abolition of racial whiteness will bring with it the end of all racial categories. Just as a dominant group needs those who are dominated by it, the dominated cannot be understood as such without a dominating group. Since racial categories have meaning only by virtue of the relations of domination they describe, if the dominant

(margin annotations: "why abolish whiteness", "1. power", "2. norm", "invisible to visible", "eliminate the dominate / no hierarchy")

group is literally abolished, then subordinate groups will also cease to exist *qua* subordinate groups. Without white people, there would be no significance to nonwhiteness, and thus with the end of racial whiteness as a category, nonwhiteness, in all of its varieties, will likewise cease to be. One could perhaps respond that some nonwhite group could assume the dominant position in the new hierarchy, but given this understanding of race that would only mean that this group would be asserting their *whiteness*. Truly abolishing whiteness would rule this out, however, and so the call for the abolition of whiteness is ultimately a call for the abolition of race generally. The emphasis on whiteness is about specific rhetorical contexts and goals, and is not meant to indicate that the aim is a world in which there is every kind of racial category *except* white.

THE AMBIGUITY OF RACE—BIOLOGY, CULTURE, AND PERCEPTION   *value*

There is a great deal that is of immense value to be found in these texts, and it will be helpful to draw some of those important insights out at this point before moving on to a critique of their efforts. First and foremost, the value of these historical accounts of the ambiguity and fluidity of racial categories, as a corrective against more essentialist accounts of race, cannot be underestimated. Though I shall later be problematizing the standard notion of racial essences, for now I am appealing only to the dominant understanding of essence and essentialism. Racial essentialism, as I am using the term here, is the view that racial categories and racial membership are determined by some mind-independent, ahistorical property or set of properties (a racial essence), which individuals either possess or lack in a strong metaphysical sense. Usually understood in biological terms, this would mean that one's race is *given* biologically, and the historical development of racial "science" has been the history of the attempt to accurately "discover" the pregiven necessary and sufficient conditions for membership in particular racial categories (commonly understood biologically as a kind of subspecies). Typically, of course, the imputation of such differences has gone beyond the strictly physical, and included moral, intellectual, and spiritual differences as well. Thus, just as the difference between being a wolf and being a poodle can be determined in strictly biological terms, racial essentialism holds that being white and being black, or any other racial category, are strictly a matter of possessing or lacking certain biological traits, whether they be strictly morphological and readily observable, or deeper and less readily apparent differences in genetic code. Even if the further step is typically added that different races have different characters and virtues both moral and intellectual, racial essentialism need not necessarily go beyond the strictly physical.[9]

Arguments against the scientific validity of racial distinctions have formed one prong of the attack on racial essentialism, and historical work on the fluidity, variation, and imprecision of racial categories and their use has been another. The work of Ignatiev and Roediger can thus be understood in part as an argument against racial essentialism, just as racial eliminativists in philosophy, like Kwame Anthony Appiah (among others), have offered the biological version of this argument. When taken together, they offer a way to explain racial categorization as an ongoing political effort to restrict rights and obligations along allegedly racial lines, and the scientific discourses surrounding alleged biological differences become simply efforts to legitimize (and naturalize) those restrictions and inequalities. Texts such as Ignatiev's, therefore, offer a compelling account of how this historical process of the allocation of racial privileges and disadvantages has taken place. They help to emphasize the historical contingency of race, and provide insight not only into how it has come to be the way it is and function the way it does, but in so doing point toward ways to redress the harm wrought by such racial categories and their use. The moral of such work is that the Irish, and every other racial group currently understood as white, came to be white through a historical process that can, in principle at least, be described and accounted for in a way that makes no appeal to racial essences. The same is true for every other contemporary racial group and their historical antecedents. Once it is understood how one's ancestors came to be whatever it is that one happens to be racially, it can be understood that the process is subject to reversal. Race, once constructed, can be deconstructed. The alchemy of race is reversible. Thus racial essentialism, as the belief that racial categories are fixed and given, is quite directly undermined both by the new abolitionists and by their philosophical cousins, the racial eliminativists.

Another insight gained through study of these texts is the appreciation of the ambiguity surrounding the concept of race throughout its long history. Even if one focuses exclusively on North America in the late nineteenth and early twentieth century, one will find simultaneous yet competing understandings of the basis of racial categories, widely varying enumerations of exactly how many different races there may be, and wide disagreements on whether particular groups are or are not members of a particular race. Roediger, for example, tells us that "[i]n 1888, according to experts, there were between two and sixty-three races" (2005, 11), while a 1911 government study counted thirty-six distinct *European* races (16). Part of the reason for this great variation lies with the ambiguity of the concept of race itself, and the varying political purposes to which it was put. According to Roediger, "race was at once biological and cultural, inherited and acquired . . . at times and to some it appeared to determine what could be expected of its bearer and her children," while "in more cheerful moments it could be molded and mitigated by reformers and by virtues of America herself" (35). Thus, the Irish immigrants discussed by Ignatiev could count as white for purposes of immigration and census while at the same time being vividly and specifically described as a particular, and inferior, racial group as compared to the "native" (Anglo-Saxon) white race (Jacobson 1998, 48–52). There could be the hope that Irish racial particularity could disappear in a "generation or two" at the same time as there was a clear sense of the biological inferiority of the "Celtic race" (Jacobson 1998, 44). As more Lamarkian understandings of heredity were gradually repudiated and replaced by the Darwinism (however dubiously appropriated) of early twentieth-century eugenic sciences, the more cultural understanding of race lost much of its purchase.[10] Nevertheless, there remains even today a strong tendency to conflate race and culture in popular discourse on race.[11]

Part of the reason for the general messiness of race concepts and their application has to do with these broader trends in science, and most importantly, the popular understandings and appropriations of developments in biology and anthropology. Further reasons for this ambiguity and confusion can be found in the different *uses* to which racial concepts have been put at different times. Matthew Frye Jacobson calls David Roediger, along with Theodore Allen, to task for their treatment of race insofar as they focus exclusively upon economic and class conflicts as the basis for the development of race concepts and their application (1998, 19). To be sure, race has been, and continues to be a useful tool for what Allen refers to as "social control," creating a kind of "intermediate buffer social control stratum" that protects the capitalist class (1994, 134–35). From the use of Italian, Hungarian, and black laborers as scab-labor at the turn of the twentieth century in order to break strikes by (less ambiguously) white workers, to the current portrayal

race used to divide the working class

citizenship

of Latin American immigrant labor depressing North American wages, race has clearly functioned in part to divide the working class and pit them against each other. At the same time, Jacobson points out, another important function of racial discourse has been in separating those fit for self-government, and thus full citizenship and participation in public life, from those too savage, barbarous, and tribal to be trusted with self-government, let alone participation in the governing of the nation as a whole (1998, 20). Both of these different uses of race can admit of cultural or biological understandings. Fitness for use as cheap labor can be understood as an innate and immutable natural characteristic, or as a contingent cultural failing that can be redressed with education and cultural assimilation. And the same is true for fitness for citizenship.

Thus, if we consider the status of a given immigrant group to the United States, such as the Irish, we see that there are a multiplicity of competing interests not only among Irish immigrants but also among those both above and below them on the racial hierarchy. Proslavery white elites might want, therefore, to justify claims to Irish whiteness, so that they can be seen as fit for citizenship, and then vote to maintain slavery. White abolitionists, on the other hand, seeing this danger, might be inclined to argue that the Celtic race is distinct from other, superior and *truly* white races, and thus cannot be trusted to govern themselves wisely or participate as full citizens in national politics (including exercising the decidedly *white* virtue of empathy in relation to the enslaved black population). The same tension can be found in the economic context, where white economic elites might wish to establish the racial inferiority of the Irish, thus rendering them vulnerable to economic exploitation and facilitating the racial fragmentation of the working class, and working class "native" whites might gain psychological and even economic advantage in the short term by affirming that racial difference. As circumstances change, however, white laborers, and even white capital, might find advantage in arguing for full whiteness for the Irish in order to better defend other racial divisions deemed more critical. Thus, as Roediger describes, the increase in the new immigrants from Eastern Europe and the Mediterranean helped to make it possible for Irish laborers to shore up their claims to whiteness by maintaining the nonwhiteness (or inbetweenness) of these new immigrants, and therefore their status as cheap laborers. Thus we can understand why Jacobson comes to state that "[b]ecause the certainties represented by race are bound in a wildly complex skein of political, economic, cultural, ideological, psychological, and perceptual strands, their movements are glacial rather than catastrophic, uneven rather than linear or steady" (1998, 18–19).

Given the ambiguity and apparent contradiction within and among these competing accounts of race and racial membership, there can be a temptation to inscribe contemporary understandings of race, and especially ethnicity, back into the pronouncements of prior generations. Thus, when an article in the *Atlantic Monthly* in 1896 draws unfavorable distinctions between Celtic and Anglo-Saxon fitness for political life, it may use the term *race*, but one may suppose that what is really meant is what we now understand as ethnicity (Jacobson 1998, 48). Race, in this view, is a more general category focusing on color, and most especially the division between whites and nonwhites, while ethnicity is a more specific term, tied typically to nationhood, that is independent from race. Thus, the Irish may be a distinct ethnic group, but they are clearly racially white. Roediger and Jacobson are both careful to warn us against this temptation. "Present political motivations—from the right, center, and left—feed preferences for projecting the firm distinction between race and ethnicity back in time" (Roediger 2005, 36), but "the prevalence of studies that read later uses of ethnicity back across the decades perhaps reflects less on that term's ability to illuminate the lives of new immigrants than on its utility in supporting mainstream ideas about contemporary race relations" (28). Likewise, Jacobson insists that "we must admit of a system of 'difference' by which one might be both white *and* racially distinct from other whites" (1998, 6). While Roediger points out that the concept of an "ethnic group" is itself a very recent invention (2005, 18), his reason for rejecting its retroactive use is that, ultimately, when someone described the Italians or the Irish as a race, they meant something more akin to our contemporary conception of race than they did our contemporary conception of ethnicity.[12] Race was, Roediger reminds us, "at once about 'stock' *and* culture—heredity *and* environment—in the early twentieth century" (32). As much as race was an ambiguous and imprecise term, it was used to mark a significant difference *in kind* between distinct racial groups that is lacking in our contemporary understanding of ethnicity, though admittedly this latter term is itself vague and contentious. It is therefore a serious mischaracterization to simply read ethnicity back into past racial discourse.

In sum, what the work of Roediger, Allen, Ignatiev, and Jacobson demonstrate is not just the historical contingency and fluidity of the meaning of race and racial membership but also the extent to which even within a given period and place there could be divergent understandings both competing for dominance and even at times working together. It is important to illuminate this struggle over the meaning and significance of race both in order to better understand the past and, as all of these authors suggest, in order to help positively shape the present and the future. At the same time, they urge us to be wary of assuming that our present understanding of terms such as *race* and *ethnicity* are somehow more accurate or otherwise superior, and reading them back into our understanding of the past. As Roediger points out, while it is clear that there were important differences between the racialization of inbetween European immigrants and the unambiguously nonwhite black, American Indian, Asian, and Latina/o populations, for all of them, "nonetheless it was an experience of racialization" (2005, 12). The task will be to understand how this racialization of light-skinned immigrants was both importantly different from and similar to the racialization of Chinese or Mexican immigrants, or the descendants of enslaved Africans. To simply eliminate such comparison by rhetorical fiat (such as by declaring the European immigrants to be "white ethnics" while the other groups are "races") is to dramatically oversimplify matters.

Jacobson's work offers yet another important advantage that is worth emphasizing before I move on to my critique of this general position. He sets out in *Whiteness of a Different Color* not only to add to the historical account of the shifting meanings and attributions of race in the United States, but significantly (and uniquely) points out that ostensibly racial differences were not simply *imputed* to groups such as the Irish or Jewish immigrants of the nineteenth century but were quite readily and immediately *seen.* The English had been "observing" a distinctly Irish physiology for quite some time, and their descendants in the New World happily kept up the practice. As Jacobson attests regarding the racial perception of the Irish, "The Irishman was 'low-browed,' 'brutish,' and even 'simian' in popular discourse; a *Harper's Weekly* piece in 1851 described the 'Celtic physiognomy' as 'distinctly marked' by, among other things, 'the small and somewhat upturned nose [and] the black tint of the skin" (1998, 48). Jews, likewise, were understood to have distinct physical characteristics that could be readily and easily identifiable, such that the nineteenth-century British (and Jewish) scholar Joseph Jacobs would write that "[e]ven the negroes of Surinam, when they see a European and a Jew approaching do not say, 'Here are two whites,' but, 'Here is a white and a Jew'" (quoted in Jacobson 1998, 181). This last quote is particularly significant insofar as it illustrates that the imputation of racialized physiognomy was not restricted to those who held these groups in contempt. That is, "[r]acial perceptions of Jewishness are not simply a subject for the annals of anti-Semitism . . . nor does racial ascription necessarily denote a negative assessment of a given group in every case" (Jacobson 1998, 175). The Irish, Jewish, and Italian immigrants, among the many others, who came to the United States in the role of racialized groups distinct from the largely Anglo-Saxon white elite were not seen as such exclusively by that elite but also understood, and *saw themselves and each other* as racially distinct.

This points toward the relationship between what Jacobson calls race "as a conceptual category" on the one hand, and as a "perceptual category" on the other (1998, 173). His point is that there seems to be a kind of reciprocal relationship between the two. As a given racial category becomes increasingly salient (as more and more Irish Catholic immigrants flood into Boston and Philadelphia, for example), people will ascribe physical specificity to that category and begin to *perceive* those physical markers. The repeated observation of these physical traits, in turn, will reinforce the sense of the group as a distinct race. But Jacobson is careful not to oversimplify this process:

> This is not to say that people all "really" look alike; rather, it is to argue that those physical differences which register in the consciousness as "*difference*" are keyed to particular social and historical circumstances. (We might all agree that Daniel Patrick Moynihan "looks Irish," for instance; but unlike our predecessors, we at the turn of the twenty-first century are not likely to note his Irishness first thing.) (1998, 174)

Perception

The key, in other words, is not whether there really are or are not sets of physical features that are consistent within and characteristic of a given race, but rather how our *perception* of relevant differences is itself conditioned by larger contexts of political and cultural meaning. Again, Jacobson is clear about this: "there is a dynamic relationship between visible 'difference' on the one hand, and deep social and political meaning on the other" (1998, 173). And like the ways in which race has been understood as significantly cultural as well as biological, this sense of race as a "perceptual category" is very much alive today. There is a tendency to treat racial categories as distinct interpretations of a kind of raw data, but Jacobson is here pointing out that the "deep social and political meaning" of racial categories shape the very way in which we perceive others (and ourselves). We do not, in other words, simply see a collection of value-neutral physical differences and peculiarities, and then interpret them as racial after the fact. Rather, our awareness of the significance and content of racial categories conditions the very way that we perceive such differences in the first place.[13] In this way, Jacobson leads us to an account of racial perception very much in keeping with the phenomenological tradition in philosophy (cf. Alcoff 2006, 187–94), a point I will explore in more detail in chapter 4.

All three of the writers upon whom I am focusing have, I wish to reiterate, made significant and important contributions not only to my own thinking but also to discourses on race and racism generally. Their work illustrates the changes in our understanding and use of race over time, the way in which race as a concept has been characterized by divergent and contradictory meanings at a single time, how it has been both biological *and* cultural, and how it has related to and conditioned the way we perceive ourselves and others. All of these are crucial insights to which I will return in the next chapter. Before that, however, it is necessary to spell out some of my contentions with their work, and how this helps to illuminate current philosophical debates about the ontological status of race.

HISTORY, CONTINGENCY, AND THE REALITY OF RACE

In philosophical circles, racial eliminativism, the view that race is an empty and ultimately harmful concept that should be eliminated altogether, has effectively become the fulcrum for debates surrounding racial ontology at least from the publication of Kwame Anthony Appiah's *In My Father's House* (1992). Since Appiah's articulation of an argument for the illusory status of race, and the moral imperative to abandon the concept, the most common starting point in discussions of the ontology of race has taken the form of either advancing or refuting Appiah's position, if not his precise argument. This is due not merely to the power of the eliminativist argument but also to eliminativism's inherent appeal to popular contemporary ideology on both sides of the political spectrum. On the right, eliminativism adds force to the argument that race no longer matters politically, while on the left, eliminativism appeals to the ideal of racial colorblindness. Like the new abolitionist argument, the basic argument for eliminativism has two components.

elimitavism

1. The first is strictly ontological—that race has no biological foundation or A
justification, and thus is not *real*. The second claim is that race, as a term B
with no real referent, has only ever (or at least overwhelmingly, if not exclusively) been used to nefarious ends, and thus the elimination of the use of
the term can only be to the benefit of humanity. The contours of Jacobson's
account of race, and especially those of the new abolitionists Ignatiev and
Roediger, are clearly consistent with the philosophical position of racial
eliminativism.

It might appear at first blush, especially given their as appeal to the concepts of fabrication and invention, that Jacobson, Roediger, and Ignatiev are
not necessarily advocating a thoroughly nihilistic ontological position regarding race (that races have no reality whatsoever), but rather something
more along the lines of *social constructivism*. In other words, we might interpret their position as the assertion that race is a real, yet historically contingent, social construction as opposed to an utterly unreal illusion. Race may
have no basis in biology, and in that sense it is not real (and thus not necessary), but nevertheless it is a historical fact (and thus a contingent one) that
it *was* invented, fabricated, or constructed, and in that sense it has garnered
at least a kind of reality. Of course, this points directly toward the question
of what is meant, in such cases, by *real* at all. what is "real"?

Charles Mills has provided a taxonomy of ontological positions on race
that places the view that race is socially constructed squarely in the genus of
objectivism (along with realism), as opposed to antiobjectivism, about race
(1998, 45). His primary distinction between objectivism and antiobjectivism
is that the latter holds that propositions regarding racial identity or membership have no objective truth-value, while the former position does allow for
objective truth about race. By "objective", he does not mean in the strong
sense of a kind of ahistorical, mind-independent understanding, but rather
the more minimal sense in which the truth value of a given individual's
propositions regarding racial membership are not simply up to that individual. In other words, racial objectivism means simply that I can be wrong or
mistaken about my racial membership, or that of others. Mills himself advocates a constructivist position on race, and characterizes it as the claim
that, in a given time and place, there are generally known and understood
rules governing the ascription of racial membership that set the truth conditions for the evaluation of claims about race. Thus, the rules regarding
racial membership may vary in Jamaica as opposed to Wisconsin, such that

constructivist

are eliminativists constructivists?

one may be *red* in Kingston but *black* in Milwaukee, but within those specific contexts, one cannot simply decide for oneself whether one is or is not a member of a given racial category, or even what categories are available. The category of red, for example, is available in both contexts, but with radically different meanings, such that a man who is red in Kingston, and who then claimed to be red in Milwaukee, would be *wrong*. This wrongness is not a matter of some deep underlying metaphysical reality to which our claims must correspond, but rather a matter of accordance with sets of historically contingent, socially constructed rules that vary from place to place as well as over time. Perhaps, therefore, the new abolitionists are better understood as advocating a constructivist ontology of race rather than a nihilistic one.

In order to evaluate this interpretation, it will be necessary to re-examine the distinction between the ontological and political commitments of both abolitionism and eliminativism. If one reinterprets the ontological claim along social constructivist lines, we find that race is not simply illusory or altogether nonexistent but rather a contingent historical construct. However, the further political claim, that race serves the sole, or at least primary, function of legitimating processes of oppression and exploitation, and should therefore be eliminated or abolished, renders this understanding of the ontological position suspect. What is really at stake here is the underlying conception of the *real*. The political argument is that race can and should be abolished, but not solely because it is harmful. Presumably, if racial categories and concepts accurately described reality, even if they were ultimately harmful and even oppressive, it would make little sense, and do less good, to advocate their elimination or abolition. In other words, the move to abolition or elimination is coherent only because racial concepts and claims are ultimately taken to be *false*—they are misrepresentations of reality—and that, in addition to the harm they have caused, is why they must be abandoned. The claim that they are harmful alone would not be sufficient reason to eliminate them, they must also be in some significant way *unreal*—or at least, not *really* real.

We thus confront two crucial and interrelated questions. First, what, exactly, do we mean by social construction, and second, what kinds of reality can be socially constructed? Typical examples of socially constructed reality include objects such as money and borders, and phenomena such as games. The value of a dollar, like the border between the United States and Mexico, is not something discovered but rather constructed or invented, and each is embedded in a social practice with public (intersubjective) rules. The value of the dollar can change over time, given the relatively slow fluctuations in inflation and exchange rates, or the more seismic shifts from the gold or silver standards, but at no time is it simply up to any given individual how much a dollar is worth, or even what counts properly as a dollar. I cannot, for example, say that my doodle of George Washington on a napkin is a dollar, and that this dollar has the same value as your car, and have those things be right simply by virtue of my believing them (even if *you* believe them too). By the same token, if I am playing basketball, and run the length of the court while holding the ball fixedly over my head, my argument that "traveling" is not *real*, and therefore I should not be penalized, will and should fall on deaf ears. This is the sense of objectivity to which Mills seems to be appealing. Just as the rules governing currency value, or basketball, do not exist prior to human invention, once they do exist, they have a kind of objectivity, and thus a reality, that one is bound to respect, even if one ultimately seeks to change (or indeed eliminate) that reality. The idea of social construction thus appeals to the way in which human behavior and interaction can generate categories of being that would not exist otherwise. I can say, "I have a dollar in my pocket," or "that was a double-dribble," and those utterances have a truth-value independent of my beliefs or wishes, as a result of the social construction of the objects and phenomena they describe. For the sake of simplicity, one might say that there is a *reality* brought about through human behavior, and the truth of these propositions is a matter of their correspondence to that reality.[14] Social constructivism is in this way first and foremost the claim that reality can be shaped and structured by human intervention. There are realities that exist, to our knowledge, only by virtue of humans having created them.

What, we must ask, is the nature of this reality? Recall that central to both the eliminativist and abolitionist positions is a rejection of racial essentialism, principally in the form of a biological foundation for racial categories. The presence of racial essences or biological foundations would obviate the need for their construction, and render impossible their elimination or abolition as *real* categories.[15] They would provide, in other words, the kind of reality that not only *precedes* human intervention but also *resists* it. It is, in other words, a permanent and durable form of reality, as opposed to the transient and changeable forms of reality that are socially constructed. Mills' taxonomy, therefore, takes the position that this latter sort of reality *counts* as real, while the claim that race has no biological foundation, and is therefore an illusion (that is, Appiah), posits instead (implicitly, at least) the view that the former kind of reality is the only one that matters (at least in cases like this). All of this is exacerbated by a hermeneutic dualism that pervades discussions of racial ontology as social construction (cf. Gordon 2004, 182–89).

We find, ultimately, that arguments surrounding the reality of race are not purely descriptive debates about what does or does not exist biologically but are also, and perhaps foremost, normative debates about what *matters* when we raise the very question of the reality of race. Setting aside, therefore, the semantic questions about whether the abolitionists can or cannot rightly be called social constructivists, we find that, even if they believe that race has a kind of socially constructed reality, in advocating its abolition, they are denying the significance of that reality, in the face of the lack of underlying biological foundation. Race, in other words, may be real, but it isn't *really* real in the sense that we are *bound* to respect it (that would require legitimation by natural science). What significance race has, for both the eliminativist and the abolitionist, is purely negative—it exists as a fabrication or invention for the sole purpose of legitimating and facilitating oppression and exploitation. Thus, even if one allows that race is socially constructed, and thus has a *kind* of reality, that reality does not matter in the face of both the harm that its constructed reality has wrought, along with the fact that it utterly lacks the more permanent kind of (biological) reality—the kind that *really* matters. Since it is not really real, and has been so utterly devastating to so many people, it should be eliminated or abolished altogether, and thus come to no longer be real in any sense at all.

In this way, we can see that whether the abolitionist or eliminativist arguments begin from nihilistic or social constructionist ontological positions, the crucial point is their ultimate advocacy of abolition or elimination. Such advocacy (in which Mills, I should point out, is not a participant), even if it admits a kind of socially constructed reality of race, requires that one dismiss the significance of that reality in light of the ultimate lack of biological reality. It is the latter fact that really matters, while the former is *merely* an invention. It is in this way that both arguments participate in exactly the sort of naturalism that my Husserlian methodology seeks to displace. Both approaches take biology, understood as a mind-independent foundation, to be the ultimate arbiter of the reality of race. But in raising the radical question of methodology, we must ask *why* this is so. We find, in this way, that both approaches assume that race must be an all-or-nothing, mind-independent, and thus *necessary* category of being if it is to be understood as truly real. Since biology cannot provide the kind of criteria necessary to understand race in this way, it follows that it simply cannot be real in any binding sense of the term. All that is left is to sort out the status of what remains after this determination of ultimate unreality—either it is completely illusory, or it is a social construction with an impoverished kind of (pseudo?) reality. Either way, there is an underlying sense in which both positions hold that a *really* real notion of race must be biological, and if such a conception of race should prove untenable, then there is ultimately no such thing, and the misguided invention of the concept must be overturned, eliminated, or abolished.

Much of the philosophical literature on racial eliminativism is committed to this biological variety of naturalism. It holds that only a biological category could provide the kind of necessary and sufficient conditions for racial membership required for race to be *real*, and when such conditions cannot be found, concludes that race must not be real at all. The new abolitionists begin from this observation, and go on to posit historical analysis as the primary methodology of racial analysis. If the biological approach takes race to be a matter of phenotypical or genotypical properties inherent in particular organisms, the historicist approach takes race to be a consequence of the *past* use of (fundamentally unreal) racial categories at a given time and place. The abolitionist position clearly not only takes race to be a contingent social construction but one that is *reducible* to the political project of white supremacy. That is, whiteness, for example, is nothing more than a position of superiority or hegemony within a racial hierarchy itself constructed by white supremacist political projects. It must therefore be abdicated by those whites committed to racial justice because whiteness *just is* a commitment to, or at least tolerance of, white supremacy. Blackness, likewise, is strictly a position of relative inferiority within that same white supremacist racial hierarchy.

This is at the heart of the abolitionist argument, and it is this basic ontological claim that must be called into question. If you reject white supremacy, according to the abolitionist, you therefore reject whiteness, and if you accept whiteness, you affirm white supremacy—by definition. It would also follow, if white supremacy is the sufficient cause of racial categories as such, that any affirmation of racial identity, white or otherwise, would be a kind of affirmation of, or at least complicity with, white supremacy. Ultimately, therefore, the abolitionist position is an appeal to a so-called colorblind account of human identity. The basic picture of human identity, in other words, is a raceless amalgam of the universal human subject. If we can abdicate, eliminate, or otherwise abolish our racial identity and yet remain fundamentally the same subjects, then race cannot be constitutive of our identity in any sense. Since it is *merely* socially constructed, and ultimately incidental to our identity, we have little to lose, and everything to gain, by getting rid of race entirely.

Lucius Outlaw (2004) and Linda Alcoff (2006, 221–23) both offer an explicit critique of the abolitionist position that is a helpful starting point here. First, they both see individual identity as in some significant sense deeply informed, if not constituted, by various group memberships, like races, regardless of the contingent social origins of those groups. They reject, in other words, the universalist and raceless presumptions of abolitionism. For Alcoff and Outlaw, there is the practical concern that racial membership simply cannot be cast off, rejected, or abolished so easily as the abolitionist position seems to demand, and the more theoretical concern that identity demands a certain degree of particularism, and race is one important way to fulfill that need. Second, Alcoff and Outlaw both point toward an account of white supremacy as a political phenomenon that *positions* or locates different races but does not simply make them up whole cloth. They reject, in other words, the reducibility of racial ontology to white supremacy. What this means, in part, is that the history of the development of white supremacy as a central organizing principle is not a story of the creation of races out of what was effectively the *tabula rasa* of an essentially raceless premodern world. It was rather a history of the *constitution*, in the phenomenological sense, of races as meaningful and significant in the ways that they were and presently are.[16] It is not a matter of how the Irish, for example, "became" white in nineteenth-century North America but rather a matter of how a particular subgroup came to endorse the dominant supremacist view of the meaning of whiteness, and in so doing came to be accepted as such within that dominant framework. It is not an act of the *creation* of whiteness but an assignation of the meaning of whiteness.

Ontologically, the abolitionist position would have one believe that, prior to the first stirrings of white supremacy (marked by the conquest of the

Americas, or the diet of Valladolid, or some other historically significant moment), there were no white people, or black people for that matter. There were national groups, linguistic groups, religious groups, and ethnic groups, the ontological status of which could in turn be subject to further critical scrutiny, but races as such are a creation of white supremacy, and so have no existence prior to that historical moment. What is one to make then, of efforts by historians to demonstrate the richness and sophistication of *black* civilizations in the ancient (and thus pre-white supremacist) world, for example? One of the methods of the white supremacist project has been the obfuscation or silencing of historical evidence of nonwhite civilization and rationality. Given the traditional link between rationality and humanity, such denials of the *history* of black peoples constitute a further denial of their humanity. The lack of historical evidence of rational development—of civilization—among nonwhite peoples has been taken as proof of their irrationality, and thus their lack of full personhood. At the same time, given this presumption of nonwhite subhumanity and irrationality, any evidence that *does* crop up must be explained away. One way to challenge this effort has been to demonstrate that it is simply false—that there were indeed highly developed nonwhite civilizations, and that, *pace* Hegel (1956, 91–99), Reason can indeed be found on the African continent. The abolitionist view would seem to render this strategy of reclaiming black history unintelligible. There were no black people, qua black people, prior to their "invention" through the project of white supremacy, and therefore there could be no black civilization prior to that same historical moment. Likewise, efforts to describe the premodern visit by Lief Erickson to North America as a pre-Columbian *white* encounter with the New World must be considered utter nonsense. My task in the next chapter will be to challenge this view of racial ontology and history by offering an alternative reading of a historical period in which exactly this sort of negotiation of the meaning of whiteness was being undertaken.

There is a certain important insight in the abolitionist position, and that is that being sanguine about the meaning of whiteness is inconsistent with antiracism, insofar as the dominant meaning of whiteness *has been and continues to be* a certain enjoyment of the power and privilege wrought by white supremacy. White people cannot continue to be white *in the same way* if there is to be any significant progress toward racial justice and challenge to white supremacy. The problem with the abolitionist position is that it assumes that the dominant view of the meaning of whiteness is the *only* view, and posits a repudiation of all racial identity as the means to racial justice. As Outlaw and Alcoff have pointed out in different ways, racial identities have been and will continue to be constitutive components of individual identity, and cannot simply be abolished. Indeed, any social ontology that takes human embodiment seriously, and emphasizes the ways in which our reality (including our bodies) is fundamentally shaped by intersubjective matrices of meaning and intention, must hold that racial identity will continue to be salient, and effectively inescapable, for quite some time to come. The question is ultimately one of whether the "radically new concept of the human" posited by Clevis Headley (2004, 104) must be a *raceless* human. If one presumes that race must by definition be oppressive and pernicious—and there is, admittedly, good inductive reason to hold this position—then it would indeed seem necessary. However, at the heart of the phenomenological tradition, of which I take Headley to be a part in many important ways, is the suspension of or bracketing of such presumptions and commitments. Why, in other words, must we presume that race is an inherently pernicious concept, and humanity would be better off without it? That is the question I will be taking up in the next chapter.

not raceless human

Is race an inherently
pernicious concept?

2

Turbulent and Dangerous Spirits:
Irish Servitude in Barbados

I first visited Barbados in the summer of 2004 to attend the initial meeting of the newly formed Caribbean Philosophical Association. While a few friends and I were exploring the city of Bridgetown on a steamy May afternoon, we turned a corner and came upon a large church. Of course, churches are quite common on the island, but what struck me at the time about this particular church was the large Celtic cross on its brilliant green roof, and the windows lining the sides of the building in the shape of traditional Celtic knots. As we neared the building, I could see on a nearby sign that it was St. Patrick's Roman Catholic Cathedral. I have since learned that this should not in the least have struck me as odd or extraordinary, but at the time it most certainly did. It was the sort of edifice I might have expected to find in any number of cities with large Irish populations (the undoubtedly lengthy list of which in North America would certainly include my own home of Milwaukee), but I did not expect at the time to see such a thing in the Caribbean. What was an Irish Catholic Cathedral doing in Barbados? My curiosity aroused, I began researching the Irish presence in the Caribbean almost immediately upon my return home from the conference.

I subsequently learned that, though there had been a large Irish population in Barbados in the colony's earliest days, the construction of St. Patrick's Cathedral did not begin until 1840, at which time the original Irish population of indentured servants and poor laborers had largely vanished,[1] to be replaced much later by a significant population of Irish soldiery garrisoned on the island, for whom the island's first Catholic church had been built. Thus, while there had been a significant Irish Catholic population on the island during the early colonial era, it was not until the nineteenth century that British anti-Catholic sentiment had cooled sufficiently that the English colonists would allow a Roman Catholic church to function openly in Barbados (interestingly, that was nearly two hundred years *after* the first synagogue in Bridgetown). The Irish were, in fact, a substantial segment of the populations of colonial Barbados, Jamaica, Montserrat, and St. Kitts from the seventeenth through mid-eighteenth centuries. However, as white indentured labor was replaced increasingly with West African slave labor in the sugar colonies of the Anglophone Caribbean, freed white indentures typically either returned to Europe or continued west to the British Colonies in North America.

What most interests me about the history of the Irish in the colonial Caribbean is their impact upon, and place within, the emerging racial landscape of the time. As they did later in North America, the Irish in the early colonial Caribbean occupied a very ambiguous position in the racial hierarchy, and one that, again as would be the case in the United States, changed substantially over the course of a generation or two. Aside from any number of important historical and sociological issues raised by this phenomenon, it also points toward crucial philosophical questions regarding the ontology of race, the workings of racial oppression, and the relation between the two. In exploring this historical moment, which is different from, but in significant ways analogous to, those moments explored in the work of Ignatiev, Roediger, Allen, and Jacobson, I will be focusing upon these important philosophical questions. This particular historical example is sufficiently analogous to the situation described by the new abolitionists to be familiar to readers conversant in that literature, but different enough to allow sufficient interpretive elbow room to explore the philosophical questions that motivate this book. What was the racial status of these early Irish servants? How did that status change over time? How did their presence condition the racial structures in which they found themselves? In short, a close examination of the early period of the Irish presence in Barbados will help to illuminate the central themes and problems with which this book contends. This chapter offers a brief sketch of this historical period, and draws out some of these

ultimate goal of the book

significant dilemmas and puzzles, which will in turn be taken up in subsequent chapters.

My ultimate purpose in this book is to offer an account of the ontology of race as it relates both to the phenomenon of racism and to the understanding and interpretation of history. While it will become clear that there are significant similarities between the historical moment I will discuss in this chapter and the accounts provided by Ignatiev et al., the Caribbean geopolitical context alters the problematic of race in very illuminating ways. In order to mount a critique of the racial ontology implicit in much of the new abolitionist work, I will be drawing out both the similarities and differences between these situations in the United States as opposed to the Caribbean, and the nineteenth as opposed to the seventeenth centuries. Since the principal goal of this work is philosophical, and not purely historical, I will keep my account relatively brief and focused. It will doubtless be unsatisfying to historians, but I believe that it is adequate to the particular purposes of this text. Ultimately, given the paucity of secondary material on this historical period, I can only hope that any historical dissatisfaction with my account will motivate others more qualified than I to fill in this gap in the historical literature.[2]

THE IRISH IN SEVENTEENTH-CENTURY BARBADOS

Barbados was first claimed for the English crown by John Powell in 1625 (Harlow 1969, 3; Beckles 1990, 7). He was not the first European to visit the island, nor even the first English visitor, but he was the first to leave some permanent mark declaring ownership. Returning to England from Pernambuco, Powell stopped on the island and according to a contemporary account, "they set up a Cross in or about St. James's Town, now called the Hole, and inscrib'd on a Tree adjoining *James K. of E. and this Island*" (Harlow 1969, 3). Two years later, a permanent settlement was established by eighty English settlers, and ten "negro slaves" that had been taken "after capturing a prize" (Harlow 1969, 4). Though Barbados had been inhabited at various times by Amerindians (Barton 1979, 21; Beckles 1990, 1–6), it was uninhabited at the time the English arrived. Eventually Amerindians were brought from the South American colony of Dutch Guiana and enslaved (Harlow 1969, 6), but they were never a significant proportion of the island's population. By the time of Richard Ligon's visit to the island in the 1650s, the population consisted mostly of plantation owners, a few white freehold-ers, and enslaved West Africans and Amerindians, in addition to a large pro-portion of white indentured servants from England, Scotland, Wales, and Ireland.

Given its position as the easternmost of the Caribbean Islands, Barbados proved to be an invaluable military possession in the age of sail, since the prevailing trade winds allowed ships from Barbados to reach any other part of the Caribbean or the Americas relatively quickly, while reaching Barbados from the west (against the prevailing winds) was considerably more time-consuming and difficult. When the island switched from producing primarily tobacco and cotton as cash crops to sugar in the latter half of the seventeenth century (Beckles 1990, 20–21; Gragg 2003, 98–105), it positioned itself as the dominant *economic* force in the British West Indies. During this time the la-bor force gradually shifted from primarily white indentured labor to enslaved African labor (Gragg 2003, 113–31). The British trade in slaves ended officially in 1804, and emancipation came in 1834, followed in Barbados by a four-year "apprenticeship" in which the formerly enslaved continued to work without pay (Beckles 1990, 95–100). As in the United States, the working and living conditions of the formerly enslaved remained quite poor, and the disparity between the white land-owning elite and the black laborers was pronounced. It wasn't until 1966, however, that Barbados gained its inde-pendence from Great Britain. Today it is one of the more economically and politically stable and prosperous islands in the Anglophone Caribbean.

The first English settlers experimented for some time with various export crops in their efforts to turn a profit from their colonial possessions. The British at this time were not heavily involved in the slave trade, and the pur-chase of West African slaves from Portuguese and Dutch traders was often prohibitively expensive for these early planters, so the bulk of the Barbadian labor force came in the form of white indentured servants. Economic divi-sions in the British Isles had always ensured a large class of impoverished la-borers, and the recent civil wars and political upheavals of the time had only expanded that pool of desperate individuals. For the promise of transporta-tion, food, shelter, and a remittance (usually some amount of cash or its equivalent, and a small parcel of land), individuals could sell their future labor and become indentured servants for periods ranging from five to ten years. The early settlers spent those first years looking for the cash crop that would turn the best profit given the growing conditions of the island. Aside from tobacco and cotton, they also grew indigo, all with varying degrees of rather limited success.

Over the course of the latter half of the sixteenth century, however, several changes in conditions came about such that the use of white indentured labor fell dramatically. First, the Barbadian planters garnered a reputation for particular cruelty to their white servants (Beckles 1989, 92). In Ligon's early account, for example, he remarks: "Truly, I have seen such cruelty there done to Servants, as I did not think one Christian could have done to another" (Ligon 2000, 65). Such a reputation, justified or not, must surely have dissuaded potential indentures, and contributed to the ongoing labor shortage on the island. Second, during this time the process of growing and refining sugar was improved, and this crop was discovered to be immensely profitable and successful in Barbados. Unlike tobacco, however, which would allow one to make a modest living on a relatively small parcel of land, sugar required huge amounts of land and labor to realize profit, and as the economy shifted from tobacco to sugar, not only was the ability to support oneself on a small tract of land lost but every available parcel of land was claimed by increasingly large plantations. The sudden lack of land, and the inability for a small landholder to make a living even if it had been available, further decreased whatever appeal indentured servitude might have held for individual laborers in the British Isles. This shortage of labor lead not only to the use of involuntary transportation to the West Indies as a punishment for certain crimes and for political prisoners but also to the practice of kidnapping laborers and sending them involuntarily to serve as plantation labor. Lastly, the British successfully entered the slave trade through the auspices of the Royal African Company (Beckles 1990, 33; Harlow 1969, 311–18), reducing the costs of West African Slave labor to British colonists. All of this combined to shift dramatically the demographics of the Barbadian labor force from primarily white (indentured servants) to almost exclusively black (enslaved West Africans) by the early part of the eighteenth century (Beckles 1990, 31–33).

Throughout the period dominated by the use of white servant labor, Irish indentures provided a significant and, from the perspective of the English planters, often troublesome, segment of that population (Beckles 1989, 38–39). While a steady stream of Irish indentured servants departed for the Caribbean both from Ireland as well as ports in England throughout the seventeenth century, Oliver Cromwell's efforts to "pacify" Ireland in particular generated a veritable tidal wave of Irish indentured laborers. Aubrey Gwynn estimated that, from 1652 to 1659, approximately 50,000 Irish individuals were *forcibly* transported to Barbados and Virginia (O'Callaghan 2000, 9), the two most significant English colonies at the time. This estimation is, given the inadequacy of the historical record, highly contentious. Whatever the exact figure, however, there is clear historical support for the fact that a significant number of Irish men, women, and children were sent involuntarily to serve periods of indenture in the Caribbean and North America, sometimes for life (Beckles 1989, 47–50; O'Callaghan 2000, 93).

Let me be clear. Compared to the millions of West Africans sold into chattel slavery throughout the colonial era, even the most liberal (and quite likely exaggerated) figure of fifty thousand pales by comparison. My point is in no way to blur the real differences between the involuntary indenture of the seventeenth-century Irish and the centuries-long transatlantic trade in enslaved Africans. Indeed there is a general danger in discussions of Irish racial history of making facile equivocations between the conditions of (at least some) Irish laborers and chattel slaves. I very much wish to avoid that. At the same time, the involuntary nature of some of the Irish indentures is significant to understanding their position on the island, and the presence of a rhetorical and conceptual pitfall does not mean that one should abandon the project altogether. Slavery and servitude, even involuntary and indefinite servitude, are not the same thing. Differences such as the relation between the subject and his or her labor, the proprietary relation between the master and the subject's labor and physical body, and the ways in which chattel slavery was understood to be a heritable condition while servitude was focused upon the individual's labor as alienable property (Beckles 1989, 7), point to the importance of maintaining a clear distinction between servitude and slavery. That is why I have been careful to employ the language of "involuntary indentures" rather than "slaves" when referring to this population. However, saying that two concepts are significantly different does not mean that they cannot at the same time also be *similar*. There is a tendency, especially in discussions of race, to conflate similar and same, and sometimes this does indeed happen in pernicious ways (this is, in fact, what I will argue is an important facet of the politics of purity). But similarity is not sameness. That there were significant similarities between the situations of Irish (especially involuntary) indentures and African slaves is an important fact, and acknowledging this in no way denies that there remained significant, even crucial, differences. With this caveat in mind, I will turn to the question of who these indentured servants were, and how they came to be transported to Barbados.

Many of these involuntary indentures in the middle of the seventeenth century were sent to the West Indies as political prisoners. In 1658 Thomas Povey, an English merchant with extensive West Indian investments, stated that the majority of Irish servants in Barbados and St. Kitts had been transported by the English state for treasonous engagements against the Protector (Beckles 2000, 227). Indeed, transportation to the West Indies, and especially Barbados, was so commonplace during the Protectorate that common parlance referred to transportation as being "Barbadosed" (Beckles 1989, 53). Correspondence from Thomas Carlyle in 1655 makes this explicit: "A terrible Protector this . . . He dislikes shedding blood, but is very apt 'to Barbadoes' an unruly man—he sent and sends us by the hundreds to Barbadoes, so that we have made an active verb of it: 'Barbadoes you'" (Harlow 1969, 295–96; O'Callaghan 2000, 89).

In addition to political prisoners, the indigent poor—"idle persons that can give no account of themselves"—were also prone to being "Barbadosed" (Beckles 1989, 47). Of course, in an Ireland ravaged by war, the distinction between political prisoners and these "idle persons" can become rather blurry. For example, after Cromwell had secured Ireland, he allowed some of the remaining Irish soldiers to seek employment in the Catholic countries of Europe (O'Callaghan 2000, 43), and many of them went to Poland, France, and Spain.[3] However, they were not allowed to take any dependents with them into exile, which left many of those dependents abandoned in a war-torn Ireland without any means of support. Given Cromwell's instructions "to arrest and deliver" all Irish men, women, and children who could not demonstrate "a settled course of industry" for transportation to the West Indies (80), this situation saw a great many of those soldiers' families sent to servitude in Barbados, St. Kitts, and Virginia. The soldiers themselves may not have been political prisoners, but a case can be made that their dependents were. Of course, according to Oliver Cromwell's son, Henry, such transportation, especially of young women, was ultimately for their own good, insofar as it kept them from a life of idleness and sin (149).

All of this was in turn exacerbated by the less formal means of procuring human cargo for the merchants bound for the West Indies. Magistrates in London, for example, were given half of the capital paid for servants by merchants who transported them to the Caribbean, which greatly enhanced the appeal of transportation as a sentence in their courts, especially for juveniles (Beckles 1989, 48). In addition to this use of transportation as a sentence for petty crime, there were the "Spirits" (Beckles 1989, 50; O'Callaghan 2000, 70; Harlow 1969, 300). This was the name given to those whose practice was to kidnap men, women, and even children as young as eight (O'Callaghan 2000, 71), and sell them to ships' captains and merchants bound for the West Indies, who in turn sold them upon arrival at their destination. Those so "spirited away" made a significant contribution to the overall servant trade, though one that is clearly difficult to estimate with any precision. According to historian Hilary Beckles, "A parliamentary ordinance of 1643 stated that there was hardly a ship leaving London for the West Indies which did not carry cargo of the Spirits" (1989, 50). When one considers that Spirits operated in ports throughout England and Ireland, it becomes clear that the trade in kidnapped servants was quite brisk. There were occasional efforts by the authorities to curtail the practices of the Spirits, but its profitability, paired with its political expediency in supplying European labor to the colonies and thus increasing the white population there (more on the significance of this latter motive later in this chapter), ensured that the practice continued to flourish through the latter-half of the seventeenth century. Indeed, in 1685, the Lord of Trade and Plantations offered the sadly familiar justification that the kidnapping of servants was ultimately to their benefit, since "in being kept to a strict performance of their duty they will in all probability live more peacefully than they did before" (Beckles 1989, 52).

Upon arrival in Barbados, Irish indentures, whether voluntary or not, were viewed by the English plantocracy with suspicion, contempt, and fear. Well prior to the seventeenth century the English had viewed the Irish with distrust and scorn, and had described the difference between these two peoples in rather stark, and often highly racialized terms (see Canny 1987). By the time of the English Civil War, the tension between the two had reached a peak, and a barrage of pamphlets helped fuel the ill will among the English toward the Irish. One such pamphlet, within a litany of unflattering descriptions of the moral and physical degeneracy of the Irish people, mentions cannibalism as one of their practices (O'Callaghan 2000, 14–15). This is especially noteworthy within the Caribbean context, since the Amerindian inhabitants of the region were thought to be cannibals by European colonists, and the name *Caribbean* itself shares etymological roots with *cannibal*. In addition to the perceived racial difference between the Irish and the English,[4] there were religious differences. The English generally did not view Catholics as proper or true Christians by (O'Callaghan 2000, 149), a distinction that further fueled their contempt for Ireland and the Irish. In short, hundreds of years of war, rebellion, and repression had gone into shaping English-Irish relations by the time of the colonization of Barbados, leading at least one scholar to argue that British colonial technique was first honed and refined on Ireland (Canny 1987).

Thus, while the planters in Barbados were in desperate need of white[5] servants—both as labor and to serve in the island's militia force in case of external invasion or internal slave rebellion (both very real fears for the planters)—they were often quite clear about the undesirability of Irish indentures. A 1644 legislative action on the part of the Barbados Assembly attempted to halt altogether the influx of Irish servants to the island. Nevertheless, despite such efforts, 20 percent of servants in Barbados were Irish by 1660 (Beckles 1989, 38), and the increased numbers did not improve Anglo-Irish relations on the island. According to Beckles, "Irish servants, then, were seen by the English planter class as an enemy within and were treated accordingly" (Beckles 2000, 230). The 1661 Barbados Servant Code mentions the Irish specifically as "a profligate race," of "turbulent and dangerous spirits," and avers that they were prone to "joining themselves to runaway slaves" (quoted in Beckles 2000, 233). A further legislative attempt in 1664 to curtail the importation of Irish servants also failed, and so the planters made efforts instead to strictly control the Irish population on the island. Irish servants were required to carry passes when they left their plantations, were forbidden to carry arms, and even Irish freemen who arrived on the Island were compelled to prove to the council that they had employment, and that their masters guaranteed their good conduct, none of which applied to English, Scottish, and Welsh free immigrants or servants (Beckles 2000, 230–31). The stricter scrutiny directed toward Irish servants lead also to more frequent and harsh punishments (Beckles 1989, 99; Beckles 2000, 231–32). The larger English attitude toward the Irish served at once to provide incentive to the authorities in England and Ireland to promote transportation, while at the same time causing the elites in Barbados to resist that influx of Irish labor.

Hilary Beckles, one of the foremost scholars of Barbadian history, offers a succinct account of the general status of the Irish in the colony:

Though the behavior of most servants and freemen was typically restless and insubordinate, sparked by their awareness that West Indian indentureship offered extremely limited opportunities for social or material advancement, it was the Irish who were perceived by English masters as a principal internal enemy—at times more dangerous and feared than blacks. (2000, 226)

Beckles's comparison of the Irish to black slaves touches on a recurring theme throughout this earlier part of the colonial period. John Scott, a seventeenth-century English adventurer, wrote of the Irish in Barbados that they were "derided by the negroes, and branded with the epithet of 'white slaves'" (quoted in Beckles 2000, 230). Father Labat, a French Priest who visited the island in the early eighteenth century, wrote that descriptions of Irish indentures as "white slaves" was commonplace (Beckles 2000, 230). Again, I am suspect of referring to Irish servants as "slaves," but the appeal to the term by contemporary European visitors is indicative of the conditions of the Irish on the island. Furthermore, Beckles himself notes that English planters, in their evaluation of servants, placed Scots and Welsh at the top, and Irish at the very bottom, below even the value of black slaves by a margin of three to one (Beckles 2000, 230). There is, to be sure, only the most dubious value in being more highly prized *as property* by the plantation owners, but the fact that Irish servants were seen as the least valuable laborers on the island is quite significant. It cannot be simply a matter of anti-Irish prejudice on the part of the English, which was surely a force, but no more so than antiblack prejudice. One compelling explanation for the extremely low opinion in which the planters held their Irish laborers is suggested by the striking number of recorded incidences of the punishment of Irish servants, especially given the overall paucity of materials from this period, which seems to point toward the possibility that the Irish may have earned their reputation for insolence, disobedience, and the evasion of work.

So who were these Irish servants who were so feared and despised by their new masters? Irish servants on the island during this period were largely Roman Catholic, Irish Gaelic–speaking (English was used almost exclusively in Ireland by the "New English" settlers, and was by no means the *lingua franca* in the Ireland of the time) men, women, and children who had lived through at least one Irish rebellion and violent English suppression of that rebellion. If voluntary indentures, they had come from conditions of extreme poverty and based their decision upon the information of merchants and brokers who were often less than completely forthcoming about the terms and nature of their servitude. If they were involuntary indentures, then they were likely political prisoners or prisoners of war, petty thieves, victims of kidnappers, or simply defenseless poor forcibly transported (for their own good, of course). In sum, they neither spoke the same language nor practiced the same religion as the English planters who owned their contracts, and more often than not understood themselves to be enemies of the English in a political struggle that had been ongoing for generations.

Thus it is no surprise that, while the Irish had a reputation among the English for rebelliousness prior to their arrival in Barbados, their actions on that island only enhanced that reputation. What is more important for my own purposes, these early Irish servants seemed perfectly willing to throw their rebellious lot in with enslaved Africans. There was enough evidence of black and Irish cooperation by 1661 to warrant its explicit mention in the servant code drafted that year. There are, in fact, recorded examples of Irish and black cooperation in the 1650s (Beckles 2000, 232), including mention of "Irish servants and Negroes out in rebellion" by the Barbados Council in 1655 (Handler 1982, 9; Beckles 1989, 100–1). A 1657 clash between the militia and one band of combined Irish servants and black slaves ended with the death of twelve militiamen and thirty runaways, with the capture of twenty more runaways, six of whom were Irish (O'Callaghan 2000, 124). The Barbadian planters were also surely worried by the cooperation between Irish servants, black slaves, and the French invaders on the island of St. Kitts in 1666 (Beckles 1898, 107–8), and further collaboration between the Irish and the French on Montserrat in 1667. In 1686 a planned slave revolt was discovered before it could be brought to fruition that involved the cooperation of Irish servants (Beckles 2000, 233–34; Beckles 1989, 111), and a planned, but thwarted, 1692 rebellion likewise was discovered to rely in part on Irish cooperation (Beckles 1989, 112; Beckles 2000, 234; Handler 1982, 26–7).

The scope and significance of this Irish cooperation with black slaves, it must be pointed out, is a matter of contention. Beckles himself seems to have changed his view on this between his earlier work (1989) and more recent writings on the topic (2000). In his earlier work, he describes combined Irish and black actual or at least planned rebellions in 1665, 1686, and 1692 (1989, 100–1, 111, and 112), cooperation between Irish and black slaves with the French against the English on St. Kitts in 1689 (107), and arrest of

Irish servants on Barbados for assisting runaway slaves (108). However, in his more recent work, Beckles takes the following position:

> What worried masters in Barbados, above all, was Irish involvement in slave revolts. Fear outran fact in this regard: no certain evidence exists that servants or freemen ever attempted to participate in a large-scale violent uprising of slaves. The reality was that the Irish, as whites, benefited, though marginally, from black slavery, and the slaves knew it. (Beckles 2000, 233)

So far as it goes, this statement is surely true. Fear may very well have outrun fact. There is indeed a dearth of evidence regarding such cooperation; Irish servants surely did benefit from their whiteness, and the slaves were doubtless aware of this fact. Throughout his more recent work, Beckles suggests that the colonial authority's concern about Irish and black cooperation was largely a manifestation of paranoia, and that the references to such acts of alliance were exaggerated in the official record. Of course, the lack of hard evidence one way or the other leaves this question subject to interpretation in both directions. Neither the fact of the Irish servants' benefit by virtue of their whiteness, nor the slaves' awareness of this benefit, nor the ultimate scarcity of evidence lead to the definite conclusion that the accounts of cooperation between Irish servants and African slaves were overblown. What evidence we have comes from testimony and interrogations following thwarted rebellions, along with statements and proclamations of Barbadian civil and military authorities. It seems unlikely that the implication of Irish servants by captured slaves in their acts of rebellion were made up out of whole cloth, and while preexisting anti-Irish sentiment among the plantocracy, along with actual acts of resistance on the island, might explain their fear of Irish rebellion, it does not, on its own, explain the recurring planters' nightmare of Irish and black cooperation. The planters seemed convinced that this was a real possibility, and again, it seems more likely that there was some evidence in support of this fear rather than to assume that the planters were simply succumbing to paranoia. Surely the St. Kitts rebellion alone should suffice to demonstrate the plausibility of this fear.

In any event, Beckles's point about lack of evidence is well-taken, and every effort should be made to avoid fanciful interpretations of idyllic cooperation between Irish servants and enslaved Africans. It is not my intention to suggest that the Irish servants, immediately upon their arrival in Barbados, set about plotting with their enslaved black brothers and sisters to overthrow the tyranny of the English plantocracy and establish a racially egalitarian utopia. Surely the fact of the matter was much more complicated than either this idealized interracial collaboration or the reduction of the planters' fears to sheer paranoia. What is undeniable, given what historical evidence remains available, is that the colonial authorities were indeed convinced of the looming threat of Irish and black cooperation against them and were taking great pains to prevent or punish such cooperation, and that there were real and documented cases of cooperation, though perhaps not in as great a number as one might like or hope.

The situation of the Irish in Barbados is complicated from start to finish. Differences between Celtic, "Old English," and "New English" Irish populations, differences in wealth, in language, and especially in religion all helped to make a neat and precise sense of the Irish experience in the Caribbean impossible. Indeed, Jenny Shaw's work makes clear that the Irish experience in the British Caribbean was quite varied, including cases like that of Cornelius Bryan, whose position in Barbados went from being flogged for speaking ill of the English to eventually owning several slaves (Shaw 2009, 64–65, 189–93). Over time, according to Shaw, a sense of an "Irish Elite" developed that enabled the British Planters to begin to sort out the "right sorts of Irish" from the larger (and threatening) rabble (Shaw 2009, 236–38). She ends her discussion by making an observation that is highly relevant to the direction my own investigation has been taking:

> It was only after English authorities and elite Irish Catholics began to work together to minimize the importance of their religious differences that island societies found themselves in a space where new ways of thinking about difference had been forged. Suddenly the means by which Irish Catholics [sic] servants and poor laborers and enslaved Africans had circumvented English notions of categories of difference through their shared labor, living conditions and common religious practices—were shattered. (Shaw 2009, 286)

What this passage points toward is the way in which notions of difference come to be interpreted in different ways over time, such that what is salient at one point may become all but trivial at another and vice versa. Equally important, Shaw's work shows the way in which this developmental process of the interpretation and assignation of difference is a matter of negotiation and contestation among numerous interested parties. Any truly adequate account of race in this context, therefore, must keep the complexity and ambiguity that results from these processes of negotiation and contestation firmly at the forefront.

RACIAL ALCHEMY IN THE COLONIAL CARIBBEAN

In 1697, just five years after a planned slave rebellion called upon "four or five Irish men" to bring the guards of the garrison's magazine to a state of drunkenness so that the rebelling slaves could seize it (Handler 1982, 26), the Colonial Office in England offered to ship Irish servants to Barbados, but in response, the council wrote the following: "[W]e desire no Irish rebels may be sent to us; for we want not laborers *of that color* to work for us" (Beckles 2000, 236; italics added). This statement brings to the foreground the ambiguous racial status of the Irish, at least from the perspective of the English, throughout the seventeenth century. What color were the Irish, that the council should reject their labor? Since Scottish and Welsh servants were very much desired by these same planters, the Irish must have been considered of a *different* color from them, somehow. This surely must strike the contemporary reader, who is likely to understand all three groups as sharing the racial status of white, and the common ethnic appellation Celt, as begging explanation. What *was* the racial status of the Irish in Barbados at this time, such that the ruling English elites could see them as so fundamentally different not only from the English but also from the Scottish and Welsh?

If one follows the pattern of argument in the new abolitionist literature discussed in chapter 1, then the answer to this question would go something like the following. Irish indentured servants arrived in the Caribbean as nonwhites, or as inbetween people, at the very historical moment when the modern concept of race was just beginning to take the form that we have inherited in the twenty-first-century United States. Over time, the Irish in the Caribbean either left for the Americas, where they began the racial transformation detailed by the new abolitionists, or remained where they were and *became* white as they increasingly came to understand their interests as tied more closely with the English planters over and against the enslaved Africans.

Part of the reason this account is compelling is because of the reduction of racial membership to a particular political orientation (affirmation of white supremacy). In this way, however, the approach assumes an ontological position I wish to call into question. Appealing though the reduction of racial membership to such explicit political commitment may be both psychologically and politically, are we really entitled to the ontological picture that undergirds such a move? The problem is not only that this analysis makes such a suspicious ontological claim, but that because of this underlying ontology, it oversimplifies the historical analysis of the concept of race itself, treating it as appearing on the scene only with the advent of modernity. Interrogating this historical narrative of the creation of race in the crucible of European modernity will go a long way toward illuminating why such ontological presuppositions are suspect.

Mervyn Alleyne makes a compelling case that, contrary to those who would argue that the modern concept of race came into being with the birth of European colonial projects in the sixteenth century, the idea of racial or color difference had existed well before that historical moment (Alleyne 2002, 32–64). Margaret Greer, Walter Mignolo, and Maureen Quilligan likewise argue that the medieval record makes a strong case for a decidedly *racial* notion of human differentiation well prior to the modern era (Greer et al. 2007, 1–24). Shaye Cohen's excellent discussion of the various understandings of Jewishness in the ancient world adds further support to the notion of a premodern racial landscape (Cohen 1999, 69–106). David Nirenberg argues that part of the motivation for thinking of race as an exclusively modern invention is that it "erects a historical *cordon sanitaire* around an ideology that has come to stand for all that is evil in western Europe" (Nirenberg 2007, 73). What is more, he points out how the evidence for the *lack* of a premodern concept of race—the absence of a biological ground—would equally rule out the possibility of a modern racial concept. He states:

> What does it mean to say that although a premodern ideology was expressed in biological terms, it was not racial because the differences it reinforced were not really biological? This could be said of any racial ideology. [. . .] If this lack of congruence does not suffice to make modern racist ideologies less 'racial', then it cannot suffice to excuse premodern discriminations from the charge. (74)

Premodern view of race

Nirenberg's point is that there is a tendency to oversimplify the modern concept of race, and then demonstrate that such a concept could not have existed prior to the modern era. But this rhetorical move both ignores the way in which race, as a concept, has continued to develop and change over time, and assumes a strict boundary between biology and culture that must itself be called into question.

Alleyne, for example, in no way argues that conceptions of the racial landscape, even if their pedigree extends beyond the colonial period into the ancient world, have remained static. In his view, "The plantation economy was therefore very important in setting the particular pattern of racism, but the *basic foundation* already existed" (Alleyne 2002, 64; italics added). This premodern racial concept, or, if one prefers, *protorace,* has been constantly evolving until it did eventually arrive at its modern and contemporary articulations. Of course, as I have been arguing, even this modern articulation is fraught with ambiguity. What is more, Nirenberg points out that concepts about human populations, like *raza* and *linaje*, that were decidedly linked to notions of genealogy and animal husbandry, were at the same time understood as culturally expressed and grounded (Nirenberg 2007, 77–82). Converted Jews in Iberia, for example, were in this way understood as a *raza* distinct from the Christians, and this racial (protoracial) aspect would make itself known through behavior, but the meaning of that behavior was made intelligible by appeal to genealogy. Again, I have already discussed the way in which the link between culture and biology was present even in twentieth-century concepts of race, which shows that these premodern discussions were different in degree, but not in kind, from their modern descendants.   *Jew as race*

There is a sense in which the view that race appears sometime during the seventeenth century is correct, insofar as a particular understanding of the notion began to be articulated and put to use during that historical moment (cf. O'Flaherty and Shapir 2007). But when the notion of a static and fixed concept of race is abandoned, this can only ever be a part of the picture. Given the ever-changing and often ambiguous understanding of race in the modern era, one can trace a lineage that well precedes the modern era. To be sure, the ways people talked about human variation in the premodern world was different than in the modern world, but they were also importantly similar. Once again, Nirenberg makes this point very clearly:

I am not making these admittedly general criticisms in order to claim that race did exist in the Middle Ages, or that medieval people were racist. Such statements would be reductive and misleading, obscuring more than they reveal. But the same is true of the opposite, far more common assertion. [. . .] In other words, the practice of defining race reductively for the purpose of summarily dismissing it from the premodern has effectively short-circuited the very processes of comparison and analogy upon which any argument about the relationship of past and present forms of discrimination must depend. (2007, 74)

This move to dismiss the very possibility of a premodern notion of race, in other words, is an oversimplification that ultimately rules out the very possibility of truly understanding the emergence of the modern concept of race. Nirenberg's point about the function of analogy is particularly astute: comparison and analogy require *some* difference, along with some similarity, in order to function at all.[6] My point here is not to claim that a medieval or ancient scholar and an enlightenment scholar meant exactly the same thing when they used concepts or terms we might broadly understand as racial. But nor were they completely distinct. The development of the modern concept of race is more a matter of the evolution and alteration of preexisting terms and concepts rather than the creation, *ex nihil*, of an utterly new category of being. Since the standard dismissal of a premodern notion of race assumes a static and fixed understanding of the meaning of such a term, my rejection of this move shifts to an emphasis on a more dynamic and ambiguous understanding of what race means and how that meaning relates to past (and future) meanings.

To return to my example, the colonial Caribbean from the sixteenth through nineteenth centuries experienced what might now be referred to as a robust period of globalization. Not only did sugar production link it economically to Europe and North America, but the slave trade linked it to Africa, and the later trade in (East) Indian servants, as well as agricultural products (such as the ubiquitous breadfruit), linked it to Asia and the South Pacific. On Barbados alone, one might find indigenous people from North and South America, Sephardic Jews, English, Scottish, Welsh, Irish, French, Dutch, and East Indian freedmen and servants, along with slaves from numerous West African peoples. To complicate matters further, by the eighteenth century, the distinction between *creole* white Barbadians (as opposed to those born in Europe) and creole black enslaved Barbadians (as opposed to those born in Africa) became an increasingly salient identity (Greene 1987). In the French, Spanish, Portuguese, and Dutch Caribbean one would find different, though equally diverse, populations. Thus, on any given Caribbean island, one would find "old world" allegiances struggling with local interests and identities, rigid racial, sexual, and economic hierarchies struggling with efforts to forge a unique colonial (*creole*) identity, and all while different European powers promiscuously declare war and peace in their efforts to secure regional military and economic hegemony.

As all of these peoples, with their respective cultures and histories, converged in the so-called New World they brought with them differing understandings of human difference, and more importantly, of the significance and meaning of various forms of difference. Clan, nation, religion, language, and color all had to be given new meaning in a new context. The old rules for what mattered had to be renegotiated. Whether one was Igbo or Akan, or from Cork or Galway, suddenly didn't matter in the way it may have before (which is not to say it was made utterly irrelevant). The notion that there are differences (and similarities) based on skin tone was not new, and as the significant markers of identity from the old country became less important, the notion of (proto)racial difference gained salience, but was not created out of the conceptual ether. Race was not invented out of scratch in order to facilitate the economic exploitation of the Caribbean and the domination of those designated as nonwhite. The processes of colonization generated conditions in which the meaning and significance of racial difference could be renegotiated and reinscribed. To be sure, there were in some cases rather seismic shifts in the meaning of these concepts and categories, and it would be a grievous error to think that the concept of race that emerged in the nineteenth and early twentieth centuries was identical to the notions of racial difference in the ancient and medieval worlds. But the fact that they are not identical does not mean that there was no such thing as race before the sixteenth century, unless, as I have tried to show, one presumes that there is one and only one understanding of what race might be.

Given the specifics of my example, the new abolitionist ontology explored in the previous chapter would hold that the Irish were not *truly* white until they openly sided with the English plantocracy against the nonwhite slaves. This is because it would only be at that moment that the Irish could be said to have openly affirmed white supremacy as a political project, and whiteness is neither more nor less than the affirmation of white supremacy, with the subsequent conferral of some, if not all, of the political benefits of whiteness. And so Noel Ignatiev will describe how the Irish *became* white in the nineteenth-century United States through a process of taking political action against black interests, and thus earning white status through their promotion of a white supremacist political agenda. But I have argued that this account is inadequate. There is some evidence that the English did not fully consider the Irish to be white, such as the above-mentioned reference to the color of Irish laborers, but there is also evidence to suggest that they were indeed viewed as white, including the dubious but widespread discussion at the time of "white slaves" and "white slavery" (Beckles 2000, 230; Beckles 1989, 52–53; O'Callaghan 2000, 94–96), and the explicit use of Irish indentures to boost the *white* population of British colonies in the Caribbean for purposes of defense.[7] The association of slavery with Irish servitude is particularly telling, as in this statement from a minister of parliament during a debate on the topic in 1659, who "pointed out that, if such conditions were allowed to prevail 'our lives will be cheap as those of Negroes . . . I would have you consider the trade of buying and selling men'" (O'Callaghan 2000, 96). This brief statement at once suggests that whites were being treated as slaves, but that slavery is really only proper for Negroes, and that Negroes, since they are fit for slavery, are clearly not men. If the Irish are white, and therefore men, then they are not fit for slavery, even if this particular minister of parliament thought that they were being so treated. It seems, in short, that the Irish during this period and in this place occupied a highly ambiguous place in the racial landscape of the time.

One troubling aspect of the abolitionist position on racial ontology is that it seems to grant absolute hegemony to the perspective of the ruling elite, whoever they may be in a given context. If the dominant Anglo population in Philadelphia decides that the Irish are white, then they *become* white, and if the British landowners in Barbados decide that the Irish are not fully white, then they are not. While it is certain that a great deal of discursive power is wielded by such elites, this view completely elides the extent to which the meanings of such important political categories are in fact a product of an implicit and explicit dialog between multiple parties with often competing interests within a given polity, which is itself struggling to articulate its identity. The question, in other words, is not just whether the

how white viewed by others

British planters viewed the Irish as white, but whether the Irish viewed *themselves* as white, and how the racial status of the Irish was understood by the black population of Barbados. Equally, if not more importantly, we must ask how these various populations understood the meaning and significance of whiteness. It isn't, in other words, simply a question of whether the Irish understood themselves to be white, but what they took that to mean. To deny the importance of these nondominant perspectives is to effectively deny those populations any agency at all within the political field, and to assume that the elites wield absolute authority in the assigning of meaning to such important and complicated issues. In other words, the account in which the Irish *become* white takes the meaning of whiteness itself to be settled, fixed, and given, dependent entirely upon the understanding of the term employed by the dominant racial elites. What I wish to emphasize, as opposed to accounts of race steeped in the politics of purity, is the way in which racial categories have always been, and continue to be dynamic, ambiguous, contentious, and indeterminate, despite their pretensions to the contrary.

On the surface, at least, the new abolitionist texts all stress the fundamental ambiguity surrounding the categories of race. All of this messiness, indeterminacy, and ambiguity, however, is trumped at the end of the day by their larger narrative of *becoming* white. That is, even as Roediger's later work describes early twentieth century Italian, Hungarian, and Greek immigrants as occupying a space of racial "inbetweenness," they are ultimately "working toward whiteness," and their "inbetween" status serves only as a temporary placeholder on the way to pure white status. The same is true for Ignatiev's nineteenth-century Irish immigrants, who eventually "become" white, and Jacobson's nineteenth-century Italian, Irish, and Jewish immigrants, who come to fully occupy the emerging Caucasian category. Whiteness itself remains, therefore, an ontologically *pure* category—one either is or is not white. Those nonwhites may include Roediger's "inbetweens" and those on the way to whiteness, but insofar as such groups have not yet arrived, they remain nonwhite in certain significant aspects, until such time as they finally become white unambiguously. The examples of these earlier immigrant groups, therefore, serve as the exceptions that prove the rule—the ambiguity of their status stood as a challenge to the racial hierarchy that *had* to be overcome one way or the other.

In other words, there is a kind of gravitational pull toward pure racial categories, such that the status of these groups simply *had*, ultimately, to be settled in a way that purged them of their racially ambiguous status. The new abolitionist texts are indeed testaments to the contingency and ambiguity of race, to be sure, but in their appeal to becoming white, they are also accounts of racial purity. Not only do they describe the political processes whereby the purity of racial categories and groups was described, reinscribed, maintained, and enforced, but they also in their own narrative of *becoming* white engage in a process of maintaining the normative purity of whiteness. Ultimately, by means of their calls for abolition, they are accepting the account of whiteness *as pure*, which in turn drives their historical narrative of racial ambiguity as a kind of threat which must be settled one way or the other. Such threats to purity can be addressed either by purging the race of those who are racially ambiguous (they are *not* white), or by purging those on the margins of that ambiguity itself (they have *become* white). In either event, whiteness stands as an all-or-nothing category that one either occupies or does not, and those who are "working toward whiteness" are clearly not there yet. The concept itself, therefore, remains static, even if there is some fluidity in the way that particular groups or individuals are sorted by those categories.

At this point I can begin to account for what I mean by the politics of purity in this context. The norm toward which racial categories (and especially, but by no means exclusively, whiteness) aspire is one of purity. Whiteness, as a category, demands clear boundaries and distinctions, and when those boundaries and distinctions become fuzzy or indeterminate, something is bound to give way. Either the boundary will shift or the challenge to that boundary will be removed, or at least redescribed in a way that is no longer threatening to the underlying purity. Racial categories like whiteness, according to this logic, are pure, unambiguous, all-or-nothing categories. One either is or is not a member of a given race. Significantly, the categories of mixed, biracial, or mestizo also function in this way—part of the point of the politics of purity is that one cannot occupy multiple racial categories simultaneously. If it appears that someone does, then a new category is invented, which the formerly ambiguous or multiply-raced individuals now *purely* inhabit. In other words, the politics of purity will not allow individuals to be white *and* black, or Asian *and* white, and so such individuals come to occupy a new, yet still discrete and exclusive (pure), racial category. If one is not purely of any particular preexisting racial category, then one must

racial purity

generate a new category, which he or she can then purely occupy. In this way, the politics of purity overrides any actual ambiguity—reworking both individuals (you were ambiguous, but now you are white) and the racial taxonomy itself (you were ambiguous, but now you are mixed race) until the categories themselves are discrete and pure, and individuals are purely of one and only one category.

The modus operandi of the politics of purity is thus such that any threat to the purity of a category must ultimately be overcome, or it threatens the entire system of categories itself. Indeed, this is at the heart of the eliminativist and abolitionist use of these historical moments of ambiguity—since these moments call into question the *purity* of the racial concepts, they call into question the *reality* of those concepts altogether. If this categorical purity is called into question successfully, then that shows that the category is, and has always been, ultimately empty, illusory, or otherwise unreal. The politics of purity operates, therefore, not only in naïve realist accounts of race but also in the eliminativist claim regarding the nonexistence of racial categories altogether. The metaphysical presumption is that *if* race exists, it must be pure—it must consist of discrete, exclusive, and unambiguous categories admitting of necessary and sufficient conditions of individual membership—and if it is not pure in this way, then it simply must not exist. Philosophical arguments for the elimination of race tend to follow exactly this pattern: describe the logic of racial reality as demanding exactly this sort of conceptual purity, demonstrate (through appeal to biology or history) that such conceptual purity is impossible, and conclude that race cannot be real. In any event, the ultimate conceptual purity of race as the norm is maintained. Naïve realism and eliminativism are thus two sides of the same ontological coin. Both points of view insist that any racial reality worth taking seriously must obey the politics of purity, and the only disagreement is whether any actual set of racial categories satisfies that criterion.

At stake in my own historical example then, is not simply a question of whether the Irish servant population was or was not white (as if that could be answered with a simple yes or no), but rather the meaning and significance of whiteness (and blackness) within a given polity at a given time. To be sure, the abolitionists are correct that there is a dominant meaning to whiteness, and it has been, and continues to be, a decidedly white supremacist one. What I wish to raise at this point is the question of why they should take the dominant view to be definitive, silencing all of the contending voices within the relevant context. Clearly, there is a presumption on their part that racial categories, including especially whiteness, can really only mean one thing, and that is white supremacist domination, which is why, of course, racial justice demands its abolition in the first place, and why white people who resist white supremacy are *race traitors*. The purity of the meaning of whiteness, in other words, is taken for granted, such that if whiteness does not mean *that*, then it does not mean *anything*, and you cannot be both antiracist and white at the same time.

Aside from the ontological assumptions regarding race that I have been pointing toward in the abolitionist literature, there is also an important teleological assumption at work. There is, in other words, the presumption of discrete and fixed racial categories, paired with an assumption that the *telos* of racial membership is directed toward whiteness (understood ontologically in the way I have been describing). In the context of immigration history, for example, the aim of full membership in the polity for certain ethnic groups is understood to be *whiteness*. Success, understood as citizenship, civil rights, or even liberation, will amount to the achievement of whiteness. Irish liberation—the cessation of Irish marginalization and mistreatment in the U.S. polity—is the achievement of full whiteness. But black liberation (think of the larger civil rights movement from Reconstruction to the present) can never equal whiteness. This is significant to two reasons. The first has to do with the difference between those groups who can have a *telos* directed toward whiteness and those that cannot. The only way to make sense of that distinction is through appeal to an ambiguous, layered, and complex understanding of *race*, such that it is possible to think about the path that *white* ethnics take toward *whiteness*—such individuals and groups are thus at one and the same time both white and not white. I will explore this point in more detail in chapters 3 and 4. The second reason in which this teleological point is significant is because it points toward a way of understanding the phenomenon of *race treason*. Those who Ignatiev might refer to as "race traitors" might be better understood as rejecting this underlying *telos* of racial membership rather than rejecting their racial membership *as such*.

To illustrate this point, we might ask ourselves whether those Irish indentures who ran away with enslaved Africans "into ye thickets and thereabouts" (as a discussion in the Barbados Assembly put it) would have considered themselves white? Would the enslaved Africans who enlisted Irish servants to aid them in planned rebellions in 1686 and 1692 have considered them white? Or were these really acts of treason to whiteness? They were, at least in part, and likely only implicitly, rejections of white supremacy, but to presume that this means they are also rejections of whiteness is to assume this very static and purified notion of the meaning of racial terms. My case against this view begins with the relatively simple claim that things are far more complicated than this interpretation of events allows.

What my historical example shows is that, on the one hand, the English plantocracy was itself rather confused about the racial status of the Irish. The Celtic race was understood to be distinct from the English race, to be sure, but whether it counted as white, and whether their shared status as whites counted for much politically, was still very much up for grabs. The Irish themselves, meanwhile, were trying to carve out their niche in their new home as distinct from their English, Welsh, Scottish, and African neighbors, and as I have suggested, there is a strong sense in which, at least at first, it was more important for them to emphasize their differences from the English than it was to establish their consanguinity with the planters over and against the African population. The enslaved Africans, in the meantime, were looking for allies, and seemed to find little contradiction in the pale-skinned Irish acting in concert with them against the English. If we abandon the politics of purity, there is no inconsistency in saying that these Irish servants were white people who worked against white supremacy (even if that was not their explicit intention) in that place and at that time. What we have, in other words, are several different and competing understandings of the meaning and significance of whiteness vying for domination within the context of seventeenth-century Barbados. The story is not one of Irish servants alchemically transmuting from nonwhite to white, as if the meaning of whiteness were a fixed point, but rather it is one of the Irish entering this ongoing contestation of the meaning of whiteness—simultaneously shaping and being shaped by that unfolding *process* of contestation. They were not *failing* to be white but rather demonstrating a different *way* to be white. They were participating, as people with a particular history and appearance (morphology in the parlance of philosophical discussions of the ontology of race), in an ongoing and extremely complex contestation over the meaning and significance of that history and that kind of appearance (and even whether it was a distinct *kind* at all).

We must understand racial membership, therefore, not as a static and

race = process of negotiation of meaning

pure category of identity, but as an ongoing context for and process of nego- tiating who *we* are (both as individuals and as groups) and how we relate to each other. In the next chapter, I will account for this in part as an emphasis on becoming over being. Furthermore, because races, like all social categories, are historical, and this history conditions their meaning and significance, their reality is manifest both politically (in how our social structures and or- ganizations take shape and interact) and individually (in how we understand ourselves and our place in the world). But, and this is the crucial point for my approach, the histories themselves are histories of the contestation of meaning, and fraught with ambiguity, such that we participate in the process of shaping the meaning of race not only in the here and now but also its meaning and significance historically. In short, we shape the history of race, as a history of meaning, by the understandings that we bring to bear on it from the present. The new abolitionist ontology insists, therefore, not only on purity for racial categories themselves (one either is or is not white) but also employs a politics of purity in its approach to history. That is, it treats the history of whiteness *purely* as a history of white supremacy, and any in- dividuals or groups who break politically with white supremacy thereby demonstrate their nonwhiteness (they become "race traitors"). What I am calling for is a rejection of purity in both of these senses. Racial memberships and the identities that go along with them never really function as all-or- nothing categories (though they certainly pretend to do exactly that), and to ignore white struggles against white supremacy is as much of an inadequate interpretation of history as it would be to ignore white affirmation of white supremacy. And this is true for all racial categories and identities. They are all fraught with ambiguity, indeterminacy, and even outright contradiction, and part of my claim is that the damage is done in large part by trying to conceive of them as purified of that ambiguity and contradiction, for it is that insistence on *purity* that links racial categories to oppressive norms.

So were the Irish in seventeenth-century Barbados white? My answer to this question requires me first to point out that the real question is not simply whether they were or were not white but rather *in what way* they were or were not white. And the answer must in any case be yes *and* no. They were white in the strictest sense in that they were able to raise the white population of the colony, and were eligible to take up the *telos* of be- coming fully white, both of which facts distinguished them importantly from the African population. Yet they were not white to the extent that they were seen as representing a "different color" from the English in such a way that their very genealogy rendered them morally and politically suspect. Their *way* of being white was also ambiguous in that they were acting, as embodied agents bearing the markers of generations of struggle with the English, in a context in which the meaning and significance of racial categories was in a robust state of contestation. Their actions, therefore, were infused with this underlying ambiguity, in that they were and were not white, and stood as contributions to this ongoing negotiation of the meaning and significance of whiteness.

What this means, exactly, will only become clear after I have spelled out in more detail my understanding of racial ontology in the next two chapters. In the end, my point is that the question is misguided as it is typically understood. There is no yes or no answer to the question of the racial status of the Irish in seventeenth-century Barbados, or of any particular group or individual in any particular time and place. The dynamic and ambiguous concept of race that I will argue for rules out any such simple and complete answers to this sort of question. Clearly, the brief sketch of the direction I wish to take offered in this chapter must raise more questions than it answers. In the next two chapters, my task will be to offer a more complete account of the ontology of race that goes beyond the politics of purity, and places the moment of contestation and negotiation front and center in our understanding both of what race is and how it operates in our lives.

Same for racist?

3

Race and Biology:
Scientific Reason and the Politics of Purity

In order to articulate an account of racial ontology that transcends the politics of purity, it is necessary to spell out in more detail exactly what the politics of purity is and how it operates. Broadly understood, the politics of purity holds that the norm toward which racial categories and racialized individuals ought to strive, or are even driven, is one of purity. The claim is not that the categories and individuals actually are pure but only that they ideally should be—it is in this way that it is the politics, and not the *reality*, of purity. The normative presumption, in other words, is that any given individual ought to clearly and unambiguously be a member of one and only one racial category, and that each category will itself be discrete and self-contained. Thus, the racial categories are themselves pure (or at least striving to be), and each individual is purely of a category (or at least ought to be).

As a political phenomenon, the politics of purity operates by addressing failures to achieve this ideal state of purity. When ambiguity is found within a category, or an individual (or group) appears who seems not to fit neatly into any particular category, then the politics of purity works to eliminate that ambiguity either by redrawing or refining the borders of the categories, or by redescribing the individual. I have already discussed in some detail larger historical examples of this, having to do with racially ambiguous or "inbetween" peoples, and the forces brought to bear in eliminating that ambiguity. However, there are far more common and mundane examples that should be familiar to most anyone who has spent a significant amount of time in North America or Europe (among many other places), such as the myriad ways in which individuals with multiracial ancestry are subtly (and often not-so-subtly) urged to identify with one and only one aspect of their racial background. Or the various discourses of racial authenticity, which view manifestations of racial identity that diverge from whatever is taken to be the "real" racial identity as moral violations. As I suggested in the previous chapter, even outright rejections of race, such as racial eliminativism and the new abolitionism, participate in the politics of purity insofar as it is precisely *because* the categories and individuals cannot live up to this standard of purity that they should be eliminated or abolished. For the eliminativist, in other words, the norm is still one of purity, but since race cannot realize that norm, it needs to be abandoned altogether as a concept.

This chapter begins with the articulation of a more in-depth account of the politics of purity. I then draw upon the Husserlian phenomenological tradition to further elaborate the politics of purity and use this to analyze critically the arguments against the biological reality of race. Finally, I appeal to this discussion of the biology of race to elaborate the failures of the politics of purity to even understand what the important questions about race and biology are. Those important questions will in turn be taken up in chapter 4.

THE POLITICS OF PURITY

The argument for the abolition of whiteness, like philosophical arguments for eliminativism, is situated in a rejection of biological realism about race. Race and races are not logically or biologically necessary but rather have been contingently and historically imposed, constructed, invented, or fabricated by human beings within particular historical contexts for particular political ends. For Roediger and Ignatiev that particular end was white supremacy—the project of establishing and enforcing the domination of whites over and against nonwhites. Races only came into being, in other words, because of the particular way in which the European encounter with Africa, Asia, and the Americas took shape. This being the case, there is no way to preserve any meaningful notion of racial whiteness, or any other racial category for that matter, without at least implicitly endorsing or preserving white supremacy. Thus, the only viable way to end white supremacy is to end or abolish the white race (or rather, ending white supremacy will necessarily entail the end of the white race). Put yet another way, what it means to be white (or any other specific race) is nothing more nor less than occupying a certain political position within a hierarchy shaped by white supremacist history and current practices. Any assertion of white identity, therefore, is the same thing as an assertion of superiority vis-à-vis nonwhites because that superiority, or at least the presumption thereof, is what *makes* one white. Thus, there is no way to be white that avoids this linkage to domination and exploitation, and in a world devoid of white supremacy, there would be no white people. By the same token, what it means to be a member of a nonwhite racial group, such as black, is nothing more nor less than the occupation of a particular subordinate position within the racial hierarchy, and assertion of a black identity, therefore, is the same as the assertion of inferiority vis-à-vis whites because that particular position of inferiority is *all* that makes one black. Thus, while the new abolitionists focus on racial whiteness, their argument applies to all racial categories, and in this way leads to conclusions indistinguishable from eliminativism generally: a racially just future must be a raceless one.

So how does the politics of purity help us to understand this line of argumentation? Beginning with the conceptual level, the politics of purity demands that every racial category have clear boundaries along with distinct and unambiguous criteria for membership. Each category must thus be *pure* in that it describes or captures all and only members of that category. In philosophical circles, the task then typically becomes the sorting out of exactly what those criteria might be, and whether they are singly or jointly necessary or sufficient or both. Skin color, facial features, ancestry, genetic background, and even such more ephemeral features as culture and language have all been tested in the crucible of philosophical literature on race.[1] Criteria that fail to draw racial divisions clearly and distinctly are understood from the start as problematic. Once such problem criteria are encountered, effort must be made to demonstrate that their ambiguity can be explained away. If the ambiguity is persistent, that stands as evidence that the criterion in question is fundamentally unsuitable as a condition for racial membership. Ideally, the aim would be something like a mathematical set—just as "the set of all numbers divisible by nine" picks out all and only numbers divisible by nine, the category of black would pick out all and only individuals who share the necessary or sufficient or both conditions for blackness. Thus, insofar as the ambiguity and indeterminacy of the categories is taken to be a problem that must be overcome, the standard view of racial categories is shaped by a normative understanding of these categories as conceptually *pure*.[2]

Of course, one response to this problem of ambiguity in the categories is to reject them altogether. The ambiguity cannot be overcome, the argument goes, and this shows that the categories cannot be *real* in the ways necessary to legitimate their continued use. This is, as I have pointed out, exactly the argument of racial eliminativists. Because no set of criteria can be found that unambiguously demarcates racial boundaries and sets the conditions for individual membership in those categories, the categories themselves must be rejected. Here the norm of purity functions so as to rule out the legitimacy of the categories altogether. Since they do not function in the ways dictated by the politics of purity, racial categories must be rejected *in totum*. Thus, the norm of purity is preserved even for the eliminativist, insofar as it is the demonstration of the lack of conceptual purity that stands as the first line of evidence for the elimination of racial categories altogether.

What is important to realize at this point is that such arguments are predicated not only upon the failures of conceptual analysis but also upon appeals to the notion that race must be nonarbitrary. That is, we could easily set necessary and sufficient conditions for racial membership that are perfectly clear and unambiguous in their sorting of human populations, but they would not be properly *racial* categories because race is meant to refer to something in some important sense deeper than the arbitrary sorting of individuals—it should not be strictly nominal. We could, for example, let *white* just mean those whose melanin content is beneath some measurable quantity, but that would be in some significant sense arbitrary, since racial categories are meant to account for some underlying reality, not generate that reality out of whole cloth. In other words, that is not *really* what white means, insofar as such a definition of white would exclude people with relatively high melanin content who presently consider themselves, and are considered by (most) others, to be white, and would include plenty of non-white people with quite low melanin content. Or, to make the case even more clearly, we could designate racial categories based upon number of freckles on the left shoulder blade, or the length of the right pinky finger. Here again, such clear and distinct (pure) categories would be utterly disconnected from the meaning and history of racial concepts. Essentially, the point here is that racial categories aren't an end in themselves but are supposed to capture something meaningful and significant. Thus, while the lack of purity in our racial categories could, in principle, be corrected through the nominalistic generation and imposition of new and unambiguous criteria for membership, it is clear that the fundamental arbitrariness and ahistoricity of such criteria would pose a serious problem.

In short, it is not simply that the categories themselves must be pure but also that such categories must map onto some significant reality. Racial categories are not like social security numbers, to borrow an example from Charles Mills (Mills 1998, 42–44), imposed arbitrarily from the *outside*, but are rather supposed to be constitutive of and *internal* to individuals in some significant sense. They must, again with thanks to Mills, allow for the question "what race are you *really*?" to be a coherent one. It is thus not simply the categories in the abstract but the underlying *reality* or race, which the categories purport to describe that must be pure. We could, in other words, construct *artificially* pure categories with relative ease, but their artificiality would make them in some sense useless precisely because they fail to map onto, in the appropriate way, any real racial categories. Indeed, this is a significant aspect of the eliminativist and abolitionist argument: the categories that we do have are completely arbitrary and thus capture no reality we are bound to respect. The emergence here of the question of reality gets to the heart of the matter, for it points to the way in which the politics of purity is not simply about an analytic norm having to do with the construction and employment of categories, but is more fundamentally a claim about how reality itself must be structured at its most basic levels.

Recall that the eliminativist argument hinges upon two basic claims. First, the ontological claim that racial categories describe nothing *in the world*—they are illusory, or *merely* constructs. Second, there is the political claim that such categories have only functioned, and can only ever function, in pernicious ways. Given that race has no underlying reality to which we are beholden, and that it has wrought, and can only wreak, harm, it should be eliminated altogether. If one reinterprets the ontological claim along social constructivist lines, one finds that the ontological position is that race is not simply illusory or altogether nonexistent but rather a contingent historically constructed reality. But the political claim, that race serves the sole, or at least primary, function of legitimating processes of oppression and exploitation, and should therefore be eliminated or abolished, remains essentially the same.

The ultimate normative argument, therefore, is that race can and should be abolished, but as I pointed out in chapter 2, this cannot be solely because it is harmful. One cannot coherently advocate the abolition of something that is *real* in this sense—it would be like calling for the abolition of gravity based upon the belief that it has only ever caused us harm. Even if this latter claim is true, there is no point in calling for gravity's abolition. As I argued earlier, while it may ultimately be the harm caused by the category of race that justifies its elimination or abolition, it is the lack of relevant reality that makes this elimination possible at all. Races are thus not merely (and solely) pernicious morally and politically but also, even if one admits that they could be socially constructed, not *really* real. Implicit in such arguments is the claim that biology alone could provide the kind of reality to racial categories that would make the eliminativist or abolitionist projects impossible. The concept of race could only be real in this deepest sense, if it were biologically grounded. This is because, it is assumed, biology does in fact provide the kind of clear and distinct boundaries that are so necessary to the politics of purity. This shows how the politics of purity operates with regard to racial categories themselves. They must be pure if they are to be recognized as real in the ways that matter, and this is because the *kinds of reality* that matter are likewise pure. As I will argue below, this points toward a way in which the politics of purity informs our understanding of the nature and meaning of reality at the deepest levels, and not just with regards to racial ontology.

Of course, since racial categories are understood as ways of organizing human populations, in order for the categories to be pure, the individuals within them must also be pure. Returning to the analogy of mathematical sets, while integers can promiscuously occupy multiple sets simultaneously (for example, 18 is in the set *divisible by 9* and in the set of *even numbers less than 20* and in the set of *even numbers divisible by 3*, and so on), individual human beings do not seem to have this luxury, especially with regards to race. If a given racial category includes an individual who is not purely of that category, then it follows that there is some element of the category that is no longer pure. Purity, operating as a governing norm, therefore demands either that the category be purged of the impure individual, or redefined to unambiguously include the anomalous element. While this particular move

political — boundaries
math

can be clearly seen in the one-drop rule dominant in the United States, it is important to point out that even taxonomies that allow for categories of admixture preserve the purity of *those* categories and the individuals within them. Mulatto, mestizo, quadroon, and so on all become independent racial categories in their own right, and insofar as they are *not* white, or black, or indigenous, they stand as affirmations of racial purity even if their roots, so to speak, are found in mixture.

Let me make two points. The first is a reminder that I am describing the *politics*, and not the *reality* of purity. It is, it seems to me, a peculiar manifestation of the epistemic myopia of whiteness that renders the dominant racial discourse in the United States utterly blind to creolization. The reality is one of the creolization of human populations, to which the politics of purity has two basic responses. One strategy, dominant in the Caribbean, for example, and especially in the Spanish- and French-speaking islands, is to generate new categories which then continue to operate under norms of purity, while another, dominant in the United States, is to preserve a traditional set of racial categories which then exhibit increasingly asymmetrical standards for membership. In nineteenth-century Cuba, for example, there could exist a myriad of racial categories capturing all the various racial combinations of one's parents and grandparents. All of these were kinds of mixture, to be sure, but individual members occupied only their specific category, and not the categories of their parents, and vice versa. While in most (but not all) of the United States at the same time, any black ancestry at all was sufficient to render one "purely" black. The important commonality is that both strategies are disposed toward outcomes in which it is impossible for any given individual to occupy multiple categories simultaneously. One cannot be both *mulato* and *alburazado* in nineteenth-century Cuba (Gracia 2005, 89–90) any more than one can be both black *and* white in nineteenth-century Virginia. We can see the same operation taking place in the present-day United States, where *mixed race* is gradually coming to establish itself as its own discrete racial category that is definitely not white, but is also not black either.[3] Again, we have instances where individuals of ambiguous or mixed status represent *problems* that the politics of purity must overcome either by shifting the meaning of established categories, or generating new categories altogether.

The second important point is that while the norm for all racial categories in the abstract is one of purity, in practice the use (and abuse) of such categories is always in the service of *white* purity. What motivates the abolitionist call for the end of the white race is the quite accurate insight that whiteness has functioned, and continues to function, within a politics of purity, as at once a kind of universal human norm, and as a specific embodiment of the highest manifestation of human reason and virtue. It is, in other words, a specific and exclusionary moral, material, and aesthetic norm passing itself off as the universal truth of the human. Whiteness is thus pure not only as a category but also insofar as it describes the *purest* manifestation of the human—to be purely white is to be purely human, and to be less than white is to be less than human. Much of the political *practice* of white supremacy has been directed toward the maintenance of white purity in both of these senses (I will explore this point more in chapter 5). The ideal of whiteness as the most rarified instantiation of humanity is manifest in the efforts to purge or distort the record of nonwhite historical achievement, and in efforts to foster and support the portrayal of nonwhites as in important ways beneath the pinnacle of human endeavor.[4] At the same time, one need only think of the one-drop rule or antimiscegenation laws in the United States, both of which explicitly focus upon white purity, and are relatively indifferent to admixture among nonwhites. To be sure, more explicitly racist cultural practices have held *all* forms of racial mixture to be morally odious, but the highest levels of censure were reserved for the so-called pollution of the white race. In the United States, mixing with whites could formally earn fines and even imprisonment under antimiscegenation laws, and informally could lead to acts of vigilantism up to and all too often including lynching. Yet the mixing of different nonwhite groups might be frowned upon, but was not viewed as threatening in the same way. Meanwhile, nineteenth-century Cuba or present-day Brazil may allow for a great many racial categories in between black and white, yet it remains the case that white stands as a racially pure category at the pinnacle of social, cultural, and economic hierarchies throughout the Americas.

Thus, in protecting the purity and exclusivity of the white race, within this framework, one is protecting the virtue of humanity itself (at least, in its purest form). It is *because* the purity of the white race must be protected that it must be made illegal for whites and nonwhites to marry. The one-drop rule could function the way it did precisely because the purity of the black race was not valued in the same way as the purity of the white race: to be *purely* white demands that one have *only* white ancestry, but one is *purely* black (in the sense that one is *only* black, not black *and* white) simply by virtue of possessing some black ancestry. Of course, depending upon the time and the place, one could be octaroon, or mulatto, or mestizo, or biracial, or mixed race, but what is significant here is that each of these mixed categories are themselves pure and discrete, such that their members are purely of them in that they cannot be mestizo *and* white or mulatto *and* black, for example. Significantly, while the number and character of different nonwhite categories may vary from place to place and time to time, the norm of the purity of whiteness is all but universal. Whether in colonial Cuba, or present-day Lima or Boston, one simply *cannot* be white at the moment some nonwhite ancestry enters the picture, and this is because it is this vision of whiteness as the purest form of humanity itself that is at the heart of the politics of purity. It is because whiteness is understood as pure humanity that the purity of whiteness must be protected, and while it may be preferable that nonwhite categories also be pure, their purity is less politically or morally imperative because the admixture of already less valuable media does less harm than the dilution of what is understood to be of the highest value.

The politics of purity thus operates to norm not only racial categories themselves but also the individuals that occupy them, and, through its norming function, serves to cast racial whiteness as the most pure manifestation of the human. But there is yet a deeper level in which the basic understanding of human agency that informs the dominant view of race is organized around notions of purity. This can best be seen in the way in which racial categories are often understood to be intrinsically contrary to individual liberty. Not only is race precisely the sort of morally arbitrary characteristic that should be precluded from properly just Rawlsian deliberations about the basic structure of society, but it also constrains our liberty and imposes norms of behavior upon individuals. Racial identities must be rejected "if one chooses freedom" (Zack 1997, 102), for if one accepts a racialized identity, the argument goes, then one is affirming a self-concept that is artificial and externally generated, and in this way one is choosing to abdicate one's freedom. Ultimately, what is at stake in this line of argumentation is the nature of the self, and more specifically, what is *internal* to or constitutive of it.

Purity here operates on the level of the very distinction between what is internal and external to the self in a kind of Aristotelian fashion (Aristotle

1987, 387–90; Grimshaw 1988), but one that does not, ultimately, admit of degrees or ambiguity.[5] A given factor or motivation or cause in our decision-making process either is or is not free in the sense of arising from the self (internal) or arising outside of the self (external). If racial being is internal, then it is consistent with human freedom, and if it is not, then it is either irrelevant because it has no impact on our decision making, or it is contrary to freedom because it influences our decision making *from without*. There are, within this schema, really only two ways in which a behavioral cause can be understood as internal. It can either be something innate (built-in or hardwired), or it can be voluntarily and explicitly chosen. That is, I am acting freely when I am acting in accordance with my nature, or when I follow the rules, for example, of an organization I have voluntarily joined. This is in part why the question of the biological foundation of racial categories is so crucial within the politics of purity. If race can be proven to be biological in this way, then it becomes clearly (purely) *internal*—it is built into our makeup, constitutive of who we are, and thus behaviors, decisions, and identities that arise from our racial makeup can be understood as free. On the other hand, if race is not biological, and it is furthermore not the case that we can voluntarily choose our racial identity, then it must be an externally imposed influence or force, and as such is fundamentally contrary to liberty. Another way to think of this is in terms of necessity and contingency. A biological account of race would prove that racial aspects of our identity are necessary and inescapable. If such a case cannot be made, then it follows that race must be contingent, and if so, there must be some compelling reason *why* we would choose to affirm it. What is more, if it can be shown that racial categories were fabricated strictly for the nefarious purposes of racial exploitation, the case for their inherent illiberality is made even stronger. To *choose* to take up a racialized notion of identity (because it is contingent, and thus *could* be rejected) therefore becomes a *choice* to take up categories that are inherently harmful and oppressive.

The primary way in which racial categories, and the identities that tend to go with them, harm us is thus by *imposing* ways of being upon us that are not internal, inherent, necessary, or intrinsic. If races are by definition contrary to freedom because they limit or constrain our actions, it can only be because they are understood as significantly *external*. They are imposed from without. This imposition is bad enough in its own right, but given the historical trends of white supremacy, this is particularly harmful to nonwhites,

Kant

since they are always positioned as inferiors within white supremacist racial hierarchies. Once again, the driving norm is one of purity. The self must be *purified* of external and contingent factors that are involuntarily imposed, or, if voluntary, are inherently harmful. What is more, since racial categories are not biological, and therefore not real in the right sorts of ways, even if a case can be made that they are not inherently morally or politically harmful, insofar as they falsely represent reality, they are *epistemologically* harmful. Either way, they corrupt the purity of the self, demarcated by a clear and distinct boundary between the internal and the external, and must be purged from our psychic life.

Lastly, the politics of purity is also bound up with our thinking about the nature of similarity and difference. It presumes an understanding of similarity that will not tolerate difference, and an understanding of difference that will not permit similarity. The two categories, in other words, become utterly distinct and mutually exclusive—they are understood as pure. It is this underlying sense of similarity and difference that ultimately drives the norm of categorical purity with regards to race. If there are properties (necessary and sufficient conditions) that govern racial categories, then it must be the case that for the relevant properties, all and only members of the particular category will share them. In this way they are all *similar*, and those who are not members of the group are all *different*. And again, if no such distinguishing features can be found, this is taken as evidence that the categories are themselves illusory or meaningless. In other words, there is a conflation between the *similar* and the *same* that drives the politics of purity. Its underlying logic is such that there must be strict identity along some domain for all members of a given category. Thus, for the category *white*, there must be some shared property common (and identical) to all members of that category, such that for two given white individuals (S and P), there is some *identical* property *w* such that, relative to that property (and thus *qua* white people), S is *identical* to P with respect to *w*. Anyone lacking the relevant property or set of properties, is likewise *different* from and outside of that category, and so they need a category of their own. Similar debates in feminist theory surrounding the scope and meaning of the category *woman* illustrate this point equally well. Furthermore, this underlying manifestation of the politics of purity is what drives much of the development of mixed-race categories. An individual (or group of individuals) is found such that they cannot be *identical* in the appropriate ways to any of the currently extant categories, and in this way they are distinct from all of them and thus require either some new category (or set of categories), or the expansion or weakening of the boundaries of one or more of the existing categories. The former strategy was more common in Latin America, while the latter dominated racial practices in the United States (though this is slowly changing).

Thus we can see that the politics of purity operates in different but complementary ways on different levels. There is the insistence on clear, discrete, and exclusive categories of being, with the demand, explored and criticized at length by those theorizing mixed race identity, that one occupy one and only one category. Each category is thus pure, and each individual is purely of one category, or, if this proves untenable, then that only shows that races do not exist at all (and either way the norm of purity is maintained). If all cannot be identical, then they must all be different. On the more individual level, the politics of purity demands an account of identity that is purged of ambiguity and indeterminacy—one that is purely internal. Racial categories, understood in this pure sense, either exist—in which case they force individuals necessarily into monolithic and exclusionary categories of identity (because the categories themselves are pure, and the agent is purely *of* the category)—or they do not exist *at all*, and thus have no bearing whatsoever on individual identity or their bearing is in a strong sense voluntary (contingent) and ultimately misguided (if not outright immoral). Clearly, if this account of race and its function were accurate, then the eliminativists would be correct. Any genuine commitment to a racially just future would indeed demand the ultimate elimination of race altogether, since it is fundamentally inconsistent with human autonomy. Just as the politics of purity demands all-or-nothing organization of the racial world, it is at the same time subject to this binary, in that the lack of purity necessitates the complete rejection of the concept.

In calling into question the politics of purity, therefore, I will be raising objections to its function at all of these different levels, from the boundaries between categories to the relation of similarity and difference. As I suggested above, one of the lynchpins that holds these different levels together is the way in which the understanding of reality operates within the politics of purity broadly. This is made especially clear in the way in which both the eliminativist philosophers and the new abolitionist historians appeal to biology in the course of their articulation of the radical contingency of racial membership. I will therefore begin my critique of the ontology of race within the politics of purity by placing this understanding of the relation between reality and biology under careful scrutiny.

RACE, BIOLOGY, AND REALITY

In his essay "Phenomenology and the Crisis of Philosophy," Edmund Husserl offers a sustained critique of *naturalism*—the belief that the methodology of the natural sciences is the best (if not only) model for understanding all of reality, including "spiritual" or "humanistic" bodies of knowledge and experience [*Geisteswissenschaften*] (Husserl 1965, 152–54). Naturalism itself is a particular instantiation of positivism, which, in the Husserlian phenomenological tradition, is the insistence that knowledge claims ultimately have some mind-independent *ground*. In the absence of such a ground, there can be no truth at all, and we are left only with "text" or "play." This particular set of concerns can also be understood as a motivating project for Nietzsche, who understood the death of God as this absence of a positivistic grounding for truth and value, and saw a looming crisis in the nihilism that followed from that absence (Nietzsche 1967a, 35–39; Nietzsche 2001, 199; Schacht 1983, 344–49). The significant point, again, is that both naturalism and nihilism preserve a positivist norm—*if* there is any truth, it must be traced to some mind-independent, necessary ground, and if there is no such ground, then there is no truth.

What I am calling the politics of purity can thus be understood largely as a manifestation of positivism in this sense. I am focusing here on its function in the context of race, but I believe it can be fruitfully applied to other contexts as well, such as gender and sexuality.[6] In the racial context, however, the position is that *if* race has any reality we are bound to respect, it must have a biological foundation that admits of necessary and sufficient conditions for racial membership, and has clear and distinct boundaries between racial groups. If no biological property works in this way, then race must not exist at all. The underlying positivism can be found in the fact that race is assumed to be strictly biological or natural, and its status as a *human* phenomenon is left to moral and political critique that has no bearing on the question of its ontology.

Husserl's response to positivism is both to raise the radical question of methodology, and to emphasize the role of human agency in the *constitution* of the world *as meaningful*. First, the question of methodology calls upon us to critically address our assumptions about the very methods we employ in attempting to describe phenomena. We must avoid what Lewis Gordon has pointed out as the tendency toward "ontologizing one's discipline," which in this racial discussion takes the form of "*biologism*, where the biologist presumes the meaning of concepts to be embedded in the organism without an account of the social processes that make those meanings normative" (2006a, 33). To avoid this kind of biologism, we must critically assess *why* the common approaches to racial ontology take biology to be the final arbiter of racial reality, the consequences of that set of assumptions, and especially how biology is even understood within that context. Second, emphasizing the role of human agency invites us to bring to the foreground the sense in which the world of human experience is not simply a matter of inert objects (like races) arranged thus and so, but is always already saturated with *meaning*. It is through this practice of meaning-giving and meaning-interpreting that Husserl understands us to *constitute* the world (Husserl 1970, 168; Natanson 1973, 93–94; Moran 2005, 52–58).

From this Husserlian perspective, the failure of the accounts offered by the abolitionists and the eliminativists, insofar as they are informed by the politics of purity, lies in their underlying positivism. That is, they ultimately insist that if race is real in the most important sense (if it is *really* real), it must lie in some mind-independent and ahistorical ground, where biology is understood as exactly such a ground. Since no such positive ground exists (race is not biological), race must be construed as illusory or as a mere construct (which may be said to be real, but it is clearly taken to be an inferior or impoverished sort of reality in highly significant ways). What is more, in advocating the elimination or abolition of race, there is a clear espousal of an abstract, featureless, and atomistic understanding of human agency (purified of external contingencies). Despite the laudable efforts of the new abolitionist historians to describe the ambiguity of the nineteenth century racial landscape, their appeal to "inventing" or "fabricating" race, and "becoming" white, treats racial categories, including especially whiteness, as all-or-nothing states of being rather than as ambiguous and conflicted processes. There is, therefore, no real room for indeterminacy or vagueness regarding racial membership. Or, if such ambiguity is admitted, it is immediately explained away as evidence for the essential unreality of race. Either way, the fundamental purity of racial categories and the ultimately disembodied subject that must be assumed to stand above and beyond race are preserved.

One way to better understand how positivism works in the context of race is by closely examining the complex relationship between biology and racial categories. Race, as a way of classifying human beings, has had for most of its history an ostensively biological foundation through its appeal to ancestry. Whether it was the less formal reference to "black blood" and "white blood," or more "scientific" appeals to genetics, as Robin Andreason points out: "Races were assumed to be biologically objective categories that exist independently of human classifying activities, and scientists worked towards substantiating this belief" (2000, S654). By the early twentieth century, races were described as subspecies of *homo sapiens*, though different conceptions of subspecies were competing for dominance at the time. By the middle of the twentieth century, the formerly dominant ways of conceiving of subspecies had been rejected, and along with it much of the scientific support for so called folk conceptions of race. In the wake of this sea-change in our scientific thinking about race, two views emerged: racial nihilism, which rejects the reality of race *in toto*, and social constructivism, which holds that race exists as a social construct with no biological foundation or legitimacy. Both of these views have been discussed at length already. Very recently, however, biologists and philosophers of science have reopened the question of the biological reality of race in ways that shed important light on the relation between racial ontology and the politics of purity.

While some philosophers of science have begun to defend the possibility of a biological notion of race (Andreason 2000, 2004; Pigliucci and Kaplan 2003; Machery and Faucher 2005; Kitcher 2007), at the heart of the contention over these efforts is a concern over *essentialism*. Naomi Zack describes racial essentialism as "the theory that there are distinct and general human biological traits that determine racial membership and cause the presence of specific racial traits" (2001, 445). Racial essentialism, biologically speaking, is thus linked to what Ernst Mayr has referred to as "typological" thinking, which ties speciation to innate characteristics that are understood to be essential to particular species as such (Mayr 1982, 38–47). The shift away from typological approaches to the understanding of species, paired with empirical research demonstrating that there is little difference between the amount of genetic variation within racial groups as there is between them (Lewontin, Rose, and Kamin 1984; Nei and Roychoudhury 1993; Templeton 1999), has been largely responsible for the current (near) consensus that race cannot be biologically real.

Among those few who have begun to articulate a biological conception of race, great pains are taken to distance themselves from essentialism both insofar as their scientific methodology eschews typological thinking, and even insofar as their account of a biologically real notion of race lends support to morally pernicious forms of essentialism in our what they refer to as our folk conceptions of race. In his recent article, "Does 'Race' Have a Future?", for example, Philip Kitcher notes that both he and Andreason "are united in accepting the biological facts to which eliminativists point; we insist on the absence of deep essential differences among biological races" (2007, 298). Kitcher goes on to distance his own account from essentialism by pointing out that eliminativism "goes astray because of a mistaken premise about natural kinds: natural kinds have essences, and, in particular, biological kinds have genetic essences" (298). Similarly, in discussing the history of the rejection of biological realism about race, Andreason argues that "Pre-Darwinian naturalists often gave an Aristotelian answer to this question: a biologically objective classification scheme treats taxa as natural kinds defined by appeal to kind-specific essences" (2000, S655). Thus, the very idea that there might be "a biologically objective definition of race" (2004, 238) raises suspicions about racial essentialism, and the task, as understood by contemporary proponents of biological realism, is to articulate a biological account of race that avoids essentialism entirely.

According to Kitcher, this view of biological natural kinds as essences entails the idea that "nature is divided, independently of us, of our cognitive capacities and our interests" (2007, 298). We can see that this view maps neatly onto the positivist tenet that reality must be grounded in mind-independent foundations. The eliminativist seems to take this positivistic view of the natural world for granted (when it comes to race, at least), arguing that *if* races are biologically real then they will have essences of this sort, and if they do not have essences of this sort, then they cannot be biologically real (and vice versa, of course). The presumption, therefore, is that biological races must function in this essentialist (positivist) manner, and that any antiessentialist must also be an antirealist when it comes to biological definitions of race. The task for those attempting to defend a biological account of race is thus to substantiate a claim for its biological reality without falling back into (or even lending inadvertent support to) scientifically outmoded and morally odious forms of racial essentialism. In short, the question is one of whether it is possible to be *both* an antiessentialist and a biological realist about race. Eliminativists are clear that the answer must be no, and those articulating a new account of racial realism must take great pains to defend themselves from charges of racial essentialism.

What is crucial to note from the first is that once again the discourse is bound up in the politics of purity. Biological realism means a mind-independent (positivistic) foundation for races, and so either race is undeniably real in this positivistic (and essentialist) sense, or it is not, in which case it is *merely* a social construct, and is thus either completely unreal, or has a considerably lesser kind of reality that is ultimately up to us, and that we ought to take pains to undo. Thus, as much as the task for the new breed of racial realists is to provide an account of race that stands up to scientific scrutiny, they must also defend the notion that biological realism about race does not *entail* racial essentialism. That is, there is a presumption that the reality of race is an all-or-nothing proposition, and to thus conflate biological realism with essentialism, such that one is either (purely) a realist, or an antiessentialist—one cannot be both.

Naomi Zack's response to the American Anthropological Association's "Statement on 'Race'" (2001) is an excellent example of this tendency to view biological realism and antiessentialism as fundamentally incompatible. While she points out early in the essay that "[s]cholars across disciplines now eschew racial essentialism" (446), she is concerned that many of their efforts to confront racism, such as the AAA's statement, "may leave essentialist assumptions unexamined" (447). Her concern has to do with the extent to which the AAA failed to draw out all of the logical implications of their rejection of biological race by taking pains to reject relationships between racial membership and other aspects of biology, as well as human behavior. Asserting that "nonexistent entities cannot be causes, effects, or objects in relationships with things that do exist" (447), she is worried that pointing out that race has no link with culture, and that intermixing of human populations ensures that we are a single species, fails to take seriously enough the nonexistence of race. She argues that "the general claim that biological inheritance does not determine human capacities, abilities or cultural identities, while it may be true on many grounds, is too broad a defense of the nonexistence of race," because "the breadth of this claim makes it seem as though future empirical findings about the link between biology and culture could confirm the existence of human biological racial taxonomy, which is not the case" (450). Her basic argument is that, once you determine that races do not exist, making further claims about the lack of links between race and culture, or the lack of pure races, is redundant at best, and indirectly essentialist at worst, since it seems to suggest that the jury is still out on the reality of race, and these further facts constitute some part of the argument against race. As a result, she concludes that "The AAA Statement on Race . . . does not precisely repudiate racial taxonomy or firmly close the door on essentialism" (460).

According to Zack, this failure to fully "repudiate racial taxonomy" is problematic because, while "[e]volutionary biologists, geneticists, medical researchers and forensic anthropologists continue to work with population typologies," it remains the case that "[m]embers of the public believe that essentialist racial typology exists, and for the most part they believe that biological scientists have factual information that grounds this typology or gives it an objective and real foundation" (460). In short, when scientists use the term "race," even if in doing so they are appealing to a population-based typology, nonscientists[7] understand that to be a justification for their preexisting essentialist beliefs about racial taxonomy.

Zack appears to conclude from all of this that *any* appeal to biological racial taxonomy, even if based upon a population typology, and not an essentialist one, does more harm than good, and so should be abandoned altogether. My contention is that there is an underlying conflation of biological reality with essentialism, and this, in turn, is informed by the politics of purity. In order to make this case, I will begin by turning to a claim Zack makes toward the end of her essay: "It is in lacking distinct essences that human races fail to exist in the kind of typology commonly assumed; and the absence of nomological force for *race*, as an explanation of more specific human characteristics, renders race useless for biological theory" (460). Here she seems open to the possibility of there being more than one typology, since only the one "commonly assumed" is essentialist. Furthermore, she seems to be asserting that if there were more "nomological force" in the concept—if it could explain "specific human characteristics," and were thus *useful*—it might be worth preserving. Her case for the uselessness of race is crucial, therefore, to her argument for its repudiation, and so I must turn specifically to her case for this claim.

"In Science," Zack quite correctly points out, "biological racial essences have gone the way of phlogiston" (451). She reminds us that contemporary biologists who use race employ a genealogical or population-based concept, such as "ecotypes" (Pigliucci and Kaplan 2003) or "clades" (Andreason 2000, 2004), and take great pains to distance themselves from their more essentialist nineteenth- and early twentieth-century forebears (Zack 2001, 452). "Nevertheless," she goes on, "such scientific use of biological concepts of race easily slides into a kind of typology that can be mistaken for the phlogiston kind of racial essentialism" (452). This happens because, according to Zack, "typology itself partly relies on what the 18th-century philosopher George Berkeley called *abstract general ideas*" (452). The problem with abstract general ideas, she explains, is that they characterize all particulars of the same group as identical in some significant sense (otherwise, they wouldn't be part of that group). Since these contemporary scientists "are speaking about populations rather than individuals," Zack points out that "their conclusions about the traits shared by such groups are no more than statistical or highly probable," and so "they become abstract general ideas in Berkeley's sense, because there is no one thing or set of things that all members of such groups have in common" (452). Since atypical individuals for any population-based typology always exist, Zack concludes that therefore "all typologies are somewhat arbitrary constructions rather than literal models of natural divisions" (452). In turn, this makes contemporary antiessentialist biological accounts of race viciously circular because "there is no consistent, objective determinant of racial, geographical, osteological or genetic, human group membership, for any group" (457). Here we see exactly the problem of identity and difference I raised earlier in this chapter: because there is no trait that is *identical* across all members of a particular racial category, each individual must instead be fundamentally (and purely) different, and the category itself must be rejected.[8]

In discussing the eliminativist argument, Kitcher mentions Plato's metaphor about science working "to carve nature at its joints" in order to illustrate a way to think about the mistaken idea that "biological kinds have genetic essences" (2007, 298). Biological divisions, according to this essentialist view, should be present *in nature*, such that science simply reveals divisions that were already there, and since these divisions are essential, their presence or absence *determines* membership within the resulting categories, such that they serve as conditions for membership that are necessary or sufficient or both. While Kitcher argues against this view, it seems to be informing Zack's criticism of biological realism. In her discussion of the use of mitochondrial DNA markers to determine population-based (allegedly nonessentialist) racial divisions she argues that "mtDNA markers are not present in all members of those populations in which they occur, so typology based on them is also a fabrication beyond 'nature'" (Zack 2001, 457). Her argument, in other words, is that population markers can never serve as necessary or sufficient conditions for group membership in particular individuals, and thus are "beyond nature." Since, as noted above, Zack dismisses all population typologies as "arbitrary constructions," we can see that she is taking biological reality to be necessarily essentialist, and all else is not only a construction but an arbitrary one at that.

Zack's presumption seems to be that biological realism must function in an essentialist way, and thus *if* race is biologically real, then essentialism will be correct. Racial essentialism is such a threat that anything even *sounding* like biological realism, in the way she understands it, must be rejected on the grounds that it could lead to pernicious racial essentialism. Zack makes this explicit in her discussion of the use of race in medicine:

> None of the scientists using populations as units for genetic research on disease suggests that all members of the populations in question have a gene for the disease in question . . . or that no members of other populations may have a particular population-based disease. This means that population membership is neither a sufficient nor a necessary condition for the presence of diseases associated with specific populations. This logical truth means that in terms of individual treatment and diagnosis for population-associated diseases, individuals have to be treated by medical practitioners as though they do not have a particular population membership. (2001, 459)

Since population-based racial categories cannot offer conditions that are necessary or sufficient or both for predicting the presence or absence of the relevant genetic markers, they are, according to Zack, rendered irrelevant. Thus, race is either real in an essentialist way because only realities that function in this way (providing clear and distinct necessary and sufficient conditions for membership) *count* as properly real (and not a mere construction), or it is not real at all, and the mere suggestion that it is real, insofar as this "logically" entails essentialism (446), counts as a tacit endorsement of racial essentialism. In this way, her argument serves as an excellent example of positivistic thinking.

Zack | biological realism = essentialism

Again, if we are to overcome the challenge posed by this positivistic approach, one important task must be to negotiate a way to think about biological realism about race that does not fall back into essentialism. There is a sense in which Zack's claim that population typologies are "arbitrary constructions" is quite correct. Once we give up on the notion that nature has a given set of "joints" at which it should properly be carved up, then the task of finding nonarbitrary (in the sense of being determined by nature itself) typologies must be abandoned. Of course, just because a given category is not ontologically given in some mind-independent way doesn't necessarily make it arbitrary, unless one is committed to the idea that the real and true must be strictly determined by mind-independent criteria (that is, positivism). From the positivist perspective, the question of the biological reality of race is one of simply consulting the natural world to see if it is capable of determining racial membership in some nonarbitrary (ontologically necessary) way. In rejecting positivism, the focus shifts away from simply attending to the inherent qualities of the empirical world to that of taking up the meaning and significance of biological racial categories as *constituted* by human beings.

As I pointed out earlier, it would be a relatively simple matter to select a set of traits and use this set to carve up "objectively" the species *homo sapiens* into races (subspecies). One could use strictly genetic markers (in which case people of the same objectively determined race might look radically different), or even straightforward phenotypical similarity (in which case one could, by virtue of one's appearance, be of a different race from one's parents). But racial categories are not an end in themselves. It isn't enough to have them, they must *mean* something, and it is this question of meaning that gets to the heart of our concern over arbitrariness, and Zack's own appeal to a lack of utility in her rejection of race. "The question," in other words, "is not whether biological 'races' exist; rather, it is which biological race concepts can be most *usefully* applied to human populations" (Pigliucci and Kaplan 2003, 1164; italics added). As Andreason points out, once one offers a set of empirically measurable criteria for racial membership (in her case, the genealogical "cladistic" race concept), then one has an *objective* account of race (Andreason 2000, S661–S663), and, she points out in a later essay, one that is "theoretically interesting" (Andreason 2004, 430). It is Kitcher, however, who best elaborates upon the implications of this shift in our thinking:

In the sense that the world contains the so-far undifferentiated totality of what is independent of us, there is just one world. In the sense that the world is a collection of objects, assorted into types, there are many worlds, and we choose the one, or ones, in which we live." (Kitcher 2007, 300)

What Kitcher is pointing to here is something very akin to phenomenological *constitution*—it is the meaning-giving moment in every act of consciousness. Rather than simply positing a world of already meaningful objects which we then passively perceive, phenomenology points toward an *active* consciousness that confers meaning in the very act of perceiving, and in this way comes to constitute the world in which we live *as a world of meaning*. This has very important implications for our understanding of race.

If we return, for example, to the study demonstrating the degree of genetic variation within and between racial groups, we see that what remains under the surface is the fact that the racial groups, as such, were assumed from the beginning. That is, to *whom* did the scientists conducting the research go when they wanted to test for genetic variation within the black group, or between the black and white groups? There had to have been some already assumed notion of the meaning of those terms. Like the Irish immigrants to the Americas, there was a presumption at one level of their whiteness even as their exact racial status and the meaning of that whiteness were being contested. The purpose of such an empirical study, therefore, could only have been to either prove or disprove the "biological reality" of these *pregiven* racial groups, as if their meaning and extension were a fixed and determinate aspect of reality (if it should be proven), or utter nonsense (if it should be disproved). So here again, we see positivism as work. *If* racial categories are real, they must be fixed, given, and determinate in such a way that there will be greater genetic variation between racial groups than within them.

Of course, in asking a purely quantitative question about the *amount* of variation, the entire question of the *significance* of different kinds of variation is ignored. Suppose that there were a single allele that enabled individuals to leap buildings in a single bound, or to move heavy objects with their mind, or some other super-heroic characteristic. If two individuals were genetically *identical*, save for that single allele, in most cases the difference, though *quantitatively* insignificant, would be far more important than all of that similarity. It is rather astonishing that this fact of the quantitative insignificance of genetic variation is taken to be so telling, since on its own it ignores all questions of the *significance* of particular manifestations of variation. The question of the biological reality of race must ultimately come to a question of the kinds of differences that *matter* when we think about the meaning of racial groups, and not just whether and how many differences there are. As I have argued, the meaning and significance of race has never been fixed and determinate but rather always characterized by ambiguity and contestation. The seventeenth-century Caribbean may have been a kind of hotbed of such contestation, but it was taking up and transforming meanings that had already existed in some form, and did itself pass along a jumble of ambiguous and contentious meanings for future generations to try to sort out. Furthermore, insofar as race has always been about bodies (though never exclusively about bodies), it has always represented an effort to divide up the human species as a collection of organisms. When that division takes essentialist forms and marks out a normative hierarchy, then it is surely worth rejecting, but we must take up the question of whether or not race is, ultimately, such an all-or-nothing proposition.

Zack rightly points out that insofar as one is attempting to offer an ideal medical diagnosis of an individual patient, race should be irrelevant, since racial membership is neither necessary nor sufficient for the possession of particular genetic traits (like sickle cell or Tay Sachs), and so any given individual might be one of the outliers within a given population (Zack 2001, 459). Having dark skin, or being of African descent, in other words, does not guarantee that one will have sickle cell, nor do *only* people with dark skin or African descent have the trait for sickle cell. Thus Zack is surely correct that it would be bad medical practice to take race into account when the sole goal is offering the best possible diagnosis of a particular individual.

But what if our task were to target scarce diagnostic or educational resources on a large scale? If we wished to educate people about sickle-cell in order to improve public health, or to diagnose as many individuals with the condition as possible so that they could seek proper treatment, then the fact that our population-based racial categories only offered *probabilities*, instead of necessary and sufficient conditions, would be much less significant. If I knew that the probability for having sickle-cell was significantly higher in the (population-based) racial group commonly referred to as black, then my diagnostic resources would be more efficacious (have more utility, in Zack's sense), if they targeted *that* population, instead of being race blind. Indeed,

cant be race blind

to ignore race simply because it only yielded *probabilities* would be in such cases highly irrational (and, one might even say, unscientific). The problem, therefore, is that Zack's positivistic understanding of biological racial reality demands too much of the concept. No, it certainly cannot tell me everything about a particular individual, nor are the categories universally predictive and without exceptions and outliers. It does not follow from this, however, that the categories are therefore unreal, or utterly useless. It shows, rather, that the understanding of what race might be and how it might function is overly simplistic, insofar as it is bound up in the politics of purity.

Pigliucci and Kaplan, who appeal to the population-based notion of *ecotypes* as their foundation for a biological conception of race, make it clear that its descriptive and predictive capacities *for individuals* will be limited at best, in part because human populations are never completely discrete. Thus, they point out that:

> This implies that insofar as we focus on an ecotype conception of race, there will not necessarily be a unique 'race' to which any given member of a population belongs. Any given individual may in fact belong to a number of different ecotypic races, and/or be a member of one (or more) intermediate population(s) within a (series of) clinical distribution(s). However, this is hardly an unexpected complication in a discipline like biology, characterized by a high level of complexity of both the object of study and the conditions that induce variation in that object. (Pigliucci and Kaplan 2003, 1169)

The fact that the categories have vague boundaries, and that individuals may occupy more than one at a given time, therefore, does not mean that the categories are useless, or utterly without meaning. On the contrary, by taking seriously this complexity and underlying ambiguity, we can begin to articulate ways in which these categories can help us to make sense of that complexity.

In the quote above, for example, the authors note that one of the complications is "the conditions that induce variation" in populations. One of those conditions, of course, is the very sociality of the human species. That is, if we think about the ways in which human populations might begin to distinguish themselves from one another genetically, there are the more straightforward causes of geographic isolation, but there is also *cultural* isolation. There is, I am suggesting, a causal reciprocity between the social and the biological that should not be ignored (see Richerson and Boyd 2005). Indeed, part of the goal of contemporary biological realists about race is to call into question the very distinction between the biological on the one hand, and the socially constructed or cultural, on the other (Kitcher 2007, 298; Machery and Faucher 2005, 1217; Andreason 2000, S664).

The standard approach to the question of the ontological status of race has been to treat the biological and the social as distinct.[9] Historically, race was linked to biological difference, but that has been proven false, the argument goes, and so now we understand the ways in which race is, and has only ever been, a social fabrication, and this makes it distinct from the natural or biological sphere. What the recent biological work on race suggests is that this dichotomy between the natural and the social is misleading. Evolutionary biology tells us that, over time, as populations spread out geographically and differentiate themselves culturally, variations in conditions will begin to favor different traits in different environments, and thus genetic peculiarities will emerge within those populations.[10] This explains not only variations in pigmentation—which have to do both with average sun exposure in a given climate as well as access to certain nutrients—but also the ability to digest lactose into adulthood, which has to do with the keeping of dairy-producing herd-animals and of course sickle-cell, which is linked to a resistance to malaria. Different cultural and historical factors, in other words, can have enormous impact on our biology over time.

At the same time, these different populations are only very rarely *completely* isolated from each other, and so even as differentiation takes place, they will continue to encounter each other, at which time the differences, both biological and cultural, will be observed, and their significance judged. Thus, even within the same geographic region, the nomadic and pastoral Massai people of Kenya and Tanzania will be culturally discrete from their geographic neighbors (Kikuyu and Luo, for example), and tend toward endogamy (though not universally). At the same time, as political climates change, the relevance of particular differences can likewise change. Thus, as Kitcher points out, the "past application of racial concepts" (2007, 310) can come to affect our behavior, including our breeding patterns, and thus, over time, our biology. In short, as "culture affects the success and survival of individuals and groups," it comes about that "these culturally evolved environments then affect which genes are favored by natural selection" (Richerson and

Boyd 2005, 4), and as these genetic advantages come to manifest themselves, they can in turn be observed by others and construed as relevant to repro- ductive behavior, thus further impacting breeding practices within and be- tween populations. Culture and biology are thus so intimately connected that it can often be difficult to parse out their mutual influence. In other words, while it may be apt to say that biology keeps culture on a tight leash, "the dog on the end is big, smart, and independent . . . on any given walk, it is hard to tell who is leading who" (Richerson and Boyd 2005, 194). In this light, understanding the question of the reality of race as a purely bio- logical one is mistaken in large part because it treats biology as distinct from human sociality (culture). That is, it supposes the underlying *purity* of biology as such.

The point of this discussion of recent work on the biology of race is not to advocate for one account over the other (ecotypes over clades, for example), but merely to point out that the standard terms of the debate over the bio- logical reality of race are inadequate, insofar as they are enmeshed in the pol- itics of purity. First, the biological and the social (cultural) are treated as separate and discrete (pure) spheres, and race is taken to be in either one or the other of them. To claim that it is *both* biologically real and socially con- structed, though present in the literature, is understood as a radical claim in- deed. Second, the spheres themselves are seen to divide neatly into the necessary (biological) and the contingent (social), such that *if* race is biolog- ical, then it tells us something *necessary* about who we are (internal), in the sense that it determines aspects of our *essential* being. If, on the other hand, race is social, then it is purely contingent (external), and tells us nothing at all about who we are, at best revealing something only about how we are perceived. Thus there is a politics of purity operating on a very basic concep- tual level in these discussions of the biological reality of race.

Third, because of this distinction between the necessary and the contin- gent, we can see how much of the noise and strife surrounding the biological reality of race is motivated by a commitment to the purity of the individual agent. This can be understood by appeal to the classical liberal vision of a life without *external* impediments to individual choice—a free agent is the one whose agency is purified of external impediments to action. From Hobbes's war of all against all, to Rawls's prioritization of the right over the good, lib- eralism has been committed to a clear distinction between the individual and the social, such that any kind of grouping of human beings at all, if it is to be other than coercive, must be either innate or completely voluntary. That is, setting aside cases of coercion, one is either placed in a group as a result of some shared property or set of properties, or as a result of choice. Being a person living with diabetes is an example of the former, being a member of a diabetes support group is an example of the latter. Since racial membership is not chosen in this way,[11] if it is to be other than coercive, it must be innate and biological. If it is neither innate and biological nor voluntarily chosen, then it *must* be coercive, and thus race must be understood as contrary to human liberty *in itself*.

There is, in short, a basic ontological individualism informing this line of thinking about race. It can be seen very clearly not only in Zack's focus upon the failure of population thinking to account for individuals in her discussion of the AAA's statement, but also in her earlier rejection of racial categories as inherently inconsistent with a commitment to human freedom. Thus, at stake in this debate, according to the terms dictated by the politics of purity, is the extent to which race is or is not a coercive force in our lives. If it is biologically real (and this reality itself is an all-or-nothing question), then it must be in some significant sense determinative for individual agents (necessary) because it describes innate properties understood in terms of conditions for membership that are necessary or sufficient or both. If, on the other hand, it is not biological, and it is not voluntarily chosen, then it can only ever be a set of *external* descriptors (contingent) that may be taken up or ignored by any given individual. It is at this point that the history of race comes into the picture, since the question, given the rejection of the biological reality of race, becomes one of whether any given agent *should* take up racial categories in shaping their identity, and the majority of the philosophical discussions of race in the contemporary literature revolve around *that* particular issue, having "settled" the biological question.

Of course, as I have shown, the proclamations of the demise of the biological reality of race are premature. The issue is not one of whether there are essential characteristics that effectively dictate the way our species can be divided, but rather is one of the ways, means, and ends we employ to draw distinctions that we take to be *significant*. It is not about a strictly descriptive account of a mind-independent reality but rather about the meaning and significance of that reality. And these issues of meaning and significance are such as to be particularly well suited to phenomenology.[12]

The central point here is that questions regarding the biological reality of race cannot be properly adjudicated simply by assuming this overly simpli-fied, essentialist and positivistic understanding of what biology and reality even are. The question demands rather that we place the issue of the meanings of race within a given context (or set of overlapping contexts) and for a particular goal (or set of goals) front and center. The question of Irish whiteness in the seventeenth-century Caribbean, therefore, is not a matter of whether the Irish population (which, of course, is hardly clearly and dis-tinctly demarcated in the first place) shared a set of necessary and sufficient conditions with other whites (English, French, Dutch, and so on). Biologi-cally, of course, they shared some traits, generally speaking, and varied from these other populations in myriad ways (again, generally speaking). What matters, however, is not whether and how much they varied or were the same but rather the meaning and significance of that variation and similarity. In my example of the Irish in Barbados, whiteness was a matter not only of pale skin (though that is surely significant), it was also matter of the way in which that pale skin was taken to be important by the English, by enslaved Africans, by other European visitors to the island, and of course by the Irish themselves. And what my example suggests is that its significance was a matter of debate and ambiguity on all fronts, though over a matter of a few generations (which were themselves *biologically* shaped by the struggles over the meaning and significance of whiteness) the contours of that debate be-came (relatively) settled into the understanding of race that was inherited in the English speaking world of the eighteenth and nineteenth centuries.

Again, we may return to the question of whether the Irish in my example were white. The expectation of an all-or-nothing, yes-or-no answer to that question is clearly misplaced. The question cannot be understood as strictly biological, where biology is understood in ultimately essentialist terms, and as utterly distinct from cultural forces and the influence of human behavior. The biological aspects of the answer are tied up intimately with the cultural aspects, and in any event, both moments yield ambiguous answers. The point is that this ambiguity should be understood as negating neither the utility of race altogether, its reality and its importance, nor even the propriety of asking the question about the Irish at all. The question is provocative, if understood in the appropriate way as an invitation to explore that ambiguity, and that interplay between the biological and the cultural within that context and under those conditions. And gaining a better understanding of the ways in which the Irish both were and were not white can only be helpful in our efforts to understand, confront, and challenge the legacies of that historical moment.

I have argued that the politics of purity effectively saturates the discussion of the relation between race and biology. Presumptions about the purity of science itself (as opposed to culture), of biological taxonomic methodology, and the nature of the usefulness and reality of biological concepts and categories lie hidden throughout much of the published work on this topic. This body of literature rightly warns us away from essentialist notions of racial reality but wrongly conflates all notions of scientific reality with essentialism. It is possible, I submit, to articulate a notion of race as real—even biologically real—that does not commit one to essentialism. The politics of purity may insist otherwise, but it is precisely this set of assumptions regarding race, reality, and biology that need to be submitted to critical scrutiny. Drawing principally upon the phenomenological tradition, I will interrogate this set of assumptions in the next chapter.

4

"Becoming" White:

Race, Reality, and Agency

I have suggested that much of the discourse on the relation between race and biology is mired in positivism. In other words, it is presumed that, in order for something to be biologically real, it will admit of necessary and sufficient conditions that effectively carve nature up "at its joints" in a way that is mind-independent. This is a manifestation of the politics of purity insofar as it demands of biological taxonomy that it produce discrete group-ings with clear and distinct boundaries, in that it takes biological reality to be distinct from cultural production, and in its appeal to these distinctions to account for liberty in terms of the internal and necessary versus the external and contingent. By making this reference to positivism, I am alluding quite clearly to the phenomenological tradition, and this is because that tradition provides such rich resources (though I do not mean to imply that it does so *exclusively*) for resisting the politics of purity and articulating a more liberatory vision of racial reality.

PHENOMENOLOGY AND THE ONTOLOGY OF RACE

Phenomenology, from Husserl on, has been characterized first and foremost by a commitment to placing human consciousness at the center of philo-sophical investigation. Since consciousness is understood as fundamentally a kind of directed *openness*—consciousness must always be consciousness *of* something—phenomenology as a philosophical approach entails two important aspects. First, consciousness must be understood more as an activity than as a state or property, and in so doing we must recognize the extent to which attending to an object of consciousness is not a matter of the passive reception of information or impressions, but is always to a greater or lesser extent an active project of meaning making. Acts of perception, for example, always entail an active moment on the part of the perceiving agent. She does not simply receive perceptual stimulus as static and pregiven quanta of data but rather she sorts, interprets, and apprehends the objects of her perception *as* (meaningful) objects. Second, since consciousness itself is always this kind of open activity, its own meaning and content is always just beyond our grasp, and thus the *task* of understanding can never be complete. It is for this reason that Husserl has been referred to as the *Philosopher of Infinite Tasks* (Natanson 1973).

It is in this sense of phenomenology as an infinite task that it can, in Husserl's view, achieve true *scientific* rigor. According to Dermot Moran:

> For Husserl, the ideal of science and its achievements can only be understood when the subjective acts giving rise to the scientific outlook are themselves examined and clarified as to their nature, and when their subjective and cultural specificities are taken into account. Phenomenology, for Husserl, was precisely the dream of a science which would keep the guiding ideal of rationality operative in the sciences secured in the clarification of the fundamental meaning-constituting acts of human subjectivity and intersubjectivity. (2000, 145–46)

Phenomenology, in the Husserlian tradition, is thus at its heart an effort to keep science honest with itself. Rather than assuming that proper science is conducted in such a way that any given investigator can stand in for any other, Husserl is inviting us to take seriously the way in which the particularities of our subjectivity, and especially the particularities of our specific *bodies*, condition our epistemic efforts (Husserl 1970, 217–18). The point is not, however, to demonstrate the relativism of science or endorse some version of skepticism but rather to enhance the rigor of scientific endeavor by making the status of science itself, as a fundamentally *human* exercise, an object of rational inquiry. In this way, phenomenology's insights about science

Royce

are very much in keeping with recent developments in feminist epistemology and philosophy of science (see Code 1991; Longino 2001). We can better understand the world by taking seriously the peculiarities of the act of understanding itself as it is, and must always be, manifest in a particular subject.

Thus, if I seek to understand a phenomenon, I must make it the object of my consciousness. But as an activity, my consciousness of the object is itself a phenomenon that impacts the meaning of the original phenomenon I am seeking to understand. Thus I must attend not only to the phenomenon in question but also to the *way* in which I am attending to that phenomenon. This is the Husserlian method of "bracketing" (Husserl 1991, 19–21) or calling into question the presumptions and inclinations that can often surreptitiously inform our attempts to understand the world around us. Phenomenology, as a *method*, must of necessity raise the very question of methodology itself. It is characterized by a constant questioning of the way in which we approach the objects of our study. What are the assumptions and proclivities I am bringing to my investigation? How do they impact the outcome of that investigation? Of course, because each raising of the question of method, each act of bracketing, is itself another act of consciousness, it too, in turn, is subject to the same set of questions. It is in precisely this way that phenomenology must be understood as an infinite task, and for this reason we must confront "the radical self-responsibility of the phenomenological philosopher" (Hopkins 2008, 21). If I should fail to be as radical and rigorous in my investigation as I am able, then I am failing to live up to my responsibility as an epistemic agent, for that responsibility is nothing more nor less than the engagement with this infinite task, a task that is (or at least ought to be) the *sine qua non* of philosophical endeavor— *reason*. As Maurice Natanson points out: "the logic of the phenomenologist's enterprise involves a meditation on Reason carried out by reason—a meditation whose task is also infinite and whose name is philosophy" (1973, 175).

At this point, the naturalism informing much of the debates surrounding the biological reality of race should be clear. The question of the reality of race is raised, and taken to be an issue simply of the presence or absence of certain biological facts. But as I have argued, certain understandings of the workings of biology, of the nature of empirical reality as such, and the ontology of the human person are all taken for granted. If something is real it must function as a mind-independent set of properties. The natural sciences, such as biology, are concerned solely with exactly this sort of reality. Thus, if

questioning of assumptions

race is biologically real, it will function as a set of properties (leading, of course, to necessary and sufficient conditions) applicable to all members of a given race, such that any particular individual will belong to one and only one racial group. Since reality must be understood only in this way, if race should prove unreal, then it must be completely arbitrary, and given its pernicious effects and its inconsistency with individual self-determination, we would be better off without it. The discussion of the biological reality of race in chapter 3 has shown, however, that biological kinds do not necessarily function in this (essentialist) way, that the "arbitrary" and the real are not necessarily incompatible, and that ultimately the purposes and meanings we bring to our efforts to understand the natural world shape that world even as they are shaped by it. In keeping with Richerson and Boyd's argument that culture and evolutionary biology are mutually influential, and Kitcher's claim that "in the sense that the world is a collection of objects, assorted into types, there are many worlds, and we choose the one, or ones, in which we live" (2007, 300), the way in which human consciousness shapes the reality it struggles to grasp must be placed at the forefront of our efforts to understand race. We must, in other words, take a phenomenological turn in our thinking about race.[1] *Also to politics*

If naturalism can be understood, in Husserl's sense, as an unquestioned commitment to the idea of mind-independent standards for scientific evaluation and criteria of epistemic success, then we can see that the politics of purity is principally a manifestation of naturalism in the context of race. Both racial eliminativism and naïve forms of racial realism are thus two sides of the same coin, insofar as they both maintain the *standards* of the politics of purity and disagree only over whether such standards can be empirically met. This leads on the one hand to an overestimation of the force of biological reality, since it takes that reality to be something utterly distinct from human consciousness, and especially human social life. Husserl, however, refers to the act of bringing meaning and significance to our experience as *constitution*—human beings constitute the world not in the sense that we somehow generate it *ex nihil* (it is not *idealism*), but in the sense that every act of consciousness of the world is always a consciousness of the world *as meaningful* in some sense. What is more, since "to live as a person is to live in a social framework, wherein I and we live together in community and have the community as a horizon" (Husserl 1965, 150), every act of constitution is fundamentally *intersubjective*—I don't simply bestow meaning on the

what are assumps of prog/Am Cy

world in a vacuum but do so in a way that relies upon, and simultaneously conditions, the meaning-constituting activities of others.

Thus, the politics of purity, as a manifestation of naturalism in the context of race, not only fails insofar as it treats the natural and the social (biology and culture) as radically distinct spheres of being and meaning but also in that it gives too much credit to the natural sciences, and too little credit to the social world. That is, as some of the philosophers of science discussed in chapter 3 have argued, the biologically real and the socially constructed are compatible, insofar as our understanding of biological categories (our understanding of the living world as meaningful) is conditioned by the intentional context in which our efforts to understand that living world take place, while that understanding and that intentional context in turn shape biological processes. The politics of purity gives biology too much credit, because it is not the case that there is a kind of biological reality that is mind-independent, and simply gives us ready-made categories of meaning that we "discover." If that were indeed the way biology worked, then race would certainly fail to meet that standard of biological reality. However, no kind of reality in this sense is available to us, and it is ultimately a failure of epistemic rigor (a failure of reason) to expect otherwise. At the same time, the consequence of this insight is not that all meaning is up for grabs and our place in the world, including our racial membership, can be completely determined by individual consciousness, because the *intersubjective* aspect of our meaning-giving endeavors conditions the contours of those endeavors in ways that cannot be unilaterally ignored. In this way, the politics of purity gives the social world too *little* credit. That is, where naturalism (and the politics of purity) would insist that things are either determined by mind-independent reality (intrinsically given), or chosen by completely independent subjects (voluntary), a phenomenological approach rejects this dichotomy. We must, therefore, approach the understanding of race as a fundamentally *social* phenomenon. The traditional sense of the term *social* treats it as simply the accumulated sum of a series of individual beliefs and decisions. Phenomenology, however, must understand the social world in a much more complex way, such that individual beliefs and decisions can themselves only be understood as meaningful within a particular community—such that the "community as a horizon" is deeply constitutive of individual acts of consciousness. The social is thus inseparable from the individual, and vice versa, which raises significant challenges for traditional understandings of rationality.

"intersubjective"   yes

The task of reason, for Husserl, is to approach "apodictic" certainty. But given the complexity of the world (as an intersubjectively constituted "Life World") we are attempting to grasp, and the sense in which reason, in order to manifest philosophical rigor, must also critically reflect on *itself*, it would be a mistake to think that the aim of reason can be conceived as a static end-state to be achieved. As Husserl puts it:

> *Reason* is the specific characteristic of man, as a being living in personal activities and habitualities. This life, as personal life, is a constant becoming through a constant intentionality of development. What becomes, in this life, is the person himself. (1970, 338)
>
> Thus the philosopher must always have as his purpose to master the true and full sense of philosophy, the totality of its infinite horizons. No one line of knowledge, no individual truth must be absolutized. Only in such supreme consciousness of self, which itself becomes a branch of the infinite task, can philosophy fulfill its function of putting itself, and therewith a genuine humanity on the right track. To know that this is the case, however, also involves once more entering the field of knowledge proper to philosophy on the highest level of reflection upon itself. Only on the basis of this constant reflectiveness is a philosophy a universal knowledge. (1965, 181)

What this means, ultimately, is that knowledge is a *process* of "constant reflectiveness," and not a kind of property that an epistemic agent either possesses or lacks. The standards of success, therefore, cannot be something fixed and static (like necessary or sufficient conditions) but must themselves be dynamic. Philosophy, reason, and knowledge cannot be evaluated, therefore, strictly on the basis of *what* they achieve, or the *content* of their claims, but rather must be judged by the *manner* in which they are undertaken.

Phenomenology insists first and foremost that we critically reflect not only upon the objects of our inquiry but on the ways and means of our inquiry itself. This includes, significantly, raising methodological questions about phenomenology qua methodology. As I have already suggested, this means that our standards of evaluation must eschew categorical proclamations, not only in the realm of epistemology but also in ontological matters. This does not mean that we cannot draw conclusions with a certain (and significant) degree of confidence, it means only that we must also be prepared to raise important questions about the standards by which we evaluate our claims. Husserl himself was trained as a mathematician, and he understood phenomenology as a search for certitude. "Phenomenological certitude," according to Natanson, "rests not only on the in-person givenness of intentional objects but on the manner in which that givenness has been secured" (1973, 98). The "givenness" of intentional objects is always secured not only by means of perception but also within an intersubjective context. If I perceive something as thus and so, yet my compatriots do not, then I must begin to think through the manner in which the object or phenomenon in question is presented to me, and how I might justify that experience both to myself and to those compatriots. It is the categories, meanings, and usages established within a given community that both shapes the way I understand the world—what Linda Alcoff, following the Hermeneutic tradition, refers to as our "interpretive horizon" (2006, 94)—and how I am able to explain, legitimate, criticize, and even alter that understanding to and with that community. In other words, once we move beyond the purely abstract world of mathematics, the question of certitude demands an active engagement not only with oneself as an embodied and historically situated epistemic agent but also with the ways and means of one's interactions with other embodied and situated agents. In this way, even paradigmatic cases of *propositional* knowledge need to be understood, at least in part, on the model of more *practical* kinds of knowing. The evaluation of "S knows that p" depends upon the *way* in which that act of knowing is undertaken and justified, not only to S, but to others within (and even outside of) S's epistemic community.[2]

By way of example, consider the question of what it means to claim that one knows how to play an instrument. In Appalachian Kentucky, there is a community of people who gather once a week at a local furniture store to play and teach gospel and bluegrass music.[3] The method of teaching is simply for the more established musicians, within a given song, to leave room for neophytes to take a more prominent role, and gently correct them as they play. Thus all of the musicians may be playing the same song, and in this way can be said to *know* their instruments, yet some are clearly more proficient than others, and none of them are so proficient as to be incapable of further learning and improvement.

Knowing one's instrument, therefore, cannot be thought of as a simple yes-or-no, all-or-nothing proposition. *Complete* mastery is an unreachable goal, but the problem is in the ideal of completion, not mastery. Mastery of an instrument may, in a sense, be possible (though again, not in the sense of completion), but part of what characterizes the master musician just is the ongoing and constant effort to improve his or her playing. To seek out the most challenging pieces to play, the most stimulating collaborators, and the most discerning critical ears. Indeed, if one were to claim that one had completely mastered an instrument, and thus stopped practicing and improving, we might be tempted to say at that point that they can no longer rightly claim to *know* the instrument—the knowledge lies in the *practice,* and once the practice has ceased, the knowledge ceases as well. The individual may still (for a while, at least), be able to take up the instrument and play competently, and thus we might still hold that she knows how to play, but insofar as she has stopped her critical engagement with her own proficiency and musicianship, what knowledge she has is but a shallow imitation of the knowledge possessed by one who remains intimately connected to the practice of the instrument.[4] Before one picks up an instrument and begins the process of learning to play, it is surely clear that the agent does *not* know how to play. So it is not the case that such questions are always ambiguous. Nevertheless, once that process is begun, then the epistemic status, so to speak, of any given musician is a matter of their continued engagement in the process of learning, and not simply a matter of their collected technical repertoire.

What is most radical about the phenomenological approach is that this must also apply, as I mentioned above, to propositional knowledge. It is one thing to say that knowing *how* to play an instrument is an ambiguous and dynamic claim, but it is quite another thing to propose that knowing *that* the earth is round must be thought of in these terms. For Husserl, philosophy, as a genuine "rigorous science," can be understood as the exercise of reason in the pursuit of knowledge of the truth (Moran 2005, 43–46; Natanson 1973, 171–74). In his *Vienna Lecture*, Husserl states:

> If inadequacy announces itself through obscurities and contradictions, this motivates the beginning of a universal reflection. . . . No line of knowledge, no single truth may be absolutized and isolated. Only through this highest form of self-consciousness, which itself becomes one of the branches of the infinite task, can philosophy fulfill its function. . . . Only through this constant reflexivity is a philosophy universal knowledge. (1970, 291)

Philosophy, in other words, is thus a form of self-consciousness, which must be understood as an ongoing *activity*—a "constant reflexivity"—directed toward universal knowledge. This universal knowledge, however, must not be understood as state to be achieved or a goal to be reached, for that would render the knowledge "absolutized and isolated." Rather, knowledge becomes itself a mode of consciousness. Knowing is thus a kind of doing or becoming, not a kind of having or being, and so one's knowing that the earth is round can be understood as more akin to one's knowing a musical instrument than traditional epistemology of the all-or-nothing "S knows that p" stripe would admit.

This has especially important implications for our knowledge of who and what we are—our knowledge of identity. If human consciousness, as Husserl maintains, is always consciousness *of* something, and in this way it must be thought of as fundamentally an active process, and not a static property, then our identity, likewise, is not something we have, but is best understood as an ongoing process. Alcoff, whose *Visible Identities* grounds its notion of identity (in part, at least) in the phenomenological tradition, aptly and elegantly defines identities as "positioned or located lived experiences in which both individuals and groups work to construct meaning in relation to historical experience and historical narratives" (2006, 42). Her reference to identity as an "interpretive horizon" captures the sense in which this describes the way that our approach to the world around us is always an approach *from* somewhere. That somewhere is conditioned by our bodies (both qua human bodies generally, and *qua* this body in particular), by the norms and practices of the communities in and through which we operate, and the history of those norms in relations to these kinds of bodies. At the same time, since the activity taking place within this context and toward this horizon is, in part, the shaping, reshaping, and articulating of our identities themselves, we not only approach the world *from* somewhere but also *toward* somewhere. In this way, while our horizons can be understood in part as a limit and condition on our consciousness, that same consciousness, as an activity, is always altering the landscape, and shifting the boundaries of that horizon within a context that is itself, since it is comprised of other consciousnesses, always in flux. In Sartre's version of existential phenomenology, this is described as the "metastability" between "transcendence" or freedom on one hand, and "facticity" or situation on the other (Sartre 1956, 50, 68). Again, one of the central implications of this approach is that the individual cannot

Royce

be thought of as completely ontologically distinct from the social. In order to manifest identity, I need a community whose meanings and norms I can use to articulate and develop that identity (cf. Mead 1934, 162–64).

What this means for our understanding of the politics of purity is that a radical shift in our very approach to the questions surrounding race is necessary. Racial reality has been treated as something static. The politics of purity views racial categories as all-or-nothing sets of properties—necessary and sufficient conditions—such that any particular agent either is or is not a member of one and only one racial category. Given a phenomenological approach, however, race cannot be properly thought of as a matter of being but rather of constant becoming. There is thus a strong sense in which raising the question of what race *is*, insofar as the logic of the question itself demands a *definitive* and static answer, already capitulates to the politics of purity. As I have argued in my discussion of the history of race, the term has meant many (often conflicting) things at different times and places, and even, importantly, in the same time and place. The discussion of biological reality, likewise, indicates that raising the question of what race is, if we are to treat it with the proper philosophical rigor, will point to a variety of different legitimate answers, depending upon the use to which the concept is being put, the context in which it is being used, and the aims of those employing the concept in the first place. Thus, in asking what race is, we should *expect* ambiguity, contention, contestation, and even contradiction in the various responses worthy of consideration. This is simply what will happen when we examine a *human* phenomenon by raising the question of its meaning(s). To conclude from this that the concept is therefore meaningless, useless, or outright nonsense (illusory), is to employ standards of legitimation proper only to the politics of purity, and not, I submit, standards proper either to reason or to science. What is needed is to move beyond the standards of the politics of purity.

If human subjectivity is understood in this way as a process situated and conditioned by embodiment, history, and sociality, then race must be understood as a significant aspect of identity, at least within the contemporary context. Race, as an embodied way of organizing and interpreting the meaning of the process of identity for any given subject, cannot be reduced to a collection of (unambiguously possessed or lacked) properties, or a state to be achieved (or avoided altogether). One's racial status is the intersubjectively constituted position from and through which one engages in the ongoing

continual reshaping & articulation

process of negotiating meaning (including the meaning of race itself). Thus, just as identity is in part a position from which I engage the world, at the same time this position is not some stable and fixed platform but rather is itself an ongoing act of engagement, and so it is also constantly moving. The racial membership of any given individual, therefore, is at once part of the situatedness of one's identity (by means of their embodiment, the intersubjective significances and meanings of that embodiment, and the histories of that embodiment), and at the same time something which they are unavoidably engaging (affirming or critiquing either implicitly or explicitly) through the very act of articulating and negotiating who one has been, who one is, and who one wishes to be. As existential phenomenology is quick to point out, even our evasion of our identity as a kind of position shapes and conditions that identity. It is in this way that race, like identity, is a matter of becoming and not being. It is always more than what it is at any given moment, since its status is always being reinterpreted and renegotiated within an inescapably dynamic context that is already rife with ambiguity. Race, from the phenomenological perspective, is a *living* process, and as such is always developing and changing. To understand race within the politics of purity—to treat it as a static mode of being (or not-being)—is to approach it as a dead thing rather than a living phenomenon.

What this means is that my being white, by way of example, says something important about where I have come from, and where I am positioned in a social world deeply informed by centuries of sedimented (though always ambiguous) racial meanings. But my whiteness is not simply a property that I have, nor does it determine in some rigid and essentialist fashion the way I manifest my subjectivity. As a human subject, I am surely situated and conditioned by whiteness, but I am also able (indeed, unavoidably compelled) to condition and alter that whiteness, to offer new critiques and interpretations of it, to model or manifest it differently, or even to affirm it, deny its reality, or evade the question altogether. As a subject in a world full of other subjects, my engagement, critique, and interpretation of whiteness is also deeply informed and conditioned by the similar (and conflicting) activities of others. This intersubjective aspect is what keeps racial meaning from being purely subjective.

As a result, what my racial membership is and means cannot be simply chosen by fiat or willed away altogether for two important reasons. The first reason is that it has informed and continues to inform my identity as "interpretive horizon" in ways both explicit and implicit. Who I am, in this sense, will always be in part a matter of my whiteness. The second reason is that, since my engagement with racial meaning must take place in an intersubjective context, I must be able to employ the term in ways that will be understood as meaningful and significant, even if my aim is to offer critiques and attempt to change the meaning of the concept. For these two reasons, the statements "I am white" or "there are six black students in my class" do indeed mean something significant, even while they do *not* pick out any racial essences. To offer a Wittgensteinian point, the idea of a completely "private language" misses the entire idea of what it means to *mean* something (Wittgenstein 1958, 94–96). Thus, while it is true that there is no mind-independent foundation for racial meaning (positivistic essence), it does not follow that the content of the concept is completely up for grabs. My whiteness has meaning and significance that is independent of my own interpretations and desires, not because it is built in to the essential structure of the natural world over and against the ephemeral world of culture, but because it is part of the intersubjectively constituted system of meaning (Husserl's "Life World") which, because it provides a context in which meaning is even possible, enables me to exist as an intending and meaning subject in the first place.

This last point is crucial. Because the politics of purity tends, as I have argued, toward an atomistic ontology of the human in which the ideal of liberty is expressed in terms of the purity of an internal self free of external and unchosen impositions and constraints, it tends toward a rather generous definition of coercion. At one extreme, but rather common, end, this can come to view even and especially language, insofar as the individual agent did not create or choose to employ it, as such an external imposition and constraint. The problem with this line of thinking is that it ignores the way in which these external factors that condition and shape our thought and action also make it possible to think and act at all. In the words of Peter Caws, "Social structures once interiorized constrain and liberate at the same time, in that we are now free to communicate but only on the condition that we use available structures of communication" (1992, 306). Caws's point is that, for all that it constrains and conditions how we conceive of ourselves, how we express ourselves, how we conceptualize our actions and their meaning, and so on, language is also what makes it possible for us to do any of these things in the first place. In this way, language at once "constrains and liberates"—it is a necessary condition of human freedom at the same time that it can be a means and medium of oppression.

In the context of race, this can be seen in the outright rejection of racialized identity as exactly such an external imposition, the ultimate implication being that a truly autonomous identity would effectively manifest itself *sui generis*. Similar arguments can and have been made in relation to gender, as well.[5] Like language, racialized and gendered identities, in this view, become oppressive forces in themselves, constraining the free expression of our autonomous identity the moment they are *imposed* upon us. Of course, just as this view of language misses its liberatory aspects and potential, so too must the way in which race and gender both liberate and constrain be explored. To be sure, raced and gendered identities can have, and certainly have had historically, an oppressive, dehumanizing, and coercive impact on the lives of countless individuals. But to reject racialized and gendered identities outright as a consequence preserves a purified ideal of the abstract, ahistorical, featureless "agent" as the ideal of autonomy. It may leave individuals who are not constrained by such external impositions as racial identity, but it also leaves individuals with no *individuality*. In the language of recognition, it is a call for recognition as *a* person, when what one needs is recognition as *this* person. It is, once again, a call for identity devoid of all difference, and an assumption that any difference—any ambiguity—calls into question the whole of identity. To avoid these mistakes, we must conceive of identity, even raced and gendered identity, in line with Caws's claim about language. As part of the position from which, and the means through which, as particular individuals whose *individuality* is in part constituted by our similarities to, and differences from, others, we are enabled by race and gender even as we are constrained by them. Any genuine challenge to the politics of purity must be able to articulate this ambiguous aspect of identity and work to realize its liberatory aspects as fully as possible.

Of course, as I have argued, none of this means either that racial meaning is fixed and determined for all time in some static sense, or even that, at a given time, it is clear, distinct, and unambiguous. The way in which racial meaning has altered over time and from place to place is already quite a familiar story. I have discussed in the context of seventeenth-century Barbados the way in which multiple and competing understandings of race were contending with each other at the same time and place, and the important phenomenological claim to make here is that none of this points toward the meaningless or illusory status of race but rather to its status as a *living* and *human* concept. Once we understand racial reality as a process, and not a set of properties, then this ambiguity and flexibility becomes further evidence, rather than counterevidence, of the reality of race.

Just as individual identity is an ongoing process that must always be coming *from* somewhere, but is also always moving *toward* somewhere else (it is, as Sara Ahmed has described it, a kind of *orientation* [Ahmed 2006]), racial reality is likewise both a starting point for human consciousness, in that it conditions and shapes our meaning-making capacities, and a product of human consciousness, in that we are always conditioning and shaping race as a larger (intersubjective) context of meaning. The politics of purity demands that this living and changing process of meaning be replaced by a fixed, static, and dead state of being (or for the eliminativist, nonbeing). The phenomenological account of racial reality must reject all-or-nothing, pure approaches to racial ontology, racial membership, and racial meaning. Ontologically, race cannot be expected to provide essential properties that carve up nature (at the joints) in some *discoverable* way. In terms of racial membership, it cannot be expected to provide clear boundaries or necessary and sufficient conditions determining how individuals fit into distinct (pure) racial taxa. And the meaning of race cannot be fixed into any single set of meanings (such as the abolitionist tendency to reduce racial meaning to some relationship to white supremacy). Rather, race must be understood ontologically as fundamentally ambiguous and always, because it is a process of human meaning, undergoing change and redefinition. It is part of the larger context of meaning from and through which we orient our lives (Ahmed 2006, 109–29). Racial membership must therefore be understood as an ongoing process of negotiation and contestation rather than as necessary and sufficient conditions describing discrete and clearly bounded categories. Finally, the meaning of race is itself always in a process of contestation and negotiation, and cannot be reduced to any single set of meanings or narratives about what race is and how it works.

The eliminativists are surely correct when they reject racial reality as a set of positivistic (essentialist) criteria for dividing up the natural world into static kinds. The problem, however, is in assuming that this is the only way that reality can be understood to function. My brief discussion of the current debates surrounding the biological reality of race shows how these positivistic assumptions are being called into question by means of an argument that our very understanding of biological reality must be grasped within a context in which that reality is shaped by human consciousness (intentionality), and not simply given to us as "things in themselves." I have suggested that this is a kind of phenomenological point, even if those philosophers of science discussed above do not understand themselves to be phenomenologists, and that this points to the benefits of a phenomenological approach to racial ontology. This approach places human consciousness at the center of our inquiry, both insofar as we must take seriously the consciousness of those agents investigating the reality of race, and insofar as that consciousness itself must be held up to critical scrutiny. This yields an understanding of racial reality as a fundamentally dynamic and ambiguous process of meaning constituting. Race is, in a sense, the *here* from which I articulate my sense of what race itself might mean, but it is a *here* that is always ambiguous and even shifting (and that shifting is in part a result of my own grappling with or evasion of that *here*). Race is thus a process that is real not in the sense of determining the structure of things in themselves, but in the sense of being an inescapable factor conditioning human subjectivity, and structuring the meaning of the social world. However, insofar as it is this kind of dynamic process constituted by human consciousness, it cannot be *determinative* of those meanings and conditions—it is itself subject to renegotiation, contestation, and critique. It may, as I put it, be the *here* from which I enter into the ongoing contestation of race, but insofar as I am indeed *participating* in that contestation, it is always retreating and shifting in response to that participation (and in that sense it is also a *there*). Racial reality thus shapes who I am as an agent, but as an agent, I am always simultaneously shaping, in some small but nevertheless real way, racial reality.

RACE, HISTORY, AND MEANING

The ontological move from static to dynamic inspired by the phenomenological tradition highlights the significance of history, and why it figures so prominently in the account I am offering here. The static understanding of racial ontology may hold that our *ideas* of race may have a history, but race *in itself* must always be the same. Of course, I am speaking here of race as an ontological category—as a set of properties or conditions. Even in the static view, we may find that new races come into being, or that evolution changes the contours of the racial landscape, but what race fundamentally is and how it operates is always the same. Either there is some underlying essential reality to it, and our ideas can be a more or less accurate account of that essential reality at that moment in our evolutionary history, or it has always been a pure fiction, and our ideas of race so much nonsense. In this view, racial reality has a history insofar as the biological conditions of our species have changed over the last few hundred thousand years, but the reality of race *as a concept*, understood in this static sense, has no history, precisely because it has always been the same. We may be able to account for a history of how race has *appeared* on the scene of evolutionary science, but what race *is* as a category of being must always have been the same.

As I have suggested above, however, the ontology of race is not about what is or is not in itself but rather about what is or is not significant and meaningful about human variation, and how that significance and meaning might be expressed, reinforced, and reflected upon. What is more, that meaning and significance—as well as the ways and means whereby they are inscribed, altered, and interpreted—are always undergoing a dynamic process of alteration. My appeal to phenomenology is meant to bring to the foreground this question of meaning and significance. Reality is not simply laid out before us passively waiting to be mastered in its essential truth.[6] Reality is constituted as *meaningful* by human consciousness within an intersubjective milieu of shared meanings. Since consciousness is always active, the reality constituted by it must be dynamic and subject to change.

The question of the relationship between biology and race makes this clearer. No matter how much similarity we may have as individuals in biological terms, it remains true that there are innumerable differences (again, the exact nature of the relations between similarity or identity and difference is crucial). Height, build, proportionality of the length of torsos and legs, and of course all the usual racial suspects of pigmentation, hair color and texture, prominence of brow, size and shape of nose, and on and on. One can choose from all sorts of differences (though adding my science-fiction candidates of the ability to leap tall buildings or telekinesis might make this point even more clear), and any one difference could be chosen as a marker of taxonomic differentiation, depending upon whether and how we find particular differences *significant and meaningful.* The differences are there. The differences are real. The differences are even biological. What makes them racial is not a matter of discerning their inherent and pregiven racial properties but rather the way in which we constitute those differences as *racial* (and indeed, as *differences* in the first place).

Returning to Barbados in its early colonial period can illustrate this crucial point. There are all sorts of differences between the various groups and individuals on the island. From the mundane differences of eye color, height, and the biographical differences relating to place of birth and family background, to the more cultural differences of religious practice, economic status (I do not wish to enter into a debate about class formation in this period, so I will eschew that term), language, and political alliances (Roundhead versus Cavalier, for example). In addition, each of these individuals and groups brought with them a certain understanding of the meaning and salience of various kinds of difference from their place of origin—understandings that often did not easily fit into their new context. Pigmentation, therefore, was one difference among many, but it was one that had a long history of meaning and significance within the European context (and beyond). Whiteness was not, therefore, simply conjured forth out of nothing as a purely political tool of oppression and exploitation. The important change occurring in Barbados at this time was not one of the generation of whiteness but rather one of the alteration of the meaning and significance of whiteness. To reduce that meaning and significance exclusively to the political project of white supremacy is to omit both the long history of whiteness prior to this particular moment, and to disavow the ambiguity and conflict that characterized (and continues to characterize) racial reality at every level.

If, as I have argued, the straightforward question of whether the Irish were white is misguided, then what *are* the important questions to ask about this example? First and foremost, it is crucial to bear in mind the ambiguity of the term *Irish* itself. Historically, the Celts were continental invaders who crushed the native Firbolg before the Romans conquered Britain. Even if one takes these Celts to be the quintessential Irish, one has to decide how to accommodate the countless Norse invaders absorbed by that Celtic population, the Norman invaders of the twelfth century and their Old English descendants (which in turn points to the genealogical ambiguity of the English, as well), the subsequent "New English" transplanted nobility of the English restoration, and of course the protestant Scotch-Irish settlers in Ulster. Indeed, as historian Robert Kee has pointed out, "many of the names we think of today as most typically Irish—Joyce,

Burke, Costello, Prendergast, Fitzgerald, etc.—are in fact the names of these early Norman 'conquerors'" (1972, 10).

However ambiguous their provenance may be, the Irish who entered the scene I described in chapter 2 did so with a longstanding relation of antagonism to the English. To be sure, there were tensions and rivalries within the Irish population, and the question of who the Irish even were (for example, the peasantry and Old English merchant and aristocratic classes, who were Irish-speaking, might have had a different understanding of this issue than the English-speaking "New English" transplants), but for those Irish indentures that are the focus of my account, the differences between Galway and Wicklow, for example, were less important in the new context of Barbados. Likewise, their biological differences took on a different meaning in their new situation. Skin color differentiated them from the Amerindian and African populations, to be sure, but as I described in chapter 2, the English in particular understood the Irish to be physiologically recognizable and distinct from the rest of Europe, as well. They were simultaneously understood as white and as not white. And the question of what they *really* were cannot be reduced either to an isolated study of their biology or to a simple matter of their political allegiances. They took up the meanings and understandings of difference they inherited and employed them in new and different ways in their new context. As a result, the meaning of those differences, including the biological ones, were altered. In the earlier period of rebellion and resistance in concert with enslaved Africans, the Irish were not implicitly rejecting or denying their whiteness but rather asserting that the significance of their pale skin was less important than other attributes, which made them similar and different in relation to the other relevant populations. They were, in other words, implicitly offering an interpretation of the meaning of whiteness, insofar as they were acting as agents who both were and were not white in a context where the significance of whiteness was still very much up for grabs.

As these meanings developed over time, and as the Irish continued to negotiate their place in Barbados, whiteness, too, changed. As economic and demographic forces evolved, and in the face of political forces both internal and external to the island, whiteness began to have increased significance for the majority of the Island's inhabitants across the board, and those inhabitants came to understand the whiteness of the Irish as *like* that of the English, and to give that similarity a significance that put the Irish increasingly at odds with the nonwhite populations of the island. Thus, the biological status of whiteness took on different meanings over time as the different parties carved out their positions in the ongoing contestation over the significance of race. And as that significance changed, it conditioned human behavior in important ways, including, of course, patterns of endogamy and exogamy, thus simultaneously conditioning the very biological differences with which those populations were attempting to come to terms.

The whiteness of the Irish was an ambiguous political, biological, and cultural position from and through which they entered into the ongoing contestation of their place on the Island, including especially their *racial* place on the island. Their fundamentally ambiguous racial position at once conditioned and was conditioned by the actions (including acts of interpretation) of the Irish, along with their *interactions* with other populations on the Island. Once we introduce the idea that reality, including biological differentiation and its significance, has undergone and is constantly undergoing change, we introduce it as a *subject* of history.[7] It is that history which enables racial reality to condition human subjectivity, even as it is constantly being conditioned and reconditioned by that subjectivity. In this way the history of race is critical to our understanding of racial reality in the here and now while at the same time our present understanding conditions our interpretation of history. One task of the phenomenologist is to make this diachronic reciprocity an explicit object of inquiry.

What is more, by taking seriously the role of human consciousness in the constitution of racial reality, we must understand how it is conditioned not only by its past but also its *future*. An individual agent, for example, has a history that conditions her identity in the present. It is both her history as an agent, and also the history of the communities to which she belongs, which shape the contours of her "interpretive horizon." But her identity in the present, who she is and understands herself to be, is also conditioned by her sense of who she is to become. And that projection toward an as-yet-unrealized future also conditions the meaning and significance of her past. The interpretive causality, in other words, is not linear and unidirectional once human consciousness enters the mix. Unlike a mechanical system, in which subsequent moments are strictly determined by prior ones, in a world of meaning—in a world constituted by consciousness—the present, as meaningful, is conditioned by the past *and* the future. I may be a budding novelist, for example, which is a way of accounting for my present identity by appeal to an as-yet-unrealized future. It is not only the present that is shaped by the future-directedness of consciousness but also the past. Because of my desire to write a novel, my history of poverty and the tepid public responses to my guitar playing is no longer the history of my failure as a musician, but is in fact the history of my path to becoming a novelist—the tempering of my terse and hard-boiled prose. In the context of racial ontology, this means not only that the history of race conditions the present, but that our present understandings of race inform its history and, equally important, our sense of the future of race likewise informs its present and its past. There is a kind of reciprocity between the racial past, present, and future rather than a strict causal directionality from the past to the future. My claim that the new abolitionist account of racial history is fundamentally an appeal to color-blindness is a clear example of this, insofar as an essentially liberal color-blind view of human liberty informs their historical understanding of the nature of race. *Because* of the projection toward a raceless future, history for the abolitionists is a matter of the creation of different racial categories as illusory constructs capable, in principle, of being unmade. *That* racial history is conditioned by the longed-for, raceless future.

One way to capture the more phenomenological understanding of racial reality, following Clevis Headley, is to think of it as a kind of *conjuring.* In his essay "Delegitimizing the Normativity of 'Whiteness': A Critical Africana Philosophical Study of the Metaphoricity of 'Whiteness,'" Headley (2004) approaches the questions surrounding the reality and meaning of race through the Africana metaphor of conjuring. This metaphor is called upon to replace the more dominant metaphor of *construction* for three reasons. First, conjuring points more toward the *immaterial* transformation of the world rather than the decidedly concrete implications of construction (91). Furthermore, rather than the implication that one is creating something new out of whole cloth, conjuring carries with it the connotation that one is transforming or reshaping already existing materials. It is in this way, in particular, that his account can be understood as phenomenological—conjuring, like constitution, is a kind of shaping of reality rather than a summoning into existence out of nothing. Lastly, and perhaps most importantly, Headley emphasizes the connection between the metaphor of conjuring and appeals to magic found in more "traditional" Africana communities. In particular, he stresses the way in which, like the magical worldview, the reality of race is intimately and inextricably bound up with the meanings, symbols, and lived experience of those who participate in that reality. In a world that is inescapably saturated with racialized meaning, we all participate in that reality, and are thus implicated in (and responsible for and to) the conjuring of race.

Headley's overall approach, and the metaphor of conjuring as he lays it out, is clearly informed by Africana Phenomenology. Objects of human consciousness are constituted (conjured) within a fundamentally *intersubjective* context (cf. Husserl 1970, 182–86). This intersubjective aspect is crucial, because it is this aspect which prevents any given individual from solipsistically conjuring or simply annihilating some aspect of reality. In order for it to work, conjuring requires the participation of a community. Both directly and indirectly, each manifestation of conjuring involves the participation of multiple agents who condition the significance and meaning of that act. The "magic" of a given act of conjuring has to do with the way we shape and are shaped by a world full of meaning and significance that cannot simply be reduced to a collection of material objects. According to Peter Caws:

> If we think of ourselves, our biological individuality is assured by purely material considerations, and the quasi-causal relations into which our bodies enter are subsequent to our being what we physically are, even though some of them are essential to its continuance. But our social individuality was produced and is sustained only by the relations into which we have come to enter. (1988, 249)

If our individuality and our sociality are intimately connected, then conjuring, in this sense, is crucial to who we are. Our interactions with others, saturated as they are by meanings and symbols that both condition and make possible those interactions, serve as the medium for those acts of conjuring so crucial to racial reality, and to dismiss that reality because it is a kind of conjuring, far from a manifestation of clarity of vision, is in fact a kind of blindness.

A stage magician such as one might find in Las Vegas is a perfect example of this. For one not familiar with the performance of stage magic, the act will appear either to be genuinely miraculous (for the outrageously credulous) or nothing more than a series of deceptions—an exercise in serial lying. The magician attempts to trick the audience into believing something impossible has occurred when in fact, of course, it has not. But this interpretation comes from *outside* the practice. For the magician and her proper audience, the experience is fundamentally different. They both understand the meaning and tradition of stage magic and the standards by which a particular performance is judged to be good or bad. The audience is fully aware that what they see is an illusion, but they throw themselves into the deception in order to experience the performance *as magic* rather than simply as a series of lies. They know full well that the magician is not truly levitating or causing solid objects to pass through each other. The magician, for her part, does not take herself to be literally deceiving the audience. She does not believe that her task is to convince the audience that the person *really* has been sawed in half or the tiger has been summoned from thin air. If, after the show, an audience member asks her how she performed a given trick, she does not count it as a failure that the person was not convinced that it was indeed a miracle. The performance of magic is *successful,* in other words, not when the magician fully deceives the audience, but only when both the magician and the audience *constitute* the performance in the same way *as* a performance of magic. If an audience member spends the entire performance pointing out over and over again that each element is a trick and lie, he has not thereby revealed some deep and hidden truth about the performance, but is in fact *blind* to the meaning and truth of the performance. Racial reality is in this way analogous to the performance of magic, and is thus aptly captured by the metaphor of conjuring. The eliminativist is akin to the lone "realist" in the audience of the stage magician—in his effort to capture the "reality" of the situation, he is in fact missing the point entirely.

Of course, there are limits to this analogy (as with any analogy). Stage magic establishes, within the theater, a context in which there is a kind of mutual agreement to embrace what might otherwise be thought of as deception. But what makes the performance of stage magic work is precisely the underlying condition that once the audience leaves the theater, things will be as they were. One might see, for example, the sawed-in-half lady sitting quietly and in one piece at a slot machine. The significance of this analogy is that if such an encounter causes one to exclaim in outrage about deceitful so-called magicians, then one has missed the point of stage magic. In the theater, in any event, to point out that magic is not real does not demonstrate that one has uncovered something important about stage magic but rather merely makes clear that one has been incredibly obtuse. What I mean to suggest by this analogy is that, in the case of race, we are always in the theater (one clear way they are disanalogous), and the magic of race is such that it permeates all our actions and interactions. To dismiss it as illusion is to miss this crucial point.

If, instead of the positivistic approach favored by eliminativists and abolitionists, we work within the phenomenological framework of the metaphor of conjuring, the ontological analysis of the racial status of the Irish in seventeenth-century Barbados proceeds in a much different fashion from the analysis of analogous periods in the United States offered by Ignatiev, Roediger, and Jacobson. Rather than viewing the world prior to the fifteenth century as fundamentally raceless (because there was, allegedly, no white supremacy), conjuring invites us to see what happened during the colonial period as a transformation of preexisting concepts and meanings into something new and different, yet not something literally generated out of the void. There were, in other words, white people before white supremacy, just as there were black civilizations flourishing in the ancient world, even if neither population thought of themselves in terms that map neatly onto what we now think of as racial categories. The "magic" of colonialism and white supremacy as a political project lies not in its having created a difference that wasn't there before but rather in having attached meaning and significance to those preexisting differences. Race in general, and whiteness in particular, were thus *conjured* during a particular historical moment, but this involves, as Headley reminds us, "a whitening *of the world*" that "oppositionally entails making blackness the diabolical other" (2004, 92; italics added). The conjuring, in other words, reworks preexisting materials. Whiteness and blackness have always been tied, however tenuously and with degrees of inexactitude often distressing to those with positivist tendencies, to morphology. The encounter between Europe and Africa was, among many other things, an encounter between people who are relatively pale, and those who are relatively dark. And as the conjuring procedure advanced, the history and mythos of those pale peoples became the history and mythos of *Europe* (this point will be explored further in chapter 5) and the white race, which is a new way of interpreting that history and that mythology, but it all existed prior to the moment of conjuring.

In other words, the raw materials of biological difference along with linguistic concepts that are at least protoracial, as I have argued, were already present, and what happened was a shaping of those raw materials, through an intersubjective act of conjuring (constitution), into something different (and in that sense new). And as the conjuring of race played out and continues to take place, this shapes, and is shaped by, our understanding of the direction in which all of this is headed, which in turn shapes, and is shaped by, our history. Thus it becomes perfectly legitimate, not only for rhetorical or political reasons but *ontologically*, to speak of pre-Columbian *black* civilizations, or to describe Leif Erickson's voyage across the Atlantic as a *white* encounter with North America. The legitimacy of these claims, however, is not simply a matter of a purely descriptive account of the biological features of the participants, though surely such features are relevant. Erickson's whiteness, for example, is not simply a matter of his pale skin but also a matter of the way in which Norse culture became integral to the understanding of Europe as a place and as a culture that was itself a significant component of the modern conjuring of whiteness. Erickson and his crew certainly did not see themselves as part of the same race as the Saxons and Celts they raided on what are now the British Isles, and the reality of their all being white is not determined by some innate biological difference. It is rather a matter of the way in which certain biological differences, in reciprocal relation with certain cultural developments (again, the hard distinction between the biological and the cultural must be called into question), came to take on a significance that conjured a new meaning to historical events. This new meaning, because it is infused with and dependent upon human consciousness, is at the same time characterized by ambiguity, and must be understood as a dynamic process, and not as a discrete and fixed set of categories. But it is no less real for all that.

The racial ambiguity of the Irish in colonial Barbados, therefore, is not about the unfinished creation of racial whiteness, but about the indeterminacy of the meaning of whiteness. That the Irish could be described both as of a "different color" from the English, and at the same time as "white slaves" should thus be understood as an effort to refine and determine what it means to be white. What is more, the ambiguity of the Irish status was in large part due to their own refusal to conform to English standards of "proper," white behavior and comportment. The Irish were, historically, remarkably bad at enacting whiteness in the ways understood and preferred by the English, and they were, furthermore, often quite content with that fact. There are two important aspects of this particular effort to assign meaning to whiteness that are illuminated by the conjuring metaphor.

First, as Headley has reminded us, this effort is fundamentally opposi-tional. Negotiating the significance and meaning of whiteness, and the place of the Irish within that concept, was also a struggle to determine the meaning and significance of blackness (and everything in between, so to speak). Second, this was a process of *negotiation*, in which all of the parties had some involvement. Just as the stage magician must have an audience who are, to a greater or lesser extent, willing to play along, the conjuring of racial reality required not merely the *fiat* of the English elite on Barbados but also the resistance, rebellion, acquiescence, and even cooperation of the Anglos, the Irish, the Scots, the Welsh, the Sephardic Jews and the enslaved West Africans, as well as the offspring of exogamous unions, all of whom were attempting to negotiate their place on the island in relation to each other. One illustration of this is the way in which the English planters on Barbados at once stressed the differences between the various ethnic groups among their servants (English, Scottish, Welsh, and Irish), while at the same time pitting them all against the numerically increasing black labor force on the island. According to Beckles, "Planters consciously designed policies to divide servants and slaves politically and to split the servant class along na-tionalist lines, in order to keep resistance focused on an individual, and hence unorganized and containable, level" (1989, 98). The Sephardic Jews, at the same time, who had been invited to the island to escape persecution in Brazil and the Netherlands in part because they brought with them tech-nical knowledge crucial to sugar production, were likewise granted certain privileges vis-à-vis the servants and slaves, but were still understood is sig-nificantly distinct from the English Plantocracy. Of crucial importance here is that all of these groups had their own role to play in this negotiation; they were not simply the passive pawns of the English elite. My contention is that the whiteness of the Irish was not a matter of whether they could *be* white, but whether they would come to *endorse* the dominant view of what it *meant*, and largely still means, to be white. It is not about being white but rather *manifesting* whiteness in a particular way. *Being white* in any event is not only ambiguous but dynamic, and must be understood not as an attri-bution of a set of static properties but rather as a sort of shorthand for man-ifesting an embodiment and history consistent in at least some respects with the dominant, yet always in the process of being negotiated and contested, meanings of whiteness. It thus picks out a real subject position that will in-evitably condition both how one develops as an embodied subject, and how one is able to interact within a given social context, but because it is dynamic and ambiguous, one's development and interactions contribute to the ongoing negotiation and contestation of the meaning and significance of racial categories themselves. The Irish in Barbados were thus white people (in this sense) who had a chance to resist white supremacy, and, at least a few of them, at least for a while, did exactly that. In those moments of resistance, they did not cease to be white, they simply manifested a different *way* to be white. More importantly, by eventually capitulating to the supremacist vision of whiteness, they helped to further solidify that vision—they were willing participants in the conjuring of racial whiteness as we have come to know it today.

Toward the end of his essay, Headley calls for a "teleological suspension of whiteness" (2004, 102), which entails "a continuously affirmed refusal to prolong the ontological and existential project of whiteness" (103). It is important to emphasize his reference to whiteness as a "project," since this is in keeping with the idea that it entails certain political and ontological *commitments*, which must in turn be reenacted, reinscribed, and reaffirmed on a daily basis in ways both mundane and profound (in the same way that stage magic requires a commitment to understand the performance *as such*). Headley goes on to argue that this "refusal to prolong" cannot take the form of rational and neutral argumentation "because our language itself is infected with the project of whiteness. After all, what would it mean to argue in favor of renouncing whiteness and its benefits by using a discourse imbued with the categories that perpetuate whiteness?" (103). This means that any antiracist commitment must be made manifest in part through a continued emphasis on the way in which racial ontology, as a dynamic manifestation of conjuring, is an ongoing *process* demanding the continued participation of all those involved in that process, willing or not. The rituals, so to speak, of racial whiteness (and racial ontology in general) need to be upset, reinterpreted, and challenged in meaningful ways. However, given the pervasiveness of racial thinking, efforts to abandon or reject racial reality outright will never be effective. What is needed instead is a critical confrontation with racial reality as a process of conjuring that can and should be itself transformed into something new (conjured differently). As Headley puts it, paraphrasing Fanon, "Moving beyond whiteness requires a radically new concept of the human, a new metaphoricity of humanity" (104).

One way to undertake this project is, following Alcoff's suggestion, to draw forth and emphasize those historical moments in the development of racial ontology in which the meaning of whiteness has been contested (2006, 223). Just as racial justice movements in North America have involved the recovery and emphasis of the history of black resistance to white supremacy in the form of Denmark Vessey, Nat Turner, Sojourner Truth, Frederick Douglass, Ida B. Wells, Rosa Parks, and Malcolm X to name a few, so too will it be important to reclaim the legacy of John Brown and Sophie Scholl, and even those Irish indentures who chose to form confederation with African slaves in resistance to slave masters. This is not meant to be a white washing, so to speak, of the history of white supremacy but rather the examination of an alternative way to manifest whiteness. It is an effort to offer a new metaphor for whiteness by pointing toward those white folks who rejected and actively resisted white supremacy. To be sure, they probably did not think of themselves at the time as resisting white supremacy, but by the same token, it seems unlikely that Denmark Vessey explicitly understood his actions as a form of resistance to antiblack racial oppression. At the same time, this emphasis on historical moments of white resistance to white supremacy clearly should not be understood as a denial of the reality of white privilege,[8] or as downplaying the reality of white supremacy and nonwhite oppression. Rather, it points toward a view of whiteness that is at once inextricably tied to a history of privilege and oppression, yet actively resisting the continued legacy of that history. It means, for the individual white person, recognizing and taking responsibility for racial whiteness and the role it has played in one's own life and the world around us, while at the same time pointing out that, as Headley puts it, "things can be otherwise" (2004, 104), and that whiteness does not *have* to be reducible to white supremacy (cf. Monahan 2003).

The presumption that race is reducible to a set of relations to white supremacy is, as I argue in chapter 1, a result in part of the fundamentally liberal individualist ontology that informs this approach to race. It emerges out of the imperative for the purification of the self that fosters an understanding of the social world as fundamentally *external* to the self. Since the ideal is to have a (purified) self unencumbered by such external influences, racialization, as a kind of imposition of an external identity, must be understood as essentially contrary to human autonomy. If we instead make a teleological suspension of this set of assumptions, we can see that part of what informs it is both the presumption that an unfettered self will be a raceless one, and that the aim or goal is a lack of fetters at all. In a context in which whiteness functions as a universal norm—as a raced perspective that need not acknowledge itself as racially particular but rather understands itself to be the universal norm of the human *beyond* race—an unfettered self will also be a white one. The abolitionists, at least, recognize this point and understand themselves in part to be recognizing the particularity of whiteness. However, insofar as their prescriptive moment entails the abolition of race, they are still pointing toward a raceless norm. They are taking for granted the idea that freedom or liberation is inconsistent with historical specificity (the ideal of the unfettered self), and that racial particularity is a clear instance of such a fetter.

The suspension or bracketing of this set of assumptions would suggest that it is not being racialized in itself that is pathological but rather the insistence that one is *not* racialized (or might at some future time cease to be racialized). In other words, the rejection of race is intended to address the problem of racism, and identifies the imposition of racial categories and racial identities (racialization) as the source of the problem. Race is the problem, and racelessness is the goal. The phenomenological approach I am advocating would instead open the possibility that the pathology lies in seeing oneself as *not* raced rather than in seeing oneself as raced. The idea that one's subjectivity is embodied, historical, and deeply socially situated is not the real threat. It is rather the effort to evade racialization and posit an abstracted, undifferentiated, and ultimately ahistorical subjectivity that needs to be taken to task. Not merely because it might be (and very often is) whiteness in the guise of the universal (raceless) human, but ultimately because it offers a flawed notion of human subjectivity as radically distinct from the socio-historical context in which it finds itself.

It is because there is a presumption of a certain norm of humanity (as I will argue in the next chapter, a purified one), that race must be understood by this eliminativist/abolitionist approach as inherently pernicious. As I argued earlier, the insistence upon a raceless humanity is simply the other side of an all-or-nothing coin with positivist racial realism, which sees racial being as shared inherent properties, on the one side, and racial eliminativism, which seems racial being as a collection of misguided concepts that can only serve to undermine our autonomy, on the other. But the phenomenological approach I am advancing here rejects this dichotomy, just as it rejected the dichotomy between biology and culture. It is not that human subjectivity is either strictly determined by essential properties or completely at liberty to choose voluntaristically between a myriad of "external" influences. Both of these views treat human agency as static and fixed, either anchored within these essential properties, or completely above and beyond such contingencies. Contrary to this traditional view, we must approach both individual and racial ontology as dynamic rather than static, and ambiguous rather than pure.

What this means for the analysis of the history of race is that we place more focus upon the *contestation* of the meaning of racial categories as opposed to the outcome of those contests. To be sure, those whites who struggled against white supremacy, even if they did not explicitly understand their actions in that way, ultimately lost their battles. But the point of understanding race as an ongoing and dialogic process is that while the battles may have been lost in the past, the war, to continue this admittedly bellicose metaphor, is *never* over, and thus never lost.[9] The fact that white persons have struggled, and continue to struggle, against white supremacy does not mean that they thereby cease being white; it means that they offer a different vision of *how* to be white, and what whiteness can and should mean. To demand that antiracism entail an abolition of whiteness is to concede ultimate victory to the supremacist vision of the meaning of whiteness. I would argue that such a concession is premature, and ultimately harmful.

This is because racial concepts are so deeply historical as to have far too much inertia to be so easily left behind. Race has had too much significance for too long, and it is precisely because that significance has wrought so much horror that we need to continue to take seriously its role in our lives, even as we struggle to make that role more positive rather than attempt to expunge it from our lives completely. The reality of race, as an ongoing process of contestation over meaning within an intersubjective and richly historical context, is constitutive of one's identity in all sorts of significant ways. Of course, since identity itself is an ongoing process, and the role and meaning of race is dynamic, we are shaping it even as it shapes us. To deny the role of race is not to capture some hitherto denied reality (that race is an illusion), but is rather to reject a *human* understanding of reality for a positivistic and ultimately antihuman one (this point will be elaborated in chapter 5).

In emphasizing the status of racial being as an ongoing moment of *contestation*, and calling for historically and philosophically rigorous engagement with that contestation, I am thus at the same time calling for an affirmation of *agency*. The abolitionist position, I have argued, concedes complete discursive power to white supremacist elites by allowing that particular interpretation of the meaning of race to function as the *only* interpretation. By calling upon and emphasizing the role that people of all races and social positions have had in challenging that power historically, in the present, and with an eye toward the future, we bring to the foreground the very agency and humanity that white supremacy seeks to obfuscate. We must, I submit, come to the struggle against white supremacy as fully embodied, historically situated subjects, which means that, like it or not, we must struggle against racism from a position that is always already raced. Fanon tells us that genuine freedom cannot be granted externally but must be *actively* taken (2008, 195). The mere fact that we are raced, therefore, does not in itself deprive us of freedom, as the abolitionist position would have it. Our freedom suffers when we *capitulate* to the supremacist *meanings* that are attached to those "facts." Antiracism, therefore, demands the struggle to participate fully in the ongoing negotiation of racial meaning—it demands, in other words, the assertion of our own fully human (and thus embodied and even *raced*) agency and that of others. In chapters 5 and 6, I will elaborate on the implications for antiracist *praxis* that follow from this account of racial ontology.

5

The Politics of Purity:
Colonialism, Reason, and Modernity

In terms of racial ontology, as described in the previous chapter, the politics of purity operates normatively to prescribe clearly bounded categories of being admitting of necessary and sufficient conditions for membership such that each individual is unambiguously a member of one and only one racial category. As a corrective to the politics of purity, I advanced an approach to race such that we understand it as a dynamic process of contesting and negotiating the position from and through which we constitute meaning in and of the world, including especially the meaning of race itself. It is a kind of orientation or horizon, and as such is a manifestation of becoming, rather than being. This means that racial categories are ambiguous, describing what are at best only ever tenuous and indistinct boundaries. It further means that individual agents can be of multiple categories simultaneously, yet, insofar as the categories themselves remain in flux, are never fully or purely of any particular category. But what does all of this tell us about racism as a phenomenon? Much of what has motivated efforts to understand race ontologically both in the past and more recently has been racism and our efforts to undermine it. That is, the racist used ontology to legitimate racial oppression by pointing toward natural divisions within the species, while the antiracist worked to undermine racial oppression by pointing toward the *lack* of such divisions. Given my effort to shift this discourse

How to undermine racism / + build democracy

away from the all-or-nothing thinking of the politics of purity, and my emphasis on the plurality and ambiguity of racial meaning from the ground up, we need to explore in more detail the way this shift impacts our thinking about racism as a phenomenon.

In this chapter, I offer an account of how the politics of purity impacts our understanding of racism as a social phenomenon, attending especially to its norming function in relation to racial whiteness, and its links to the hegemony of a particular understanding of reason. I will begin by exploring how racism can be understood on a more individual level, and then I draw some implications for our understanding of the meaning and function of racism, before situating that account within a broader social and institutional context. Ultimately, I will argue that racism is intimately connected to the politics of purity, insofar as it has functioned as an effort to *purify* the self on the more individual level, and to purify humanity as a whole at the more social and political levels. I must stress at the outset that I see this distinction between the individual and the social more as a kind of heuristic device, and that the understanding of these levels as strictly distinct is in fact, I will argue, a further manifestation of the politics of purity.

BECOMING ANTIRACIST: REFLECTIONS ON INDIVIDUAL RACISM

According to my students, people, by and large, are not racist. They may acknowledge racism's continuing potency and relevance, but they are certainly not racist, nor are their friends. The general sense of confidence my students express about the moribund status of racism seems predicated upon exactly this sense of their own (and their friends') lack of racism. There may be a few individuals out there committing hate crimes and offering racist rants, but they are the exception to a generally nonracist rule. To be sure, my students usually are not, at least at first, sensitive to distinctions between individual prejudice and systematic or institutional racism, and this alone might be sufficient to cast their prognostications about racism's imminent demise into doubt. However, I would like to set this aside for the moment, and look closely at their claims about their own lack of racism. Not because the beliefs of my students are of interest in their own right (they may be, though I'm certainly not committed to arguing for that position), but rather because they are indicative of a broad set of views about racism that are worthy of attention because of their dominance within racial discourse in North America.

By way of an appeal to Nietzsche, and specifically to his critique of dualistic ways of thinking, I will argue that a significant conceptual error is being made within this dominant discourse.

Nietzsche's critique of dualism is in significant ways analogous to Husserl's critique of positivism, and in this way builds upon my ongoing critique of the politics of purity. I appeal to Nietzsche here both because I believe his metaphors and linguistic idiom better capture what is going on at this more basic, individual level, and to demonstrate the sympathies between the phenomenological project and other critical theoretical approaches. Again, I am focusing in this section on how we understand racism at the level of individual agents. This is artificial, in that I ultimately do not believe that there is a purely individual level to a phenomenon as complex and deeply intersubjective as racism, but I believe that as long as this artificiality is born in mind, it can be instructive, insofar as the radicality of the shift in thinking brought about by the critique of the politics of purity can be seen quite clearly in this simplified context.[1] In due time, I will abandon this overly simplified approach, and I want to stress that I am not at all here advocating an understanding of racism that reduces it to a matter of individual beliefs and intentions. It is simply a heuristic device that will, rest assured, be set aside once it has done its work.

The dominant view of racism at this individual level, informed as it is by the politics of purity, tends to treat racism and the lack thereof as if they were states of being which, though they may admit of degrees in the finer details, at root stand as all-or-nothing propositions. One either is or is not a racist. Thus one may say that David Duke is *more* racist than my grandmother, who in turn was more racist than my grandfather, but in point of fact they all are (or were) racist, the difference is simply a matter of how virulently and explicitly the racism is manifest in each particular case.[2] So, just as the politics of purity understands racial membership as a matter of the presence or absence of certain conditions that are necessary or sufficient or both, this account of racism treats it as a kind of contingent property that either does or does not inhere in particular individuals. Racism, within this view, can thus be broadly understood as the presence of conscious or even subconscious mental states that can themselves be properly described as racist. It would certainly be possible to enter into a lengthy and very complicated discussion of what mental states might even be, and what it would mean for such states to be racist, but that would be a distraction at this

point. By *mental states* I mean the ordinary, so-called folk psychological understanding of beliefs, ideas, and meanings, which in turn inform and guide
our actions, and by *racist* in this definition, I mean only that the mental
states in question attribute pejorative moral, epistemic, cultural, or anthropological characteristics to others based upon alleged racial membership
(Jorge Garcia's volitional account of racism would be an example of this
[1997, 29–31]). What is important about this admittedly fast and loose account, and the reason why the contentious fine details are not relevant, is
that mental states, whatever they may be, constitute the truth of one's
racism as a state of being. In the case of subconscious mental states (again,
setting aside questions of how best to understand the meaning of the term),
for example, a sudden slip of the tongue (like a well-placed "those people"),
or an involuntary action (like checking to make sure the car doors are locked
while driving through the "inner city") can suddenly reveal to others, and
even perhaps to oneself, that one is in fact, and has been all along, a racist.
Of course, this would assume a certain degree of sensitivity to and consciousness of racism on the part of the observer, and one must not underes-
timate the power of self-deception. Nevertheless, assuming some basic
racial-epistemic competence on the part of the observer, the revelation of
such mental states is at one and the same time a revelation of *being* racist.

Thus, from the perspective of any given individual, on this account, the
attribution of racist mental states to that individual becomes an effective al-
legation that one is racist at one's core, so to speak. Claims that one's speech
or actions are racist become immediately linked to the heart of one's being
(or at least one's implicit conception thereof). What these mental states
show is that one is a racist as a state of being, whether one realizes it or not,
and this is largely why people (like my students) are often so threatened by
the very idea that they may harbor racist beliefs or attitudes. Any particular
manifestation of racism thus becomes, in retrospect, the revelation of one's
underlying racism. You may have thought that you were not a racist, but
then you did or said something that shows that you have been mistaken all
this time. Racism is thus ultimately an all-or-nothing proposition. One
either possesses racist mental states consciously or unconsciously, in which
case one is racist, or one lacks them utterly, in which case one is nonracist.

To be nonracist within this account, therefore, means to be without the
appropriate (or, since I am talking about racism, inappropriate) mental
states. We believe that Bob is not a racist because we never witness Bob

saying or doing racist things. Provided we have no good reason to suspect that Bob has some secret life in a white supremacist organization, this counts as good evidence of his nonracism. Subjectively, the same process is at work. Bob knows that he is not racist because he does not detect within himself any racist mental states. In short, if we understand racism as a state of being, as a kind of contingent property, then nonracism must be the absence of racism—the absence of that property. One is a racist when racist mental states are present, and one is nonracist when they are absent. The conformity with the logic of purity is clear here.

As mentioned above, this means that *any* failure, any revelation of racist mental states, puts the lie immediately to any claims of nonracism. You may have *thought* you were nonracist, but that you did x or said y shows that you were mistaken. One can readily see how this approach to nonracism would be conducive to a kind of pessimism, especially in a social context so deeply saturated with racist institutions, symbols, and structures of meaning (here again, the social immediately threatens the artificial simplicity of this individualistic analysis). To grow and mature within such a context would seemingly ensure one's ultimate racism.[3] Within a deeply racist world, one is all but doomed to possess racist mental states. Despite all of one's best efforts, it seems reasonable to always suspect that squirreled away somewhere in every individual (of every racial background) is some tenacious racist mental state, eating its way like a termite into the nonracist self-concept we have worked so hard to construct. To be sure, there is no reason to rule out in principle the psychological possibility of eventually achieving nonracism, but there does seem to be a very reasonable case for a rather robust pessimism. Why bother exerting oneself in the effort to purge oneself of racist mental states when the odds are so heavily stacked against us? Why not do just enough to *pass* for nonracist, and let the rest take care of itself?

Of course, arriving at this pessimist conclusion requires no small amount of self-scrutiny, and careful reflection upon the forces arrayed against the would-be nonracist. In the absence of this self-reflective discipline (which is surely more common), this conception of racism is more likely to lead to complacency rather than pessimism. That is to say, as long as one is convinced that one has purged oneself of racist mental states, then one *is* nonracist. The work is done (I have achieved nonracism—mission accomplished!), and one need not worry about it again. At least, one need not worry about it again until such time as one is forced to confront some failure or another—

Should have
Royce have kept quiet

that slip of the tongue or involuntary act. This risk of *exposing* oneself, in effect, gives one a clear incentive to avoid those situations that are likely to elicit such failures. If I believe myself to be nonracist according to this static view, but I suspect, however dimly, that there could be lurking racist mental states just waiting to spring themselves on me and shatter this belief, then it is clearly in my interest to play it safe—to avoid any and all situations conducive to stirring up those mental states. This risk aversion dictates that one should avoid talking about race, or mixing socially with other races, or in any way sticking one's neck out such that hidden racist mental states might reveal themselves to oneself, or, even worse, to others. If I, for example, as a white person surround myself with other well-meaning, "nonracist" white people, then we are collectively far less likely to unearth that hidden racist mental state, and thus we may continue to congratulate ourselves on our lack of racism. Anyone who has witnessed a group of such well-meaning people talk their way *around* issues of race has a clear example of this sort of behavior.

Another result of this way of understanding racism is an often energetic or even aggressive defensiveness when it comes to issues of race (again, a phenomenon many of us are likely to have encountered, or even enacted). If I hold myself to be nonracist, this belief can be challenged either by subjective manifestations of racist mental states, like a thought or image passing fleetingly through my head, or it can be challenged by an external, public manifestation, like an utterance or gesture witnessed by others. I can defend myself against the former by avoiding situations or people that I suspect might cause such mental states, or by avoiding introspection altogether. But when some other person accuses me of racism, my strategies for self-defense must be different. Again, the threat here is so significant in large part because this view of racism holds that the revelation of some racist mental state or mental states by some other indicates that I *am* a racist.

Thus, rather than taking up the observation or challenge and assessing its plausibility so that I can address the mental states in question (during which process, at least, I would continue to be racist until I have purified myself of the racist mental state, and which admission would throw further doubt on any future claims to nonracism), a more common and psychologically appealing strategy is to deny the original accusation altogether. I may argue that my utterance or gesture was in fact *not* racist, for reasons x, y, and z, or that you thought you saw something that wasn't really there, or even better, that it is *your own* racism that leads you to interpret my perfectly innocent statement as racist ("Why are you always playing the race card?"). If one thinks of racism as this sort of all-or-nothing status one either occupies or fails to occupy and one takes racism to be wrong, then there is a compelling incentive to deny vociferously any and all accusations that one is racist. Clearly, sometimes such accusations can indeed be erroneous; arising out of ignorance, malice, or simple misunderstanding. My point is not that one should treat every such observation as equally valid but rather only that this way of thinking about what racism is provides a strong motive to treat every such observation as a threat to one's *status* as nonracist—and this threat demands a strident defense.

All of this constitutes, I submit, a compelling set of reasons to be suspicious of this static view of racism predicated upon the politics of purity. It brings with it a tendency toward pessimism as well as pernicious forms of complacency, risk-aversion, and defensiveness. What, then, should be offered in its place? In the spirit of the dynamic account of racial ontology I offered in the previous chapter, I suggest a Nietzsche-inspired account of a dynamic view of racism and *antiracism* (as opposed to nonracism) consistent with my developing critique of the politics of purity. I wish to stress that my use of "Nietzsche inspired" is quite deliberate. I make appeal to certain aspects of Nietzsche's thought to develop these insights regarding racism, but this does not mean that I take any position regarding Nietzsche's own racism or lack thereof. Nor do I take myself to be offering an exhaustive or authoritative interpretation of Nietzsche. I believe my reading of Nietzsche's fundamental positions to be consistent with the spirit of his texts, and try to make the best case for that interpretation I can—no more, no less.

One of the major themes throughout Nietzsche's corpus, but most especially in *Thus Spoke Zarathustra*, is a critique of dualism. In *Beyond Good and Evil*, for example, he tells us that the true philosopher must reject "faith in opposite values," and embrace the great and "dangerous maybe" (1966a, 10). Perhaps the best way of capturing this suspicion is by way of Nietzsche's emphasis on *becoming* over and against *being*, which clearly resonates with Husserlian phenomenology's understanding of life as a constant becoming. In *Zarathustra*, for example, Nietzsche writes:

> God is a thought that makes crooked all that is straight, and makes turn whatever stands. How? Should time be gone, and all that is impermanent

a mere lie? To think this is a dizzy whirl for human bones, and a vomit for the stomach; verily, I call it the turning sickness to conjecture thus. Evil I call it, and misanthropic—all this teaching of the One and the Plenum and the Unmoved and the Sated and the Permanent. All the permanent—that is only a parable. And the poets lie too much.

It is of time and becoming that the best parables should speak: let them be a praise and a justification of all impermanence. (1966b, 86–7)

And in *Twilight of the Idols*:

You ask me about the idiosyncrasies of philosophers? . . .

There is their lack of historical sense, their hatred of even the idea of becoming, ... They think they are doing a thing *honor* when they de-historicize it, *sub specie aeterni*—when they make a mummy out of it . . .

What is, does not *become*; what becomes, *is* not. . . . (1968, 45)

Nietzsche thus places an important emphasis on change—growth, decay, going under, going over, creating, smashing, and overcoming—over and against more static notions of being. He thereby calls into question ossified notions of truth, value, morality, and identity while embracing more fungible, transient, and fallible versions of these concepts. He favors experimenta-tion—indeed, the philosophers of the future are the "attempters" (1966a, 52)—and uncertainty over complacency and a self-deluded (and often self-serving) claim to certainty.

One can see this emphasis on becoming over being at the heart of Nietz-sche's critiques of slave morality, truth, science, and philosophy. The moment these concepts posit some eternal, rigid, and unchanging essence "behind the world" (1968b, 17) they become targets of his ire. But a morality that creates value "in the world," a truth that is flexible and fallible, a science that is open to creativity and artistic interpretation, and a philosophy that is *ex-perimental*, all of these earn his respect. Value, for Nietzsche, emerges out of change, and so any theory, concept, or system that seeks to avoid or suppress change cannot be valuable.

Yet another way to see this at work is through Nietzsche's frequent appeal to *overcoming*. Life, we are told in *Zarathustra*, is "that which must always overcome itself" (1966b, 115). Likewise, the meaning of the *Übermensch* is that humanity is something that must be overcome (1966b, 12). The narrative of Zarathustra himself illustrates both this aspect of becoming, and over-coming. He is constantly changing—coming down from the mountain and "going under," then returning to his animals and his mountains, then coming back down, seeking friends, then leaving them, then seeking new ones, and so on, all in an effort to push himself and others to ever greater heights. Zarathustra proclaims that humanity itself is "something that must be overcome—[it] is a bridge and no end" (1966b, 198). Thus, it is only through this ongoing process of overcoming oneself that the full promise of humanity can be approached (though surely never achieved as an end *state of being*). Humanity itself thus serves as an example of becoming—we are always, Nietzsche reminds us, becoming what we are.

Self-overcoming, as a manifestation of becoming, is central to Nietzsche's conception of humanity, the *Übermensch*, and life itself. Of course, since self-overcoming is explicitly not an end state, it can never be a *fait accompli*—one is never finished overcoming oneself; that would be an appeal to being. For one to think that one has overcome oneself is to misunderstand the very meaning of self-overcoming. Such self-assurance and conceit becomes itself something that must be overcome. This is of particular importance in relation to racism, as I will show later.

One final important aspect of Nietzsche's thought is his emphasis on creation and self-expression (value creation), which is closely linked both to self-overcoming and to his rejection of dualism. The revaluation of all values is thus a project of creation. We are urged by Zarathustra to smash old tablets of values and erect new ones, all the while realizing that these, too, must one day be torn down and replaced. It is in this destruction of old values and erection of new ones that human *being*, and life itself, is overcome, and the full promise of humanity emerges. But insofar as this full promise is realized only in this *process* of overcoming and value creation, it can never be an end state, and each instance of overcoming only opens the way for yet further such instances.

What this means is that we must—if we are to become what we are through this ongoing process of self-overcoming—avoid stasis and complacency. The danger for humanity, according to Nietzsche, is "the spirit of gravity"—one of his favorite recurring metaphors. The spirit of gravity refers to becoming mired down in ossified, transcendent, and fixed truths, beliefs, or values that serve as a kind of psychological, aesthetic, epistemic, and moral ballast. They weigh us down and inhibit the free-flowing movement that is necessary for the kind of self-creation and self-overcoming that Nietzsche endorses. Such truths and beliefs become so central to us that we simply cannot abandon them, and at that moment they become a loadstone around our necks. They come to define us as a kind of *being*, and retard the processes of becoming that are the real source of value in the world (in this way it is akin to Sartre's spirit of "seriousness"). When we become mired down in the spirit of gravity, genuine creation and self-overcoming are all but impossible.

This concern with the spirit of gravity, however, does not entail that we should cast off all reference points and ideas. This, indeed, is the problem of nihilism—the rejection of timeless and eternal truths does not obligate one to nothingness. This is analogous to the previous discussion of racial ontology. Within the context of the politics of purity, the realist about race seeks to fix its meaning in static structures and properties, while the eliminativist, in finding no such static structure or properties, holds that race must therefore be rejected altogether. Nietzsche's critique of the reliance on fixed and transcendent notions of value and truth as well as the rejection of all truth and value that comes with the *death* of such gods and idols, thus has very strong affinities with Husserl's critique of positivism. There are, to be sure, numerous significant differences, but both thinkers identify the insistence on mind-independent, fixed, and ahistorical foundations for truth and value, and the subsequent rejection of all truth and value that issues from the collapse of such foundations, to be a point of *crisis* that must be overcome through *true* philosophy. The task, for both thinkers, is to articulate ways of thinking meaningfully about truth and value that avoids the pitfalls of positivism and nihilism—and they advance this project, at least in part, through an appeal to a fundamentally *dynamic* understanding of human existence.

One way to see this point is though appeal to another of Nietzsche's favorite metaphors—dance. He repeatedly holds up dance as a symbol for exactly the sort of exuberant, creative, self-expressive activity that he takes to be the full flourishing of humanity. Dance just *is* change and movement. When the movement and change cease, the dance is over. To be sure, there may be pauses and respites from the action, but these, if they are part of the dance, are there only to heighten the meaning and significance of the kinetic change taking place around them. Like a dramatic pause in music, what makes it dramatic is the contrast from the ever-changing sounds on either side of the pause. What is most significant, however, is that dance is

dance + gravity

impossible without gravity. Imagine, if you will, attempting to dance in zero gravity. There may be a certain grace to floating weightless, but one is hard pressed to think of it as dance, and what grace there is seems to have more to do with the circumstances in which the body finds itself rather than with the movement and directed energy of that body. Dance is made possible through resistance and occasionally, but only ever temporarily, *surrender* to gravity.

Dance is thus a perfect metaphor for self-overcoming and Nietzsche's rejection of dualism. That is, if we take seriously the metaphor of dance (and the frequency of its appearance in Nietzsche's corpus seems to facilitate this), we can see that viewing the spirit of gravity as a threat is not the same thing as a call for the complete elimination of gravity as such. The truth of self-overcoming and value creation (as kinds of *dance*) emerges out of resistance to this metaphorical gravity and exists only through resisting and working within and against it. To say that self-overcoming requires this gravity, however, does not mean that it requires the *spirit* of gravity. The latter is an attitude (one Nietzsche takes to be a manifestation of weakness and a kind of surrender) that actively endorses the weighing down of humanity with fixed and given essences and values, and my point here is that self-overcoming may require active resistance to this attitude, but that such resistance does not necessitate the annihilation of this sense of gravity as such. While we may need gravity in order to dance, the recognition of this fact in no way entails an affirmation of the *spirit* of gravity. Likewise, where the politics of purity would insist on fixed and given categories of racial being, resistance to the politics of purity does not require that we abandon all notions of race altogether. The point is rather that we must understand them quite differently, and resist the all-or-nothing tendencies of the politics of purity for a more dynamic account of racial reality. As I argue in the previous chapters, the appeal to boundaries and distinctions between human populations may be helpful ways of capturing certain aspects of human life (the targeting of sickle cell diagnostic resources, for example), the failure is when we either treat these categories as static and unambiguous, or dismiss them altogether.

I would now like to return to the question of racism and antiracism. If instead of thinking of racism as a manifestation of being, as in the static (pure) approach, we think both of racism and antiracism as *processes* of becoming, a radically different picture emerges. First, racism cannot be a static property that a particular individual either possesses or lacks but is rather a way of becoming. It is a kind of esteeming or valuing that expresses the self-hood of the subject in starkly dualistic and static terms, and is therefore always already a misrepresentation both of the subject herself and the object (or objects) of the racist mental states. As a kind of valuing, a kind of action, racism is thus a manner of becoming attempting to pass itself off as a kind of being. It is not a fixed property but a way of valuing which should be overcome for several reasons. Following Lewis Gordon, we can also see strong affinities here with the Sartrean notion of the "spirit of seriousness" (1993, 133–37). The serious agent attempts to fix value and meaning in static essences and thus racism, as a form of seriousness, attempts to establish the value and meaning of racial being in racial essences. The white person, from this perspective, is virtuous and good not as a matter of anything she may have done, but simply because of what she *is*. It is, in Gordon's account, a *bad faith* flight from one's freedom and the responsibility for self that emerges through that freedom. In the Husserlian framework, racism natu-ralizes and treats as fixed things a phenomenon that is fundamentally a matter of intersubjective constitution. In the Nietzschean approach I am sketching here, racism is a manifestation of the spirit of gravity, retarding human growth and change by attempting to fix our meaning and value in allegedly natural essences. In all of these instances, since the very meaning of humanity is a matter of change, growth, transcendence, becoming, and self-overcoming, racism must be understood as antihuman. But of course, since racism itself is a kind of action—it is a way of evading, of fixing, of under-standing—it must be understood fundamentally as a manifestation of be-coming that attempts to pass itself off as being, and is therefore (ironically) a very *human* act of inhumanity.

It should be noted that my linking of racism to the appeal to fixed and static racial categories is not meant to reduce all instantiations of racism to naive biological essentialism. It has been increasingly common, for example, to explicitly deny any inherent racial essence, while affirming that there are cultural differences between particular groups that make them more or less fit to occupy various social positions, or at least generate enormous disad-vantages for individuals within the suspect culture. The Moynihan report (1965) is an excellent example of precisely this move. In Ladelle McWhorter's recent discussion of the report, she points out that he "was careful to assert that the pathology he had identified was not a racial trait" (2009, 288). Rather, it was a result of the psychological damage of the legacy of slavery and its crippling impact in particular on the culture of the family (and its fostering of matriarchal as opposed to traditional patriarchal familial structures).[4] The rhetorical descendants of the Moynihan report may now point to a "culture of victimhood," but the basic idea is the same: until other cultures adopt the virtues of the dominant culture, they will suffer the inevitable consequences (and since those consequences inevitably include criminality and the wanton abuse of social welfare programs, even the members of "good" cultures will suffer).

Thus, not all instantiations of racism follow a strictly biological line, but at the same time, even such "cultural" examples of racism are manifestations of the politics of purity for two interrelated reasons. First, Moynihan's account, and subsequent formal and informal appeals to "cultures of poverty" or "cultures of victimhood" take for granted a facile distinction between cultural boundaries. The procedure is to identify distinct cultures and their particular traits, singling out those traits that disadvantage or harm the members of a given culture. Second, the cultural taxonomy, despite its pretensions to the contrary, maps relatively easily onto traditional biological (racial) taxonomies. It eschews the explicit appeal to biological essence as the *cause* of cultural difference, but the identification of the discrete cultural groups is typically predicated upon the identification of biological racial groups. As Appiah has pointed out, there is an implicit assumption of biological race in the very identification of cultural groups (1992, 32).[5] Moynihan's account of "pathological" Negro families did not include the broken homes and informal matriarchy of impoverished rural whites because his study was focused first and foremost on "Negroes," and he knew perfectly well how to identify them (just as the study of gene variation across racial groups depends upon an assumed account of how to differentiate those racial groups). We can therefore see the politics of purity at work here, ultimately, in the presumption of clear and distinct boundaries between both the individual cultures themselves, and between cultures and biology. The more cultural accounts of racism may avoid the explicit appeal to fixed racial essences, but insofar as they rely on fixed and discrete cultural taxonomies that assume a hard boundary between the biological and the cultural even while they implicitly appeal to biological variation, they are intimately bound up in the politics of purity, and subject to many of the same critiques as the more traditional versions of racism.

Ultimately, just as race itself must be understood fundamentally as a dynamic process rather than as a state of being or set of properties, so too must racism, even in its cultural variant, be thought of as a kind of action rather than as a static position. I do not mean that racism must be explicitly voluntary, or that it must always be understood as a rational commitment to domination. Rather, I take quite seriously Shannon Sullivan's important insights into the way in which racism is a matter of habit, such that we may not always be explicitly and intentionally manifesting racism, but insofar as we have the capacity to undermine and redress bad habits, we must nevertheless take responsibility for them (Sullivan 2006). In the phenomenological account sketched in chapter 4, and developed in greater detail by Linda Alcoff (2006), the ontological status of race is a matter of the ways in which our racial embodiment, within a racialized social context (a Husserlian *Life World*), conditions the way in which we understand and interpret the world around us and our place within it. For Sullivan, this is the way in which race assumes the "status of ontology" (Sullivan 2006, 32), because habits, including racial habits, are constitutive elements of the self. But again, just as within the phenomenological tradition our interpretive horizons can shift and move, our habits, though they may condition and constitute the self, do not fix or define us.

> That habit is constitutive of the self and that habit is subconscious (or unconscious) does not mean that the self—or its habits—is incapable of change. Nor does it mean that a particular self has always and must always be constituted by means of its current habits. At minimum, this is because one of the particular habits that can be developed is that of openness to the reconfiguration of habit. (31)

It is because of this capacity for "reconfiguration" that we remain, despite the force of habit, responsible for those habits—responsible, in short, for who we *are*. Of course, who we *are* within this framework, is always a work in process—it is always a matter of process—and thus it is better to say that we are responsible for (and to) who we are becoming.

What is more, in the "openness" to reconfiguration we find the key to understanding how to account for racism within this more dynamic framework. If racism is not a matter of the simple presence or absence of certain sorts of beliefs, attitudes, and actions, then what could it be? The racist, it is clear at this point, cannot just be the one who holds members of a particular race in low esteem (to put things deceptively mildly). If this were so, then there is a strong sense in which "you are a racist" would be trivially true for everyone currently alive—at least, everyone living in a Western industrialized society, or living in a society that is directly and indirectly connected economically, politically, and culturally to a Western industrialized society. Aside from the problems of pessimism and risk-aversion this approach would engender, it treats racism as a static state of being. As a process, as a manifestation of becoming, racism cannot be about what is, but must be about the kind of *change* taking place—for better or for worse. The racist, therefore, is not simply the one who holds racist beliefs, but the one who makes no effort to confront and alter those beliefs. By the same token, the antiracist is not the person who utterly lacks such beliefs but rather is the person who manifests an "openness to the reconfiguration of habit" in the direction of overcoming (again, as an ongoing process and not as a state to be achieved) racism. This is why *antiracist* is more appropriate than *nonracist*, since the latter term implies a state to be achieved, while the former points toward constant action. The key point here is that one's racism or antiracism is not a matter of the presence or absence of particular mental states but rather lies in the *manner* in which one confronts such mental states.

On this limited individual level of analysis, racism can be understood as a resolute stance to avoid the instability, uncertainty, danger, and risk that would come from abandoning the comforting falsehoods of racist symbolism, beliefs, interpretations, and actions. Racism offers fixed and ready sets of meanings and values (I am virtuous, civilized, and rational, while you are vicious, barbaric, and irrational)—it offers stasis and clarity. The world, however, especially the world of meaning and value, is characterized by dynamism, instability, and ambiguity—including the meaning and value of race itself. Racism can thus be seen as a kind of *closure.* It is both an epistemic closure, in that it understands itself as already possessing all of the relevant answers, and a normative closure, in that it sees the value and meaning of racial categories, and the individuals that occupy them, as fixed and given (essential). For Nietzsche, this is antihuman insofar as humanity is understood as a constant process of self-overcoming. From a more Husserlian perspective, racism is antihuman insofar as it attempts to fix or ossify life, which is the constant becoming of meaning, understood in part as the *openness* to new horizons of meaning (and, as Sullivan points out, to the reconfiguration of habit). For both of these approaches, therefore, the flaw with racism lies in part in its attempt to treat human existence as static—to substitute being for becoming, and close off possibilities for change and development. Racism stands, in the end, as a failure to confront and overcome what Nietzsche might describe as a certain kind of spiritual weakness—a need for stability and determinacy, as opposed to dynamism and ambiguity.

In short, within the context of the politics of purity, both racism and nonracism are directed toward a kind of security, both in the psychological sense and in the sense of being fixed and stable. For the racist, there is the security of having fixed and given meanings and values that assert one's place in the world as part of a normative hierarchy. Even if one isn't at the top, at least one can find someone who is lower down on that hierarchy. If one is at the bottom of that hierarchy, it provides a structure whereby one can simply assert that one has been mistakenly placed within that hierarchy. For the nonracist, meanwhile, there is the security of a kind of ethical superiority that comes with the knowledge that one lacks pernicious racist mental states. Of course, from the Nietzschean perspective, this drive toward security is ultimately motivated by *insecurity*. Instability, ambiguity, and indeterminacy are so threatening that one throws oneself into these ossified systems of value. For the racist, this underlying sense of insecurity is relatively clear and well accounted for in Gordon's discussion of bad faith (Gordon 1993). For the nonracist, within this account consistent with the politics of purity, the insecurity engendered by the confrontation with one's own relationship to racism helps motivate the sense of oneself as having obtained a nonracist state of being. As nonracist, in this sense as *purified* of racist mental states, one places oneself above the concerns of those poor souls who have yet to achieve this enlightened state. But instability and ambiguity constantly threaten the false sense of security that emerges here (which is what motivates the risk aversion I discussed above), because they are what characterize the *human* condition.

At the same time, while I am taking great pains here to emphasize instability and ambiguity in response to the politics of purity, this should not be taken to such an extreme that racism is understood as utterly devoid of any consistency or even *metastability*. Indeed, the ways in which racist meanings and practices can become ossified and habituated over time most certainly creates a sort of metastability that adds considerably to their potency. But this metastability is not the kind of permanence and unchangeability of the politics of purity. Instead of a fixed and mind-independent collection of properties, like an ancient fossil fixed in stone, the metastability of racism more resembles a standing wave. There is a kind of constancy, but it is a constancy of and in motion, and one that takes active maintenance (energy, to continue with the physical metaphor of the standing wave). Racism is dynamic and unstable insofar as the world cannot live up to the standards of fixity and stability it sets, but it is still itself *relatively* stable in a given time and place (or rather metastable), just as racial categories themselves, though always dynamic and in a process of constant revision, are relatively stable in a particular moment and location. My emphasis on instability, therefore, is in part meant to undermine exactly the sort of all-or-nothing dualism of utterly stable and fixed (positivistic realism) versus totally unstable and irregular (eliminativism), which dualism is itself clearly in line with the politics of purity.

It is in this way that racism can be understood as harmful both to the racist and to the object of her ill will, though obviously to different degrees and in different ways. Insofar as racism stands as a kind of commitment to epistemic and normative closure, as an effort to define oneself and others essentially within a closed and fixed normative framework, when we are better understood as open-ended and dynamic, it is dehumanizing. Thus, racism stands as a kind of failure to more fully realize one's humanity by turning away from confrontation with openness and ambiguity and instead clinging vainly to *purified* notions of humanity and value. This point is not meant to generate sympathy for the racist, or to draw attention and effort away from those who have been, are now, and will continue to be on the receiving end of systematic racism. The men in the white hoods in photographs of lynchings may be failing to live up to their full potential by clinging to their racism, but that should neither comfort the victims of their violence, nor should it detract from efforts to address the violence and exploitation that results from their racism. In short, the realization of the harm that racism causes to the racist can be important for understanding how racism functions and perhaps even for motivating antiracism on the part of those who have for so long been its beneficiaries, but this information is not meant to draw attention or resources away from the wretched of the earth.

As a final note before moving on to a more fully realized account of racism, one important point that has emerged through this investigation of individual racism is precisely the way in which such a narrow focus on individual psychology is oversimplified. The dominant understanding of racism is very much embedded in I/thou relationships in which one person expresses negative attitudes or takes harmful actions toward some other individual. I have attempted to interrogate this basic view on its own terms, but throughout this discussion, we have seen how repeated appeal to a larger social context is necessary in order to render these individual actions intelligible. The meanings, values, terms, and hierarchies that give our beliefs and actions force in the world do not come from any particular individual. Individual A is only able to harm individual B by using racial epithets, for example, because those epithets have a socially embedded meaning and normative significance and force. Thus, while this sort of focus on the individual level can be instructive and illuminating, our investigation cannot end there. Indeed, much of the substance of the critique of the politics of purity that I am developing here takes the form of a critical attitude toward the very distinction between the individual and the social as such (an argument I will make in more detail later in this chapter).

Thus, just as our understanding of race itself must be critically informed by the contending meanings operating in a given time and place, as well as by their historical precedents and antecedents, in addition to their future-directed orientations and aspirations, so too must our understanding of racism be critically informed. Genuine antiracism, therefore, cannot simply be the reactionary rejection of all things taken to be racist. It is not solely about attempting to overcome racism, it must also strive for better and better understandings of how racism is to be understood in the first place. With this brief account of a dynamic understanding of racism as a manifestation of becoming in place, I can now sketch some of the more important social aspects of racism as part of this effort toward critical reflection.

RACE, REASON, AND PURITY

I have argued that racial categories, and the identities that correspond to them, have attempted to present themselves as discrete and pure (or at least as normatively driven toward purity), but in fact have always been and continue to be indeterminate and ambiguous. Likewise, the human condition itself is one of confrontation with uncertainty, and responsibility for the ways in which we engage in that confrontation—our status as conscious subjects (that is, our status as *agents*) always places us in the position of moving beyond a given set of circumstances and meanings. Given these two claims, the presumption that racial categories are in themselves harmful entails an account of human agency that is overly abstract and ahistorical. What harm they do results from their use to deny human agency by appealing to fixed and static notions of meaning and value. This is the lesson of the politics of purity. I have argued that racial categories must rather be understood as sites from and through which we contest the meaning and significance of our own identity and that of others within a richly historical and fundamentally intersubjective context. My race, rather than defining and constraining my agency, is simply a particular facet of that agency that situates and conditions the meaning of my own identity and my relation with others, and in so doing it enables my agency as much as it limits it. Most importantly, since racial categories—as ambiguous, dynamic, and ineluctably historical complexes of meaning—are themselves always in the process of developing and changing, they are a product of my own agency even as they condition it. The problem, therefore, is not that racial categories exist but rather that their existence functions in a manner consistent with the politics of purity—that they are understood in fundamentally positivistic terms, both by traditional racial realists and by eliminativists and abolitionists.

The harm of racism, similarly, lies not in its offering of content for interpretation and the assignation of meaning and value, but in presenting those interpretations, meanings, and values as fixed and given. Racism, therefore, is best understood not as the simple application of racial concepts, but as the appeal to racial concepts specifically for the purpose of evading indeterminacy and ambiguity both within ourselves and the larger social world. As I mentioned above, it is in this way (in part, at least) that racism is antihuman, and it is through the exploration of the meaning of the antihuman that we can best understand the power and function of racism as a phenomenon.

If one thinks of the antihuman as dehumanizing, and racism has certainly been *that*, then it can be approached first and foremost as a denial of the agency (or subjectivity, or consciousness, if you prefer) of those designated as racially inferior. Traditionally, two important markers of agency (and thus genuine humanity) have been *reason* and *freedom.* The ancient Greek tradition of philosophy clearly linked rationality with humanity, from Socrates's admonition that the unexamined life was not worth living, through Plato's prioritization of the rational part of the soul in the governance of both individuals and societies, to Aristotle's identification of human beings as *rational* animals. In Western philosophy, the history of this association of reason with humanity has been explored, and critiqued, quite thoroughly and effectively by feminist philosophers (see especially Lloyd 1984; Tuana 1992).

Similarly, the *sine qua non* of humanity has been associated with freedom, as well. Christian thought identified freedom as that which distinguished humanity from the animal world, over which, of course, we were given *dominion*, a fact that will become quite relevant as this discussion develops. In the phenomenological and existential traditions, especially, it is freedom that defines humanity. It should be stressed, in addition, that freedom and reason are often directly linked. The Cartesian Ego, as a paradigmatic case, is both a *thinking* thing, and, as nonmaterial, a *free* thing. Hegel, likewise, linked freedom and reason in their "absolute" forms.

In the philosophical literature on race, this link between racism and the denial of rationality and freedom is nothing new (Fanon 2008, 96–102). The emphasis, however, is more often on the way in which nonwhites are construed as less rational, and thus less human, and this is surely an important and pernicious aspect of how racism functions. But it is also crucial to recognize that while racism denies, by fiat, the rationality and freedom of nonwhites, it similarly posits, as given, the full rationality and freedom of whites. Of course, the immediate question that must be asked at this point is *what understanding of Reason is operant here*? In a world in which humanity is equated with freedom and reason, this is the same as affirming the absolute humanity of whites and the absolute inhumanity of nonwhites, so this question of the nature of reason lies at the foundation of our understanding of racism.

One important aspect of the harm of racism, therefore, is that it generates what Lewis Gordon has identified as the category of the *not-self, not-other* in the place of the proper moral relation between the self and the other (Gordon 2000, 85), or what Charles Mills has referred to as the division between humans and subhumans (Mills 1997, 32–33, 55), and the resulting psychological, physical, economic, environmental, and political devastation that division has wrought for at least the last five hundred years upon the nonwhite populations of the globe. This devastation, of course, has had a corresponding psychological, physical, economic, environmental, and political improvement (the "wages of whiteness," indeed) in the living conditions and security of white populations.[6] What is equally important, however, is the extent to which such devastation and improvement is both a cause and a consequence of the positing of fixed and given meanings and values for racial categories and the individuals that fall within them. That is, it is because whites are viewed as always already fully human that they are in part able to secure political, psychological, and economic advantage, and as a result of that advantage, they are then able to justify and explain their status as the fullest realization of humanity. Likewise, because nonwhites are understood as inherently subhuman they are less able to secure such advantage, which fact is taken as evidence of their subhumanity. Thus, while it is crucial to recognize and address the ways in which racism has harmed and advantaged different populations in different ways, it is also important to recognize that undergirding this process of harm and advantage is the insistence on fixed and given meanings and values vis-à-vis these different populations, which— insofar as humanity is fundamentally dynamic, ambiguous, and indetermi- nate—is the radical inhumanity at the core of our racist interactions with each other.

Thus there is an irony at the heart of this analysis. Again, it is one that has not gone unnoticed in other analyses of racism (Gordon 1995, 136), but it is worth stressing. First, in the moment of positing another (or even oneself) as subhuman, one is treating that other as an agent. Put simply, one does not need to *dehumanize* anything that is not already human. Even if this under- lying humanity is disavowed explicitly, and perhaps only dimly suspected implicitly, it remains the case that *effort*—direct and indirect, conscious and subconscious, individual and social (institutional)—is necessary in order to maintain the *illusion* (for such it must always be) of that subhumanity. Even at the height of chattel slavery in the United States, effort had to be made, both individual and institutional, to maintain the appearance of subhumanity and full humanity between white and black. Steps were taken to impose di- visions between house and field slaves, to forbid the bearing of arms, to pro- hibit literacy, to separate families, to impose white male sexual dominance, to control the practice of religion, and on and on. Thus, even as the popular white sentiment held that slaves were little better than animals, and that slavery actually was a benefit to them, there were systemic efforts under way both to convince whites that this was true, and, importantly, to convince the enslaved black population that this was true. The *imposition* of inhumanity, in other words, is necessitated by the fundamental humanity of the objects of that imposition.

Secondly, the moment of presenting oneself as inherently or essentially a full human, insofar as it posits a fixed and defined essence, is itself an act of inhumanity. One implication of the understanding of human beings as fundamentally a matter of *process* rather than product (as manifestations of be-coming rather than being) is that humanity is not something that one simply possesses or lacks but is rather something that develops, ultimately, in a process of *maturation*. Thus, just as, with regards to our conceptualization of race, one must understand racial membership more as a matter of both/and rather than either/or, so too there is a sense in which one's humanity is a matter of course (one is a conscious agent), and another sense in which one's humanity is a work in progress (one is always remaking one-self). The implication of the racist understanding of full humanity is that it is in a strong sense a *fait accompli*—for the white supremacist, one's whiteness *just is* one's complete and definitive humanity. It is a matter, once again, of closure versus openness. Humanity, as a process, is always undergoing mat-uration, to the extent that it can be understood as healthy and vibrant, while the positing of some essential and fixed definition of humanity—like the racial whiteness of white supremacy—forecloses that maturation. In this way, just as the positing of intrinsic and essential subhumanity denies the agency of the other, so too does the positing of intrinsic and essential *hu-manity* deny the very agency it attempts to pin down—precisely because it treats it as though it is susceptible to being pinned down at all. Again, the point is not to bemoan the harm that white supremacy has brought to white people, nor is it to belittle or sideline the real devastation that racism and global white supremacy have wrought on nonwhite peoples. The point is only (though this is a significant point) that racism is saturated through and through with inhumanity. I will argue that it is from this inhumanity at its *root* that all of the subsequent harm of racism flows.

While eliminativists and abolitionists understand race itself as a product of European enlightenment modernity, I have argued that race (or at least a kind of *protorace*) preceded the sixteenth century, and thus cannot be prop-erly understood as a creation *ex nihil* of European modernity. As a dynamic, ongoing process and site of contestation and negotiation, race has existed in myriad (and often competing or even contradictory) forms well before Columbus's 1492 voyage, or the famous 1550 debate at Valladolid (cf. Lewis 1959). What is at stake is not the presence of race concepts as such but rather the uses to which they have been put, and the meanings and values they have accrued. Thus, there is an important truth lurking in the view that race was invented during the enlightenment, which is that during this time a particular view of the meaning and significance of race gradually came to dominate most others, eventually asserting itself as *the only* understanding of race, such that four hundred years later it becomes difficult to conceive of how race could be anything other than this dominant view. This view of race is tied to a set of projects peculiar to European modernity, themed around the threefold *purification* of reason itself, of humanity, and of the globe. The "conjuring" of race I describe in chapter 4, therefore, is bound up with the ongoing project of the politics of purity. To make this relationship clear, I will start with the relationship between rationality and humanity.

It is in the Ancient Greek intellectual tradition, as suggested above, that the understanding of reason as *essentially* human has its roots, especially with the thought of Plato and Aristotle. For the Ancients, however, reason was understood as practical and holistic. Humanity may be the "rational animal," but we were still in important ways *animals*. Aristotelian ethics, for example, is clearly predicated upon an understanding of rationality as the *telos* of humanity, yet *excellence* in rationality is a matter of *practical* reason—it is about trial and error along with rough guidelines and models, not absolute and exhaustive rules. The virtuous life is surely a rational life, but it is reason as manifest in a constant *practice* and engagement with lived experience through habituation. While the Christian emphasis on the divine, virtuous, and pure spiritual realm over and against the sinful, corrupt, and base realm of the physical certainly began to push the Greek understanding of reason in a different direction, this process, which I will describe as one of purification, reached its climax with the emergence of European modernity. Reason at this point came to be understood in two distinct but interrelated ways, which can be roughly captured by the distinction in early modern philosophy between rationalism and empiricism.

In the rationalist tradition, reason is purified insofar as it is purged of any association with or dependence upon the physical world.[7] The ideal of the *rational* in this tradition is abstraction and universality. Reason yields universal principles and rules on the model of mathematical proofs and precepts of logic. The methodology is to abstract from all particularity and subjectivity, allowing the light of pure reason to illuminate the darkness and confusion of the (merely) empirical world. Equally significant, the rational agent is not influenced by his own more "base" nature—including emotions, instincts, drives, appetites, and so on. Reason is distinct from these animalistic aspects, and in this way humanity is no longer properly understood as the rational *animal*. In the empiricist tradition, on the other hand, reason is purified

Project of purification of reason

through removing biases or particularities of judgment in our understanding of and approach to the empirical world. The ideally rational agent must in effect bracket her agency-she must approach the world as an impartial, ideal observer, and only then can she be understood as fully rational. These approaches differ in their understanding of the manner of our approach to the empirical world, but their similarities, relevant to the project of purification, far outweigh their differences.

Firstly, both approaches see the mental or subjective as radically distinct from the physical or objective; one approach holding that truth is a matter of the strict formulation of *a priori* universal precepts, while the other holds that truth emerges from the passive and detached *a posteriori* observation of the empirical world. In both cases, the *mixture* of the mental and the physical is irrational—either the empirical intrudes upon and corrupts the purity of our understanding of the basic structures of the world, or our biased subjectivity corrupts the purity of our perception and thus our grasp of the fundamental laws of nature. Secondly, both approaches point toward a standard of explanation that holds mechanistic, mathematical understandings of the world (both natural and moral) as its guiding *telos*. The natural world is governed by laws that are universal and accessible through pure reason (whether through a priori abstraction or detached and disciplined observation), such that understanding these fundamental laws offers a *complete* understanding of the natural world. Likewise morally, the aim is to arrive at universal and exhaustive laws and principles governing action—either consequentialist utility calculus, deontological duties and imperatives, or the preference-maximizing reasoning of *Homo economicus*. The ideal goal, in other words, is the achievement of a closed and complete set of principles and rules for fully describing the natural world and exhaustively prescribing the world of human action. From the early Greek account of a holistic notion of reason as an ongoing engagement with the practice of virtue we gradually arrive at this purified account of reason as the realization of a closed and complete set of rules and descriptions.

Thus, part of the project of European modernity was this process of purifying our conception of reason from the corrupting influences resulting from the *mixture* of the mental and the physical. Hand in hand with this project was the purification of the concept of humanity itself. The fully or genuinely human agent is the one who best manifests this purified notion of reason. To the extent that individuals or groups are less completely and

Go together

[handwritten: purified categories]

purely rational, they are more like animals and less like human beings. As they developed together, these processes of purification lead to an effort to provide a taxonomy of human subdivision according to rationality. Because pure reason insists on complete and exhaustive principles of organization, such a taxonomy, if it is to be fully rational, must yield categories that are discrete, fixed, and closed. White, propertied males became the embodiment of pure reason (though *embodiment* is somewhat ironic here, since it is precisely in the alleged irrelevance of their bodies that they were purely rational), while women, nonwhites, and the poor became *essentially* impure of reason.

In the case of gender distinctions in particular, the association of masculinity with reason and femininity with passion and instinct, of man with mind and woman with body, is not new to modernity. And I am not suggesting that such a hierarchy as regards race or property standing emerged only with the dawn of modernity. Such concepts, distinctions, and associations existed well before the modern era, but modernity did rarify (and reify) these distinctions and associations. The emergence and refinement of scientific methodology, for example, provided a new set of tools for analyzing and evaluating the world, providing an easy way to classify and categorize a normative hierarchy of human subdivisions predicated upon (purity of) rationality. What is more, these methods stood in their own right as further evidence of the rationality of those who employed them. In this way, European modernity marks a historical epoch in which the associations of Africans, Asians, and the indigenous peoples of the newly "discovered" world with unreason and thus subhumanity could be clearly and distinctly articulated in a manner that was understood to be objective, scientific, and dispassionate—virtues that served as further evidence for the purity of reason, and thus the essential humanity, of those performing the descriptions and ascriptions. For those being described and categorized as less rational and less human, the future was bleak no matter what they did. If the peoples associated with unreason acquiesced, then that only demonstrated the propriety of their categorization, whereas if they resisted the "objective" determinations of "pure" science and reason, then that, too, simply demonstrated their irrationality.

Once reason has been understood in this purified manner, and humanity itself has been divided up along a hierarchy of purity, it becomes clear that the geography of the globe is able to take on a new logic. Insofar as different peoples occupy and control different parts of the globe, and different peoples have different capacities for pure rationality (and thus different degrees of genuine or pure humanity), it turns out that different parts of the globe are themselves more or less rational according to the qualities of the people who dominate them. The geography of the globe is thus at the same time a geography of reason,[8] which point Hegel makes especially clear (1956, 91–99; 1971, 35–54). Since the proper position of the less rational (the subhuman) is dependence, and the proper position of the purely rational (the fully human) is independence and control, it is incumbent upon the purely rational to expand the sphere of their influence, thus bringing the light of reason into the darkest corners of the globe, and providing the intellectual, cultural, and moral resources upon which those inherently dependent souls can ultimately rely (thus fulfilling their innate nature as dependent).

Pure rationality, therefore, is also made evident through *control* (dominion) over the physical world—the triumph of reason over nature is manifest both by demonstrating the absolute rationality of the natural world and by demonstrating the human capacity to bend nature to our will. This last point is crucial for two reasons. First, if the population of a particular part of the globe is not understood to be properly demonstrating their mastery over it, then that is evidence of their irrationality and thus their unfitness for self-government.[9] Second, as irrational, such people are not rightly conceived of as fully human, and can be understood in a significant sense as part of the natural environment—a resource to be developed, exploited, and in their own turn controlled. Thus colonialism, as the assumption of dominion over the resources of the globe, both environmental and (not fully) human, is not only a legitimate project but an imperative one. To fail to bring reason in its purest and most fully human form to the rest of the globe is a failure to assert one's *proper* place as master of the physical world, and thus is a failure to be fully rational. Once the purified conceptions of reason and the human are established, therefore, colonialism becomes an inevitable and self-justifying project.

It is important to stress that this did not happen all at once, or in a mechanistic way. It is part of what Enrique Dussel has referred to as the mythos of modernity that there is something fixed and essential about Europe and Europeans that legitimates and explains their mastery of the globe (Dussel 1995). But in rejecting that myth, and the politics of purity that informs it, I must seek a different account. European modernity cannot be understood as an event or as a state, but must instead be understood as an ongoing process and project. It is a mythos indeed, but it is one that emerges only in and through the telling and re-telling of that mythos. The year 1492, for example, did not mark the year at which the purified notions of reason and the human sprang fully formed into existence and began to organize the political, philosophical, and scientific activities of Europe for centuries to come. Indeed, where exactly *Europe* begins and ends is part of the ongoing process of modernity—Europe emerges through the articulation of a distinctly *European* history.

The year 1492, returning to the example, was pivotal not only because it marked Spain's encounter with the Western Hemisphere but also the expulsion of Jews and Moors from Spain in the course of the *reconquista* of the Iberian Peninsula for Christendom. Nelson Maldonado-Torres characterizes this as:

> The year in which the conquest and colonization of the Americas began and the moment to which one can trace the emergence of a firm imperial Europe conceiving itself as the center of the whole world and as the telos of civilization. Modern anti-Semitism, modern anti-black racism, and modern colonialism find a common historical referent in the end of the Spanish reconquista and the beginnings of a new form of conquest in the Americas. (2008, 3)

There is no denying that 1492 was an important year, and what is crucial to recognize is that it has two interrelated aspects. On the one hand there was an *internal* purification of Iberia manifest in the *reconquista*, and on the other hand the projection of conquest and colonization into the Americas marks an *external* effort to purify the rest of the world. Europe thus came to understand itself as *European* through the repetition of both of these moments, internal and external, of purification. Europe becomes Europe, in other words, through the articulation of its own mythos as the center of a rationally organized globe—the zero point of the geography of reason.

Dussel points out this two-fold aspect of European modernity when he states that: "Modernity appears when Europe affirms itself as the 'center' of a *World* History that it inaugurates; the 'periphery' that surrounds this center is consequently part of its self-definition" (1995, 65). Just as race must be understood as a dynamic and ongoing process of contestation over meaning, we must approach this account of European modernity (and *Europe* as such) as an ongoing and dynamic process. In part, Europe as such must be understood as dependent upon the effort to account for itself. Geographically, in other words, our understanding of where Europe is must be accounted for in part as a result of those people we now understand as European articulating and justifying the meaning and significance of that term. The Spanish, for example, affirmed their European status not simply by occupying a certain part of the globe, but both by purifying the Iberian Peninsula of Jews and Moors and by engaging in acts of colonial conquest.

But of course, as with racial membership, this cannot be understood as all-or-nothing, as a *fait accompli*. Because of the centuries long and quite intimate contact with Moorish Muslims and Sephardic Jews, Northern Europeans were apt to see the Spanish as at best marginally European. Especially as the protestant reformation swept through England and Northern Europe, casting Roman Catholicism as overly hide-bound, ritualistic, and authoritarian (as opposed to the innovative and liberal Protestantism), Spain came to be understood as a kind of European hinterland, despite the fact that Spanish conquest not only set the stage for European colonialism as a whole but also indirectly financed much of the economic and political development in Northern Europe.

Two important points emerge from this example of Spain as European. The first is that one's status as European or not, and even what European *means*, must be constantly reaffirmed, renegotiated, and contested. The second point is that from the perspective of Europe as the center of a *pure* world order, *periphery* has a double meaning. There is clearly the periphery *external* to that center, Asia, Africa, and the Americas. But there is also the periphery *internal* to that center. Spain, Italy (recall my earlier reference to the maxim that Africa begins at Naples), and Greece, for example, are suspect as a result of their proximity and intimacy with Africa, while Eastern Europe is suspect as a result of their proximity and intimacy with Asia. England, Scandinavia, and the rest of *Northern* Europe, meanwhile, border only the ice and ocean, and thus are free from the corrupting influence Africa and Asia.

There are other internal threats to the purity of reason (and thus the Human) that must be controlled, such as women, homosexuals, and working-class people, for example, and in the process of maintaining mastery over those who are less rational, one simply reaffirms the purity of one's reason. Indeed, since purity must always be mythical (because the human condition is of dynamic ambiguity rather than static purity), it appears on the scene only through the process of myth making. It requires the constant retelling of the myth of purity. In this particular case, Europe emerges on the world stage as disparate peoples take up the task of articulating and asserting a distinctly European identity. The purity of European modernity, in other words, is parasitic upon the alleged impurities that exist both inside and outside of Europe. Without such impurities, there would be no occasion for the telling, retelling and acting out the myth of purity. Without non-Europeans (both within and without Europe) to dominate and control, there could be no Europe at all.

At the same time, these internal and external moments of purification should not themselves be understood as pure. That is, what is or is not internal or external is ambiguous and fluid. Indeed, each act of purification is necessitated by, and stands as an ironic affirmation of, this ambiguity. Those internal threats to European purity that I have used as my examples so far, such as women and homosexuals, are also importantly external, in that they remain outside the bounds of the (allegedly) pure category. External acts of purification, likewise, are internal insofar as they serve as a declaration that the colonized land, for example, was rightfully and properly *ours* all along, and thus implicitly internal. Colonialism is an assertion of the rightful dominion of the colonizer over land and resources (including *human* resources) that only ever contingently had any appearance to the contrary. Thus, the attempt to portray this distinction as fixed and distinct stands itself as an example of the politics of purity.

By way of a further illustration, there is a particularly compelling scene in Ralph Ellison's *Invisible Man* (1994, 195–98) that is illustrative and instructive here. The unnamed protagonist finds himself working in a paint factory, renowned for the purity and vibrancy of its white paint. He discovers through the course of his tenure at the factory that this brilliant shade of white is achieved when a single drop of a black substance is added to the white paint. Upon adding this black substance, the paint becomes even whiter. The whiteness of the paint, in short, requires the presence of a modicum of blackness in order to appear whiter than white. This moment in the novel is illustrative of the way in which impurities are an important and ultimately indispensable aspect of the ongoing assertion of purity, for it is in the *act* of such assertions, occasioned as they are by the presence of impurity, that purity is made to *appear* in the first place.

European modernity, therefore, is best understood not as a historical event unfolding in a particular locale nor as a collection of precepts or ideas but rather as a matter of the *process* of attempting to articulate the meaning and significance of Europe, both as a place (the geography of reason) and as a people, as the highest manifestation of the purity of reason, and thus of humanity itself. As such, it is dynamic, ambiguous, and contentious. It emerges through and is shaped by these different internal and external efforts at purification. Some are momentous and some are ordinary, but all constitute the effort to articulate a distinctly European identity characterized in particular by the politics of purity. Of course, the politics of purity, we have already seen, offers a normative framework that insists on clear and distinct boundaries describing fixed and static concepts, and in this way is contrary to the fundamental structure of human existence as directed beyond such clear and fixed boundaries and categories. Racism, as the fixing of human value and meaning in rigid, discrete, and hierarchically arranged categories, has thus been central to the development of European modernity.

On the individual level, racism needs to be understood not as a state of *being* but rather as a moment of *becoming*, and as dehumanizing (antihuman) to the extent that it purports to define and fix value and meaning. On the larger social and political level I am now describing, racism is about the articulation and elaboration of an intersubjective framework of meanings and symbols that serves both as the elaboration of this model of racism on a grand scale, and as the necessary context that makes individual manifestations of racism meaningful, and thus even possible *as* racism, in the first place. In other words, as I have already suggested, we must question the very distinction between these individual and social levels of racism as such.

Much of the popular discourse on racism, however, seems to take this distinction for granted, and tends to take the form of an advocacy of one or the other (again, here is the all-or-nothing approach of the politics of purity). Either racism must be understood strictly as a matter of individual attitudes and choices, or it must be understood as fundamentally institutional or systemic. This view can be criticized in two important ways. First, we can point out that neither of these levels is intelligible without the other, thus blurring the distinction altogether, and second, we can point out that the distinction assumes an understanding of human ontology that is deeply implicated in the politics of purity, and must therefore be abandoned.

To make this first point clear, I will return to my previous discussion of individual racism where I argue that within the politics of purity we find a fundamentally static conception of racism. Just as the ontology of race, consistent with the politics of purity, treats race as a set of necessary and sufficient conditions that agents either possess or lack, so too is racism understood as the presence or absence of certain beliefs or attitudes within a given agent. Against this understanding of racism as a matter of being, I have advocated understanding it as a manifestation of becoming, in which the defining moment of racism has less to do with the presence of absence of pernicious beliefs and attitudes regarding racial groups, and more to do with our openness to confronting and working to overcome those beliefs and attitudes.

The interdependence of the individual and social levels of racism is manifest first in the fact that one's individual beliefs and attitudes about races are only tenable and intelligible within a social context that gives them meaning and force. By way of contrast, suppose that I happen to seriously dislike Bob, a white man who regularly frequents the coffee shop in which I am now writing. I may never have spoken with Bob, and Bob may never really have done anything directly harmful to me, I simply find his presence annoying and distracting, or maybe I just don't like the cut of his jib. Suppose I find some way to make my dislike known to him. It may be something relatively subtle, like cutting in front of him in the line for a refill, or refusing to shift my chair out of his way as he tries to negotiate a path across the seating area to the restrooms. Or it may be something more overt, like complaining loudly about him to my neighbor in the line ("Can you believe this guy?"), or telling him rudely to get out of my way as I make my way across the seating area ("Would you get out of my way?"). Bob will eventually catch on to my dislike, either over time if I take the subtle route, or quite quickly if I take the more overt route, and it will surely cause him some concern, and may even be hurtful.

Now suppose that Bob is black, but the rest of this scenario is the same (that is, his blackness is not part of my dislike for him). Even if my actions and utterances remain identical, my whiteness paired with Bob's blackness adds a new dimension of meaning to our interactions. I may not be burning a cross or using racial epithets, but my words and actions take on a racial meaning that transcends my own intentions. Whether I wish it so or not, my actions and words take on a meaning that suggests an assertion of racial dominance. They are those of whiteness as such, and Bob comes to stand in for blackness as such. If we push this example even further this becomes clearer. Suppose that, whether I realize it or not, my dislike of Bob is at least in part because he is black, and I resent a black presence in *my* café. Suppose further that my overt manifestation of my dislike for Bob takes on a more explicitly racial dimension ("Can you believe this guy?" becomes "Can you believe these people?"). In this case the racial meanings of my actions are unambiguous, and the way in which they will be interpreted by and impact Bob are significantly different than in my first description of the example when Bob and I are both white. In the latter two cases, however, whether I intend it or not, there is a racial aspect to our interaction that cannot be ignored if one wishes to render that interaction fully intelligible.

The point of this set of related examples is that the meaning and force of racism is only possible within a social context that generates and legitimates such meaning and force. For example, the very category of *black* has meaning not simply because I intend it, but because it is available to both me and Bob (and all those around us), and it affects both of us (and any witnesses to our interactions) the way it does because of the power it holds within our larger social context. If for example, Bob were a white person of Lithuanian ancestry, it probably would not occur to him that my ill will was directed toward his Lithuanianness, and if I said in line "Can you believe these people?" and meant "these people" to be Lithuanians, it seems unlikely to me that anyone would have any clue what I meant (including Bob). Indeed, even if I said, "Get your Lithuanian behind out of my way!" most people (including Bob) would likely interpret my utterance as a bizarre eccentricity rather than as a threat to Bob and an assertion of my own non-Lithuanian superiority. This is because the idea of the Lithuanian, in the context of a café in Milwaukee in 2009, does not have centuries of oppressive use and meaning informing it. It does not appeal to a rich cultural and political symbolism affirming the inhumanity of Lithuanians, and the superiority of non-Lithuanians.[10] What this shows is that the meaning of my actions is conditioned by my social context in ways that are beyond my intentions. Even if I don't have racial motivations for my dislike of Bob, if he is black and I am white, my actions will carry a racial meaning whether I wish it so or not, and if I should have such motivations and intentions, then their meaning is dependent upon a social and historical context that makes them meaningful.[11]

It is in this way that the individual level of racism is always already social. In the phenomenological sense, it is intersubjectively constituted. The meanings, symbols, and interpretations available to me are inextricably linked to a particular social context. Holding racist beliefs, in other words, is unintelligible outside of a social context that makes the content of such beliefs intelligible. At the same time, the social milieu that gives meaning and force to racial concepts, meanings, and values, needs the constant reaffirmation and representation of those concepts, meanings, and values *by individuals*. Thus, the distinction between the individual level and the social level as regards our understanding of racism must be understood as somewhat blurry at best. Just as racial categories cannot rightly be understood as pure and discrete, there is no clear boundary between the individual level and the social levels of racism as a phenomenon. It may, from time to time, be instructive to focus our attention more toward one or the other (as I attempted to do at the beginning of this chapter), but truly attending well to these phenomena will require that we recognize their constant interplay and admixture.

On a more abstract level, part of the difficulty with understanding racism as a phenomenon stems from a particular conception of human agency itself. In discussing the politics of purity, I pointed out its insistence on clear boundaries between the internal and the external, the self and the other. The view that racism must be effectively reducible either to individual beliefs, preferences, and practices on the one hand, or institutional, systemic, and political structures on the other hand, is itself a further manifestation of the politics of purity. The best response must be not so much to attempt a negotiation between these two extremes but rather to articulate a rejection of the distinction from the start. In chapter 6, I shall undertake exactly that task, but before that, I will fill out my account of racism.

RACISM, MIXED RACE, AND THE PRACTICE OF PURITY

I have articulated an ontology in which racial reality must be understood as an ongoing process of negotiation and contestation over the meaning of race, such that my racial position always situates and conditions the place *from* which I engage in that process, but because the process is ongoing, that position is never fixed and determined. At the same time, as a process of negotiation, the categories that shape it are ambiguous and plastic, such that we are, as individuals, always both more and less than the category or categories that situate the locus from which we engage in the negotiation and contestation of racial reality. Racism, as a social and political phenomenon, should not, therefore, be understood simply as the belief in the reality of races or the meaning of racial categories. The reality of racism, as an oppressive and dehumanizing force on the political landscape of the last five hundred years, must be understood rather as the interpretation and portrayal of the meaning of racial reality as demarcating clear, unambiguous, and fixed categories of Being directed toward the division of the world into the truly free, fully rational, and genuinely human on the one hand, and various incarnations of the irrational, unfree, and subhuman on the other. Racism is in this way a set of *projects* directed toward the assertion, legitimization, and maintenance of (racial) purity. Indeed, the politics of purity saturates racism as a phenomenon much in the same way that it has colored traditional approaches to racial ontology. Unlike racial ontology, which can be meaningful beyond the politics of purity, racism, as a practice of exclusion and domination, is inseparably bound up in the politics of purity—purity, both the purity of the white race and the purity of the Human—is the *telos* of racism. What follows is a brief sketch of the relationship between racism and the politics of purity.

Racism is the practice of purity, and whiteness functions as its normative center of gravity, such that it is directed toward the establishment of whiteness as the norm—the *purest* manifestation—of the human, and all other races are situated at greater or lesser degrees of distance from that normative center. Understood in this way, racism is an attempt to establish whiteness as a kind of concretization of a purified notion of the human as inherently rational, virtuous, and independent. By virtue of one's being white, one is essentially all of these good things,[12] and the farther one is from whiteness, the farther one is from full humanity (and all of those fine things). Metaphorically, the farthest one can be from whiteness is blackness, and more often than not, this has proven to be the case in localized racial hierarchies in which black people are present.[13] In every racial schema, in other words, in which there are categories in between white and black, black typically (though not necessarily always) occupies the bottom rung of the racial ladder. This observation has led Lewis Gordon to point out that racism functions as a normative injunction both to be white, but equally importantly, to *not* be black (1997, 59). This dualistic (Manichean) normative framework is at the heart of the politics of purity. Gordon uses it to raise questions about mixed-race identity, arguing that it can manifest itself as an

dualism again

effort by nonwhites to distance themselves from blacks by establishing mixed race as a distinct (and, as I argue, conceptually pure in its own right) category. That is, if it is impossible for one to be white, one can at least assert that one is not black. Ronald Sundstrom, though he is ultimately quite critical of Gordon's overall position, admits that multiracial identity can be a kind of manifestation of "racial opportunism that depends on anti-black racism", and Minkah Makalani's research into web sites advocating mixed race identity presents a compelling case that, at least for those voicing their views in such fora, Gordon's worries are legitimate (Sundstrom 2008, 116; Makalani 2003). The debate over mixed race identity, and especially Sundstrom's treatment of it, is particularly instructive and helpful to my elucidation of racism and the politics of purity, and so it will be worthwhile to devote some effort to an analysis of it.

The driving norm of racism, according to the view I am elaborating here, is the purity of the white race, understood as the rarified and most pure manifestation of the human. The purity of other racial categories is only important, ultimately, because their purity helps to maintain white purity. That is, in order for whiteness to maintain itself as discrete, self-contained, and uncorrupted by other racial categories and identities, it must preserve the clarity and force of the *borders* between the races generally. To be sure, the bulk of political and juridical energy is directed toward the protection of white purity—antimiscegenation laws and less formal taboos against interracial dating, for example, tend to be far more concerned with mixtures involving whites and any nonwhite, than mixtures involving two different nonwhites. Nevertheless, all things being equal, purity across the board operates as a clear norm. This is due to the way in which the politics of purity operates at the most abstract levels, demanding an individual ontology that will admit of membership in one and only one racial category.

This is why, in a racial context informed by the politics of purity, the category of mixed race itself often functions as another discrete and pure category, in the sense that people who are of mixed race cannot at the same time be white, or black, or Asian. Indeed, while some of the impetus behind calls for mixed-race identity stems from a belief that it points us toward an ultimately raceless future—that it is ultimately a kind of antiracist practice in its own right[14]—another significant motive is the extent to which people of mixed ancestry, especially when that admixture is visible, feel excluded from the standard racial categories and the communities that occupy them. As

Sundstrom puts it, "Multiracial identity is an identity derived from specific experiences of being born into, and living among, the gaps of racial and ethnic categories" (2008, 111). These experiences can be powerful and significant forces in the processes of identity formation, and can all-too-often be quite traumatic. The exclusion from traditional racial categories (and the sides of one's family that correspond to them) can cause real psychological harm, and at its best, the articulation of multiracial identities is an attempt to account for that experience, address this kind of harm, and challenge those traditional categories. One of the real strengths of Sundstrom's treatment of this issue is that it emphasizes the point that at the heart of these philosophical debates surrounding racial categories are real children, whose path to adulthood is being profoundly shaped by the kinds of resources we do or do not make available to them in terms of their understanding of their identity. It is for this reason that Sundstrom emphasizes his claim that "multiracialism cannot be largely a genealogical matter; rather, it is an experience" (2008, 114). Sundstrom's focus on this *experience* of exclusion is an important corrective to facile efforts to dismiss multiracial identity[15] both from the right and the left of the political spectrum, and there are two important points to be made about it.

First, the articulation and affirmation of mixed-race identities has historically, and continues in the present, to function well within the bounds of the politics of purity, despite its surface appeal to mixture. As mixed or biracial categories gain ground as terms of identity, they become themselves pure and discrete categories, such that individuals either are or are not members of them, and if they are, they cannot simultaneously be members of other categories. One is of mixed race or of some particular mixed race (for example, black/Asian, black/white, Tiger Woods's self-referential "Cablinasian"), and therefore *not* any one of the usual categories. To be biracial in the United States, or *mestizo* in Mexico, is to *not* be black, or white, or indigenous. Within the politics of purity, mixed racial categories emerge as a response to racial ambiguity and mixture that ultimately reasserts conceptual distinctness and the purity of racial categories.

Clearly, there are plenty of racial categories that are explicitly built around racial mixture. Creole, mulatto, mestizo, the South African category of colored, and Latino/Latina—all have built into them an explicit understanding of racial mixture. My point is that once established as legitimate categories, they quickly organize themselves around conditions for purity such that

modernity

creole or Latino/Latina are both understood as distinct from all other racial categories. Maldonado-Torres has described European modernity as the proliferation of a domination or war paradigm (2008, 1–19), and we can understand this aspect of racism as a further manifestation of that paradigm by appeal to a military analogy. Racism functions through efforts to carve up the racial landscape into clearly bounded territories controlled by one specific group. The politics of purity insists upon the integrity and purity of these territories, and racism can be understood in large part as the effort to maintain that integrity and purity, with whiteness functioning in this metaphor as a kind of hegemonic superpower, allowing the lesser states to squabble among themselves as long as they pose no threat to that hegemony. Let that hegemony be threatened, however, and blood will be spilt. In short, it is precisely in setting themselves up as categories distinct from nonmixed racial categories that mixed-race identity is often a further manifestation of the politics of purity. The biracial, the creole, and the *mestizo* are thus mixed in the sense that they are composed of different elements, but insofar as they maintain a clear border between themselves and those other elements, they continue to employ the logic of purity.

The second important point about the experience of exclusion emphasized by Sundstrom involves the role of the *visibility* of the racial mixture. Sundstrom describes one critique of mixed-race identity as predicated upon the fact that most nonwhites in the Americas are genealogically "mixed" to a greater or lesser extent,[16] and so the generation of a separate mixed category is "superfluous" (Sundstrom 2008, 112). Given this fact, it seems that what often separates those calling for the recognition of mixed-race identity and status from much the rest of the black (for example) population in the Americas is simply the *visibility* of their mixture. While this fact can be used to mount a political critique on mixed-race identity similar to that launched by Gordon (1997, 51–71),[17] and it can be used by racial eliminativists or advocates of "colorblind" liberalism to argue against the use of racial categories of identity altogether, it also can explain why the recognition of mixed race as a legitimate racial category is so important.

Within the present racial climate, dominated as it is by the politics of purity, those of visibly mixed ancestry surely have good reason to describe themselves as in important ways on the outside of the primary catalog of racial categories. Of course, Sundstrom's emphasis on *experience* is clearly not limited to those who *appear* mixed. Individuals with a racially mixed genealogy may certainly look, given the dominant notions of what different races look like in a given *milieu*, as though they are strictly of a particular *traditional* racial category. Such individuals may certainly still experience the "personal-familial-social rupture" (Sundstrom 2008, 115) that can accompany life in a family of racially mixed genealogy. Without denying or minimizing the importance of this, it is also true that individuals who are *visibly* mixed have a further set of experiences having to do with their interactions with others both in and outside of the family. That such individuals fail to fit neatly into any of the standard categories is inscribed in their bodies for all to see, which fact can be exploited to their advantage (though such advantage will always remain limited, given that they cannot ever be *fully* white), but it can also function to alienate them from the groups and communities that constitute the particular elements of their heritage. The calls for the articulation of a distinct category of *mixed race* can thus be understood in part as an effort to better capture a certain reality—the reality that the dominant racial categories do not capture the variety and richness of racial reality, and that people who visibly fail to fit neatly into the standard categories stand as a kind of living, breathing threat to the racial order of things (cf. Gordon 1997, 63). However, the point I wish to raise here is that insofar as the calls for mixed-race identity fail to challenge the politics of purity, insofar as they offer up yet another category of racial being to which one can belong *instead* of any other category, they fall short of the critical goal of effectively challenging racism.

While Sundstrom's discussion of mixed race identity is sophisticated, nuanced, and highly productive, his distinction between genealogy and experience needs to be more closely examined. As I have already argued in relation to biology and culture, such easy distinctions are more often than not manifestations of the politics of purity. Sundstrom's critique of the tendency to reduce the notion of mixed-race to genealogy is quite telling (2008, 114), but as he elaborates his own account of the role of experience, it becomes clear that it remains inextricably linked with genealogy. "Multiracialism, then," Sundstrom states, "is linked to interplays between genealogy, social forces, and the phenomenology of race" (115). Clearly, the social forces and phenomenological aspects[18] come into play precisely for those who have a mixed genealogy, and most acutely for those whose mixed genealogy is *visible*. It is largely (though certainly not exclusively) because of my ancestry that I look the way I do and have the family life that I have, and so it is partly because of my ancestry that I have the experiences I do and the interactions with "social forces" that I have. At the same time, however, what counts as rendering my ancestry *visible* is itself not a straightforward matter of by biological morphology but also a matter of the socially conditioned ways and means of *seeing* race in a given context. Here again, there is a dialectical relation between the genealogy and the experience that does not admit of a neat and clean distinction between the two.

What is more, the fact that individuals have different experiences that impact their sense of who they are (their identity) is undeniable. Thus, Sundstrom's claim that "[d]enying the existence of multiracial experience, and thus multiracial identity, is patently false and absurd" is quite compelling (114). It is important to raise the question, however, of what it is exactly that makes a given experience multiracial. Sundstrom is surely right that it is not strictly a matter of genealogy, but nor could it strictly be a matter of experience, since one's experiences are conditioned so deeply by one's genealogy, and the way that genealogy is rendered *visible* within a given social context. According to Sundstrom, multiracial identity is "derived from specific experiences of being born into, and living among, the gaps of racial and ethnic categories" (111), and while, as I have argued, this is not simply a matter of positivistic biological taxonomy, the location of these gaps is not completely independent of biology, either, as Sundstrom seems to admit in his later formulation, which includes a role for genealogy.

Thus, Sundstrom's basic line seems to be consistent in many important ways with the account I am offering here. That is, his advocacy of mixed race identity, though it certainly can run the risk of falling into the politics of purity, need not do so. His account ultimately emphasizes the interplay between genealogy, experience, and larger social forces, such that multiracial identity has the potential to turn our racial discourse away from the "individualist" norm and toward the "communal, political, and social" (127). However, to the extent that mixed-race identity simply assumes its place among other racial categories in conformity with the politics of purity, it will fail to "repair the ruptures around race" about which Sundstrom is so rightly concerned (126). Given the power that the politics of purity holds within racial discourse and the social forces that condition the meaning and function of race, appeals to and advocacy of a mixed-race identity will always be subject to the kinds of political effects against which both Gordon and Sundstrom warn us. But as long as such advocacy is paired with an *active* critical awareness of and resistance to this tendency, I believe that it can be consistent with antiracist practice. It is not simply whether or not one affirms a mixed race identity, but most importantly *how one* does so, and as I will argue in the next chapter, a primary aspect of such affirmation must include an emphasis on the ambiguity and plasticity of the categories themselves, such that affirming a mixed-race identity does not at the same time stand as a rejection of one's membership in more traditional racial categories. The aim is not, as the title of Carolyn Battle Cochrane's documentary suggests, to assert that one is "Biracial, Not Black, Damn It!" but to allow for the claim that one is "Biracial, *and* Black, Damn It!"

This brief foray into the politics of mixed-race identity helps to illustrate the essential claim that the boundary between the individual and the social must be called into question in a radical way. The assertion of mixed-race identity, if undertaken in the positive sense I have described here, points toward something significant about one's particular experiences, one's social situation, and even one's genealogy. All of these aspects, in turn, mutually inform each other, and have the particular meaning and significance they do for the agent in question as a result of the social milieu which constitutes that meaning and significance. The danger lies in reducing these issues either to questions about the individual in the abstract, or to the straightforward dictates of dominant social norms for racialization. This blurring of the distinction between the individual and the social is also inextricably linked to the project of the purification of reason, and so I will now take up that aspect of racism.

COLONIALISM AND THE GEOGRAPHY OF REASON

The metaphor of racism as a kind of global political struggle for territory has often been far more than a mere metaphor. European modernity, and the colonial projects that informed and supported it (both intellectually and materially), can be understood as the effort to purify the world for whiteness. The "geography of reason" has always also been a racial geography, precisely to the extent that reason has been understood in racial terms, and colonialism was an effort to establish Europe and North America at the center of a globe whose organizing principle was this racialized understanding of rationality. Of course, to the extent that reason was at the same time understood as the defining principle of humanity, colonialism can also be understood as the purification of the world for reason. There are places where reason is present in the form of domination by whites, and places where reason holds little or no sway. This latter is the realm of darkness (the dark continent), of under-development, and of *raw* resources (both material and human) to be exploited. Indeed, we can observe here a link between environmental destruction and the politics of purity. The insistence on a clear division between the internal and external aspects of the human agent places the natural environment in the position of radical Other (indeed, the *natural* itself becomes antithetical to the *human*), and the reduction of reason to instrumental rationality insists that the purest manifestation of reason, and thus humanity, is the *efficient* use of natural resources to further our own narrow interests. Exploiting resources efficiently, therefore, becomes yet another way in which a practice of domination serves the function of demonstrating one's rationality. The politics of purity thus points toward new ways to understand the link between racism and the rampant devastation of the environment. Both, on the global level, can be understood as ways to demonstrate one's status as a fully rational (pure) people over and against the natural world and those (impure) subpersons who are inextricably bound up with it. *instrumental reason*

The function of whiteness as the normative center of gravity for racism, therefore, has significant and far-reaching implications. Racism has taken the form of the advancement of a particular interpretation of whiteness and its significance, and that interpretation has been bound up intimately with the politics of purity from its most abstract level (philosophical anthropology) all the way through its use of colonialism as the concretization of the project of purity on the peoples and natural environment of the globe. Indeed, since racism, understood in this way, equates the human with the rational, and views nonwhites as inherently irrational, it effectively views nonwhites as part of the natural environment—as part of the background scenery for the grand narrative of the rise of European modernity, to paraphrase Fanon (1963, 51). The point is that all of the projects and manifestations of racism can be understood as directed toward the affirmation, legitimization, and maintenance of white purity and normativity, along with the understanding of reason and humanity upon which they are predicated.

Racism can thus be understood as the *practice* of purity. Individuals, operating within a larger social context that both gives meaning and legitimacy to their actions, and is in turn constituted and legitimated by those actions, work to reinforce and realize a vision of the world as racially pure. That is, racism is directed toward the reinforcement of an interpretation of the world—both the social and the natural world (and of course these must be understood as strictly distinct within the politics of purity)—as manifesting a racially pure hierarchy. Where the world fails to live up to this ideal, steps must be taken to correct its course. People must be reminded in direct and indirect ways of "their place" within this world, resources must be seized and transferred to those who can put them to the best (most rational) use, borders must be protected, and so on. I have suggested that European modernity and the colonial enterprises of the enlightenment can be understood as a sustained and ultimately global effort to practice the politics of purity both internally and externally. The external manifestation takes the form of expanding the dominion of the white, the rational, and the fully human—of the *pure*—and thereby freeing the globe from the corrupting influence of the impure while simultaneously putting those impure peoples in their proper place by making good use of them as slaves, servants, laborers, and finally (in the present era of globalization) as consumers.

The project of racism, understood in this way, is about establishing a clear boundary between the world of reason, virtue, and full humanity, and ensuring that this world remains pure. It is directed both toward *realizing* this vision of purity through conquest, economic exploitation, domination, and oppression, and reinforcing this vision through the ongoing interpretation and reinterpretation of history (the rise of Western Civilization as the flowering of human reason), the present (the struggle between the civilized lovers of freedom and reason on the one hand, and the barbarous forces of tyranny and tradition on the other), and the future (the inevitable triumph of market liberalism and the "end of history"). Internally, racism as the practice of purity demands the identification and domination of those impurities that reside within the borders thus established. Within the individual agent, one establishes one's purity by demonstrating that one's reason dominates one's emotions, passions, and subjective biases. This is the enlightenment vision of the fully realized human subject—independent, autonomous, and free. And just as one makes this purity clear by controlling such impurities as emotion and natural inclination, the demonstration of the purity of a people or race demands the control and domination of those impurities that are internal to it. Thus, the natural environment, animals, the poor, women, homosexuals, and of course the racially suspect must all be kept under control and in their proper place *within*, for example, a given nation state.

Purity is, as I have tried to make clear, fundamentally a myth, and must therefore be actively *maintained*—it cannot simply be assumed as a given (though it will certainly attempt to pass itself off as such). To maintain this sense of purity requires the constant assertion of that purity through repeated acts of domination. If the paradigmatic white male bourgeois head of household firmly maintains his position at the head of his household, then he maintains his sense of security in his own purity (as the rational mind in the body of the family). If eighteenth-century white European males maintain dominance over their own poor, they prove their fitness to dominate the rest of the globe by demonstrating their purity. Thus, the practice of purity needs to manifest itself both internally and externally, each of these aspects reinforcing and legitimating the other (though despite pretensions to the contrary, the purity of these two aspects themselves is also a myth). What is more, it demands constant reiteration. Since it is a myth of purity and stability, it is constantly under threat from the reality of ambiguity and plasticity. As a result, racism, as the practice of purity, *needs* these threats in order to function, for it is only in the act of eliminating such threats that the myth of purity is told and retold, and thus maintained at all.

All of this means that as the practice of purity, racism must be understood as fundamentally ironic insofar as it is a constant process of becoming attempting to establish itself as a fixed aspect of being. It offers an antihuman vision of the human. In its insistence on purity and the determinacy and certainty of being over and against the indeterminacy and ambiguity of becoming, racism offers us an understanding of human existence that fundamentally misunderstands what it is to be human in the first place. It is, in effect, an *interpretation* that attempts to preclude any further interpretation. In the Sartrean language of bad faith, it is a manifestation of freedom directed toward the denial of that very freedom (Sartre 1956, 67–70; Gordon 1995, 41). Racism can in this way be understood as consistent with Simone de Beauvoir's characterization of the serious man, whose "dishonesty issues from his being obliged ceaselessly to renew the denial of this freedom" (1948, 47). As such, and this is a crucial point, it requires constant reiteration, reaffirmation, and re-presentation. Racism, in other words, even though it portrays racial meaning as fixed and static, cannot be understood itself as a kind of fixed state of being. It must constantly evolve and change to meet the ongoing challenge posed by its confrontation with a fundamentally ambiguous and changing world of human meaning. Racism is not, therefore, a matter of the simple presence or absence of certain beliefs or mental states, nor is it a failure of rationality, nor is it a matter of the presence or absence of certain political institutions or policies. All of these accounts would treat racism as a thing, when it should be understood as an act, or even better, a *way* of acting. Racism is not a state of being, but a process or practice of becoming (one directed, again ironically, toward the *closure* of the continued possibility of becoming).

To make this clear, racism must be understood as attempting to accomplish two things. First, it seeks to establish the meaning and value of the dominant racial group as *essentially* virtuous, rational, and autonomous—as the purest manifestation (the norm) of the human. Second, it seeks to establish the *inhumanity* of those outside the dominant group—they must be portrayed as a fundamental *corruption* of the human; as vicious, irrational, and dependent. Both tasks are incoherent at their roots. The first task is an interpretation that denies that it is an interpretation—it is a manifestation of human freedom attempting to portray itself as essential to the *nature* of racial membership. Since this is an incoherent position, it requires constant maintenance. If I am convinced of the meaning and value of my own whiteness, for example, then I will find "evidence" for this belief everywhere, and when counter-evidence should seem to appear, it must be dismissed. It is, in this way, like religious fanaticism.[19] If I believe God will heal my affliction, then if I get better, it is "evidence" of God's plan for me, and if I fail to get better, then it is still "evidence" of God's plan for me, in that my faith is clearly being tested. Racism is the *practice* of offering exactly this sort of "evidence" for its own truth. Racism is manifest, for example, whenever we promote the idea that a particular group is representative of some universal norm (when we describe "a man," "another man," and then "a *black* man," for example), or when the demands among the racially disadvantaged for fair treatment are interpreted as insistence upon *special* rights or consideration. These mundane acts, taken altogether, are part of the ongoing effort to pass oneself off as essentially positioned by one's racial being. The point here is that it is precisely because the very notion of having such an essential being is false that such *constant* efforts are necessary in the first place.

The second task of racism is, at its root, an effort to dehumanize a human being and as such its incoherence is clear. One need not objectify or dehumanize what is really an object. One need not dehumanize a chair or an automobile. One only sets out to dehumanize that which we recognize, however dimly, as human. Sartre famously claimed that even the slave is free (1956, 549–50) in that she always has the option of rebellion (with the probable conclusion of death),[20] and this is easy to dismiss either as a trivialization of freedom or as utterly ridiculous. Whether one wishes to call it "freedom" or not, Sartre is surely correct that the slave always has the option of rebellion, with the likely disastrous consequences of mutilation or death (or both), and we would do well to remember those who did indeed take this path, including Frederick Douglass, Denmark Vessey, Nat Turner, and those enslaved Africans in Barbados, St. Kitts, North America, and throughout the western hemisphere who struggled to throw off their chains and assert their humanity in the face of colonial inhumanity. Sartre's point here is not that slaves are ultimately to *blame* for their enslavement but rather that, while we may certainly celebrate those who chose to rebel, in choosing *not* to rebel, the slave is still manifesting her freedom—her *humanity*. The only way to truly reduce another person to an object is by killing them. Of course, then you no longer have a slave, but a corpse.[21]

What racist oppression requires, even in its most dire and overt forms, such as chattel slavery, is thus constant maintenance and vigilance. If the enslaved were truly most happy and best suited to servitude, then it would not be necessary to break, brutalize, threaten, cajole, and manipulate them into submission. If the enslaved were truly no better than brutes, it would not be necessary to pass laws prohibiting their literacy or the practice of religion. In short, the most dire and egregious cases of dehumanization are always in this way riddled with irony—every act that dehumanizes another is at the same time an implicit assertion of the humanity of the other—if they weren't human, it wouldn't be necessary to dehumanize them. As I mentioned above, even as the masters tell themselves that all is right and proper, that God is on their side, and that the slaves are in fact happier and better off, they are also struggling to maintain white militias in the colonies so as to protect against slave insurrections, to break up strong family units and crush nascent leadership among the enslaved, to forbid literacy, the bearing of arms, and assembly among the enslaved population. In other words, they are acting in ways that openly contradict the stories they tell themselves and their children. To hold that people can be fully and completely objectified or dehumanized is not only an untenable belief, it is to deny them any agency whatsoever. Yes, conditions are arranged such that choosing to rebel offers almost certain disaster, and the point is that under such conditions it seems perfectly reasonable, and even perfectly *human*, to choose submission over torture and death. It is in *that* sense that we can understand racism's dehumanizing task as fundamentally incoherent and, consequently, as requiring constant maintenance and reaffirmation.[22]

My emphasis on the necessity of maintaining racism as the ongoing practice of purification is not meant, on the other hand, to imply that racism functions in a manner that is always explicit, deliberate, and easily identified. I do not mean to oversimplify or give short shrift to the ways in which racist practices can become habituated, ossified, or attenuated such that their maintenance, as I have described it, can be conducted on a kind of autopilot. Again, Shannon Sullivan's account of the habituation of whiteness is an excellent articulation of exactly this sort of phenomenon (2006, see especially 63–93). The main point here, as fits with the recurring theme of this discussion, is that one should not approach the question of the deliberateness of racist practices as an all-or-nothing proposition. It is not either clearly deliberate and explicitly intentional or clearly subconscious and unintended. To demand such a conceptual approach to racism is at once to affirm the politics of purity and to oversimplify both the human psyche and the phenomena of racism themselves. With this complexity informing the understanding of racism I am developing, it is now possible to begin to take on the question of antiracism.

Since racism, understood as the practice of purity, must be thought of as an ongoing process of becoming, and not as a state of being (or a collection of individual or social properties, or of necessary and sufficient conditions), we must conceive of antiracism in similar ways. There is not some state to be achieved either as an individual or as a society such that racism ceases to *be*. There is no "postracist" future waiting to be articulated and realized. Such a conception of antiracism maintains the static conception of human life endemic to the politics of purity. It is not a genuine challenge to the politics of purity but is rather the simple *negation* of the static conception of racism. It is not an expression of a genuinely antiracist practice, it is simply, to use the idiom of formal logic, ~(racism).[23] If one understands racism as a state of being—as the presence or absence of the properties that serve as necessary and sufficient conditions for *being* racist—then antiracism must be the simple negation of those properties. But in focusing our understanding around a critique of the politics of purity, such an understanding must be rejected. Just as racism, as the *practice* of purity, demands constant maintenance and reaffirmation, so too must antiracism, understood as an ongoing *practice* of critiquing and challenging the politics of purity. Most importantly, like any good critical process, it cannot take the form of a simplistic and reactionary rejection of the object of criticism. It must be a radically reflexive and self-critical project that takes seriously the ways in which the object of critique is itself ambiguous and constantly changing. Antiracism, therefore, must be understood as something one does not something one is, and an antiracist society is not something to be achieved but something to be *enacted*. In the next chapter, I will attempt to articulate the implications of this understanding of antiracism as a process of becoming organized fundamentally around a critical (and self-critical) attitude toward the politics of purity.

Antiracist praxis [handwritten]

Creolizing Subjects:
Antiracism and the Future of Philosophy

My account so far has focused upon the way in which the politics of purity serves as an organizing theme and driving force behind racial reality. The politics of purity is to be understood as informing both the ontology of race itself and the practice of racial oppression (racism), emphasizing the way in which these two moments are constitutively interrelated and interdependent. If, as I claimed in the Introduction, this project is motivated by a desire to confront and address the problem of racial oppression, then it is necessary at this point to offer an account of antiracist praxis—of liberation and racial justice. Indeed, this will serve as the ultimate arbiter of the value of this project.

The politics of purity, I have argued, constrains our thinking about antiracism and liberation in several ways. First, it demands that we understand race ontologically as either a real biological essence (of an Aristotelian sort), or as presenting what is at best only a provisional and impoverished sort of reality that we are, in the end, better off without. I have linked this to what is ultimately an understanding of the human subject that is guided by notions of purity. Either a given characteristic or property is *internal* to the agent, and thus inevitably shapes our agency, or it is *external* to the agent and only shapes our agency as a coercive force or as a voluntarily affirmed identification. Liberation, on this account, is a matter of purifying the self of external influences that are neither explicitly affirmed nor chosen, such as, in this dominant view, race.

Second, because of its presumptions regarding the distinction between the internal and external and between what is essentially real and what is not, the politics of purity demands that racial categories be exclusive and distinct, and that individuals belong to one and only one such category. When categories become challenged in their purity, or when individuals present themselves who do not fit clearly in one and only one such category, then this is understood as a threat that must be overcome. A new category must be generated, an old one redefined, or the individual redescribed (most often a combination of the three), so that the norm of categorical purity is at least approached, if not wholly achieved. This taxonomic purity of racial categories is necessary for maintaining the sense of ontological purity of the subject, insofar as this all-or-nothing, discretely bounded account of the racial landscape is the only way to describe that landscape that is consistent with the rigid internal/external understanding of the subject.

Third, the positivistic foundation underlying the politics of purity construes racism as the ongoing practice of the purification of reason and thus humanity. This practice disguises itself as a kind of static property or status, but this deception can only be maintained through the ongoing repetition of the mythology of purity. This repetition takes the form of the domination or control of that which threatens the purity of the norms of reason and humanity that serve as the organizing center of gravity for racial reality. Such threats may be internal or external to the agent or group (though of course *purely* neither). Internal threats to individual purity might be emotions or subjective biases—the sorts of things that were called into question during Sonia Sotomayor's confirmation hearings. The concern over whether she will represent pure and objective judicial reasoning on the bench, or allow the specificity of her experiences, especially her racialized and gendered experiences, to corrupt her judgment is focused on exactly this internal threat to the purity of reason. Internal threats to collective purity, like the purity of a nation or race, take the form of subpopulations who must be controlled or dominated by those who "best represent" the ideals of the nation or race.[1] Thus, a nation or race may demonstrate its rationality and purity by asserting domination over its own poor, women, disabled, homosexuals, elderly, and so on.[2] At the same time, purity can be asserted, both on the individual and the collective level, by exerting control or domination over external manifestations of corruption. For the individual, this means dominating those whose purity is suspect, for the collective, this means dominating those outside of the group whose purity is suspect.

What may be an external practice of purification on the part of an individual may be an internal practice from the collective perspective. The white man who dominates his female domestic partner is using this externally directed manifestation of control as a demonstration of his own purity (he is not controlled by the impure but rather controls it), while at the same time his whiteness means that he is affirming the purity of whiteness by demonstrating its capacity to control its own internal threats to purity. Furthermore, a given action of domination can be a practice of purity in multiple dimensions. In this particular example, there is also a purification of gender at play—as a man, he is also dominating his partner as a collective *external* threat. Thus, in this one act, there is at the same time an individual purification of an external impurity, a collective purification of an internal impurity (within the domain of whiteness), and a collective purification of an external impurity (across the domains of male and female). The main point is that it is through these actions, complex and ambiguous as they are, that the politics of purity manifests and legitimizes itself. It can only achieve the myth of stability and necessity through the constant repetition of these dominating responses to perceived threats—its apparent stability is maintained only through constant response to instability.

Fourth, the politics of purity conditions our thinking about antiracist practice insofar as it both demands of individuals that they attempt to become *nonracist* by purifying their psyche of racist content, and in its insistence on a clear and distinct boundary ontologically between that which is internal and external to the agent. Because of its clear division between that which is self and that which is other, it makes it virtually impossible to think coherently about institutionalized or systemic racism. The politics of purity relies on a positivistic conception of an effectively atomistic subject who either possesses or lacks "racist mental states" as a discrete individual. This, in turn, means that racism is understood as an all-or-nothing status possessed or lacked by all and only individuals. It fosters a conception of the human that is purified of contingency and sociality, and thus rendered abstract, ahistorical, and disembodied.

Given that I have stressed the way in which much of the politics of purity can be understood in terms of an emphasis on states of *being* often conceived in dualistic terms (such as white/nonwhite, racist/nonracist, internal/external, voluntary/involuntary, and so on), as opposed to ongoing processes of *becoming* that are saturated with ambiguity and contingency, it cannot be sufficient simply to negate these four constraints on our liberatory thinking. That is, simply *negating* the terms we seek to critique may be tempting, but it cannot challenge the dualistic all-or-nothing thinking that lies at the heart of the politics of purity. At the end of chapter 5 I argue for rejecting the view of antiracist practice that can be expressed in terms of formal logic as ~(racism) because it is oversimplified and dualistic. So, too, must I reject the temptation to simply describe liberation as the negation of the central tenets and themes of the politics of purity, or again, in the idiom of logic, simply posit ~(politics of purity). I argue in chapter 5 that the struggle against racism must be understood as an ongoing practice of antiracism rather than as a nonracist or "postracial" state to be achieved, and so too must my alternative to the politics of purity be offered in the spirit of an ongoing and often ambiguous process—an infinite task. This means that any genuine critique of the politics of purity cannot begin and end at this simple negation, but must, in the phenomenological spirit to which I have been appealing all along, continue to engage in the ongoing *critique* of the politics of purity, and this is not the same as an outright negation (this important distinction should become clearer as this chapter progresses).

In this spirit I offer my account of the *creolizing subject*. If my diagnosis points toward the politics of purity as central to the pathologies of race and racism, then creolization may be a start toward addressing that root cause. Again, I do not offer this as a simple contradiction of purity, and certainly not as a state of being. That is, I am not saying that instead of striving to *be* pure we should strive to *be* creole. Rather, what I will be articulating here is a vision of the human that emphasizes and affirms dynamism, plasticity, and ambiguity. Above all, it must open up an ongoing process of becoming rather than *define* a fixed state of being.

Of course, as I have mentioned briefly already, a concept of creolization and the creole exists already *within* the politics of purity, and so care must be taken to distinguish that understanding from the concept of the creolizing subject that I wish to elaborate in this chapter. In its sense consistent with the politics of purity, *creole* (and other similar terms such as *mestizo*, *biracial*, *mixed race*, and so on) stands as a discrete and pure category, over and against what are taken to be the discrete and pure constitutive elements from which the creole is formed, whether that be a creole language, a creole culture or practice, or a creole person. The creole, in all of these cases, stands apart and distinct from its constitutive historical, cultural, or ancestral elements. The creole individual is not understood as white, or black, or Amerindian, or Asian, for example, but the distinct amalgamation of (at least some of) these. The logic of this amalgamation may be understood differently from place to place and from time to time, such that there may be a single category capturing all who are "mixed" within that context, or there may be increasingly complicated taxonomies describing possible combinations of ancestry. The point is that the normative ideal remains one of purity, such that the creole, in this sense, in no way challenges that norm but rather simply generates and occupies a particular category (or set of categories) within that larger framework governed by the politics of purity. My understanding of the creolizing subject, however, is meant to challenge that norm of purity at the most radical level, and so must offer a different account of creolization.

Within the politics of purity, the creole emerges historically as a challenge to the norm of purity that must be overcome, either by establishing it as a pure and discrete category in its own right, or by absorbing it into a preexisting (pure) category. In many parts of Latin America and the Caribbean, the former strategy prevailed, while in the United States, at least until the late twentieth century, the latter strategy dominated. However, I do not wish to suggest that it can never be legitimate or meaningful to identify oneself, or someone else, as creole (or *mestizo*, mixed, and so on).[3] Indeed, especially within the Americas, the category of the creole came to serve the very important function of articulating an identity that differed in significant ways from the categories prescribed by the colonial (and eventually postcolonial) semiotic regimes. When Trinidadian calypso musician Young Tiger pointed out that he "stood his ground like a young creole" in his song "I Was There (At the Coronation)" (1953), his appeal to a creole identity situated him in an important way within the context of attending the coronation of Queen Elizabeth II in London. In my earlier engagement with Sundstrom's account of mixed-race identity, I argued that mixed-race identity can be a perfectly legitimate and even liberatory way of identifying oneself or others, provided such identities are offered in a way that challenges the politics of purity. Again, it is not *that* one employs such terms or takes up this sense of identity but rather the *way* in which this occurs. And so long as the manner in which creole identities and categories fail to radically challenge the politics of purity they will over time become rigid, ossified, and discrete in ways that do not merely capitulate to the politics of purity but ultimately reinscribe and reinforce it. It is this tendency that my own articulation of the creolizing subject seeks to overcome.

My understanding of the creolizing subject seeks to disrupt the norm of purity at its roots by placing at the forefront that emphasis on *becoming* which I have suggested is at the heart of the phenomenological method I have employed so far. This is why I use the term *creolizing* instead of *creolized*. It isn't that an individual or practice simply *is* creole in the sense of a status or property that one has achieved or possesses, but rather that creolization is an ongoing process or activity—it is a way of becoming, rather than a state of being. Equally important, it is a process undergone on and by *subjects* in three different senses of the term. First, in the more *subjective* meaning of one's own sense of agency (*I* am creolizing), second, in the more *objective* meaning of a subject one observes or describes (*he/she/they* are creolizing or *it* is creolizing), and third, in the more methodological/disciplinary sense of a subject of study (*philosophy* is creolizing). The creolizing subject, in other words, is meant to capture you and me as subjects in the world, you and me as objects in the world, and you and me as *thinking* about particular subjects in particular ways. What I am arguing for is the notion that, in the place of purity, an ongoing process of creolization ought to be the guiding norm for all three of these moments.

THE CREOLIZING SUBJECT

Gloria Anzaldúa's powerful account of her own confrontation with *mestizaje* offered in her landmark *Borderlands/La Frontera* (2007), is an important work to which the account of creolizing subjectivity I am offering here is deeply indebted. Indeed, the final chapter of her book, "*La Conciencia de la Mestiza*/Towards a New Consciousness," offers some of the same prescriptions I am arguing for here. Noting that, "the *mestiza's* dual or multiple personality is plagued by psychic restlessness" leading to "*un choque*, a cultural collision," she urges a "tolerance for ambiguity" (2007, 100–1). *La mestiza*, finding herself betwixt and between a variety of borders, cultural boundaries, and normative locales, must counter this "cultural collision" by generating a new understanding of *la mestiza*.

The new mestiza copes by developing a tolerance for contradictions, a tolerance for ambiguity. She learns to be an Indian in Mexican culture, to be Mexican from an Anglo point of view. She learns to juggle cultures. She has a plural personality, she operates in a pluralistic mode—nothing is thrust out, the good the bad and the ugly, nothing rejected, nothing abandoned. Not only does she sustain contradictions, she turns the ambivalence into something else. (Anzaldúa 2007, 101)

This embracing of ambiguity leads her ultimately toward "a massive uprooting of dualistic thinking" (2008, 102). Anzaldúa captures elegantly exactly the sort of resistance to the politics of purity that I wish to advocate with my notion of creolizing subjectivity. It is in the spirit of furthering her project, in articulating that "something else" into which the contradiction and ambivalence is turned, that this chapter operates.

I described the politics of purity as insisting on the existence and maintenance of a clear and distinct border between that which is internal to the agent, and that which is external. I take this distinction to be a central organizing principle of the politics of purity, and thus any effort to address purity must take this way of understanding human agency head on. From its Aristotelian roots, the internal/external distinction has become important both for identifying what is *essentially* human about us as a species (reason, for example), and for ascertaining when our actions are or are not autonomous or voluntary. Internal characteristics or aspects are necessary in the sense of being inescapably constitutive of our agency and identity, while external characteristics or aspects are contingent in the sense of being incidental to our agency and identity. As I argue in chapter 5, this can manifest quite clearly in the enlightenment ideal of the autonomous and self-governing agent, purified of all contingent and *external* influences. The logic here is one in which the agent, dedicated to this notion of autonomy, identifies where the boundary between the internal and the external lies (paradigmatically in thinking or reason), and struggles to describe the methodology by which one may ensure that this boundary is never crossed. Thus Descartes identifies the "thinking substance" as central to his agency (internal), and offers an epistemological method by which we can protect that thinking substance from all external interference, arriving at absolute certainty with regard to our knowledge claims, Kant identifies a method for ensuring that moral reason is purified of external interference via the categorical imperative, and Rawls employs the veil of ignorance to ensure that morally arbitrary factors will not corrupt the purity of our deliberations about justice. What is crucial here is the way in which this functions in a dualistic, all-or-nothing manner. A given characteristic, feature, or aspect is either internal or external—it cannot be both. This norm of purity in turn demands an atomistic conception of social ontology, since individual agents, having clear boundaries, must regard all other agents as *outside* of that boundary, such that each is a discrete atom.[4]

The creolizing subject, however, is actively engaged with the ambiguity, permeability, and plasticity of the distinction between the internal and the external, the self and the other. In this way, the creolizing subject is displacing the atomistic social ontology we have inherited from European modernity. As I argue in chapter 5, the politics of purity is a manifestation of becoming attempting to pass itself off as being (and is in this way antihuman). Purity takes itself to be a state that one can occupy or achieve (being), but in actuality it requires constant effort in the form of ongoing practices and rituals of purification (becoming), like domination, colonialism, and epistemic closure. The creolizing subject, however, openly affirms and celebrates humanity as an ongoing and open process. The critique of the politics of purity does not mean simply the affirmation of the creole in a way that preserves the same static logic of being (in the manner of ~(purity)). Creolization, like purity, is never a state that can be achieved, but demands ongoing effort and engagement with the norms around which it is organized. The difference between creolization and purity, therefore, is not simply a matter of the presence or absence of mixture and ambiguity, but is rather a matter of the *way* in which one confronts and engages that mixture and ambiguity. The politics of purity disavows creolization through a historical and anthropological project predicated upon preexisting *pure* categories of being, and through an ongoing psychological and political project of purification when creolization cannot be simply ignored. The creolizing subject, on the other hand, acknowledges and affirms the way in which individuals and groups have always been creolizing to a greater or lesser extent linguistically, culturally, psychologically, politically, and even biologically. Understanding who *I* am, who *we* are, and *how* we interact and relate to one another requires, for the creolizing subject, this ongoing critical engagement with all these different levels of ongoing, dynamic, and ambiguous processes (including, especially, the process that is *me*).

Within the politics of purity, the strict and determinate boundary between self and other serves to demarcate what is clearly and necessarily *me* from what is clearly and necessarily *not me*. I need to be able to tell what I am from what I am not, and within the logic of purity, any ambiguity poses a challenge to this fundamental distinction, and thus to the coherence of the self, that must be overcome. Once I understand myself in terms of being rather than becoming, ambiguity cannot be tolerated, for it prevents me from answering the question of what I am. The creolization of the subject plays out, therefore, at this most fundamental level as an ambiguation of this most basic distinction—that between internal and external, self and other. It is, as I have already argued, a shift from being to becoming. What is *me* and what is *not me* is never clear cut. It is more both/and than either/or, and the creolizing subject meets this ambiguity head-on. It is ultimately an effort to emphasize agency by replacing the question of *what* I am with the question of *who* I am, which can never be answered with a static description, since who I am is fundamentally an ongoing process. As such, the boundary between internal and external, to the extent that it functions at all, is always shifting and permeable.

Note that I have not claimed that the creolizing subject rejects the border between internal and external entirely, for that would be the method of straightforward negation, of ~(purity). What I am advocating is not an indistinct amalgam in which all are one and the same in some monistic fashion, or in which all attempts to distinguish and demarcate are dismissed as oppressive machinations. Recall that I have suggested that the politics of purity functions in part as a reification of difference—the same (self/internal) and the different (other/external) are understood as discrete, mutually exclusive, and exhaustive categories of being. To call for the eradication of all borders, for the overcoming of all difference, is to advocate for a world in which all is the same—a world in which individuality is erased and all is *purely* one. If creolization is a mixture of different elements (which are themselves mixtures of different elements), then it is necessary, if the call for creolization is to be coherent, that some sense of distinction, some understanding of borders and boundaries, some manner of difference be preserved. The problem with the politics of purity, therefore, is not *that* it places a border between internal and external, between self and other, but rather the *way* in which it understands the nature and force of that border. The border must be understood not as a fixed, reified, distinct division, but as a shifting, unstable, and ambiguous site of contestation. How the creolizing subject understands the boundary between the internal and the external is itself a statement about who she takes herself to be, which in turn is always already a statement about who she takes herself to have been, and who she takes herself to be becoming. As such, it is subject to constant reassessment and renegotiation, not only because her own understanding of that border is subject to change but also because her understanding is always situated within and conditioned by an intersubjective context that gives force and meaning to that understanding.

This understanding of agency thus stands as a clear rejection of the ontology of atomistic individualism. The subject cannot be understood as fully distinct and discrete *as a subject*. That is, one can understand human beings as distinct and discrete only insofar as they are abstractions—whether as strictly physical beings with a unique physical spatial and temporal description, as hypothetical signatories of a social contract ordered to serve (effectively pregiven) individual interests, or as consumers with discrete sets of preferences and desires seeking the maximization of individual satisfaction under market discipline. One of the clear lessons of phenomenology, however, is that, as human subjects, we are wielders of meaning, and meaning is a fundamentally social endeavor. The problem with so much of the philosophical discourse on individual and social ontology is that it is ultimately positivistic. To be sure, the contemporary discourse does not typically employ the internal/external distinction explicitly, but one can see it operating, for example, in the debates between liberalism and communitarianism. Rawls's "veil of ignorance," to elaborate one such example, is often criticized for precisely this reason. In bracketing what is "arbitrary from a moral point of view" (1971, 63), he is offering an account of what is ultimately *internal* to moral agency, an account that critics like Michael Sandel and Iris Young accuse of being overly abstract (Sandel 1998; Young 1990). This debate remains positivistic insofar as it treats agency as a fixed and static entity and debates only where to draw the line between what is constitutive of individual agency, and what is incidental to it—that is, what is inside and what is outside.

The phenomenological turn, however, in emphasizing an understanding of human subjectivity as a process or activity, and not as a static thing, points out that the very act of raising the question of individual and social ontology is itself part of this ongoing activity of human subjectivity as meaning-constituting activity. To *mean* something, furthermore, assumes some sense of communication, which, as I describe in chapter 5, is only possible within a community of fellow meaning-constituting agents. If the self is ultimately a meaning-constituting *activity* organized in part around interpreting and giving meaning to this process itself—the constant question of *who* one is—and that activity, in turn, is always conditioned by the communities in which one undertakes this ongoing task, then the self must be understood as a constantly changing, ambiguous, and shifting site of contestation and negotiation. It is, in short, constitutively social, but not in a way that *determines* the "content" of my agency. For, while I must engage in this ongoing process of contestation and negotiation with others, I am at all times very much an active participant in that process. Furthermore, to the extent that my subjectivity is shaped by a social context that is rich with difference and distinction, and I recognize and affirm the challenges, opportunities, and possibilities that this brings with it, rather than struggling to simplify and purify that context, my subjectivity is *creolizing*.

One may thus very well be designated as creole or mixed, and yet fail to be a creolizing subject in the sense I am employing the term. Likewise, one may be designated as racially "pure," and yet manifest a creolizing subjectivity. It is only because the politics of purity has held sway over our thinking for so long that this strikes us as begging explanation. If we accept the politics of purity, then whether one is or is not creole must be understood as a clearly demarcated and defined state of being. But creolizing subjectivity, for any given agent, is not a state that one achieves, but a way of understanding, communicating, and critically appraising one's subjectivity. At this most basic level of the distinction between self and other, between internal and external, this means taking seriously the way in which these distinctions are meaningful, but must always be understood as not only fluid and plastic but as fundamentally ambiguous and indeterminate. Our answers to questions about what is or is not inside or outside of these boundaries must be not only provisional and subject to constant reevaluation and revision, but must be understood as admitting of both/and rather than either/or answers. As a meaning-constituting subjectivity, I am always coming from some particular set of perspectives, in a particular sort of body, with a particular history, but insofar as I am actively engaging in practices of meaning-constituting, in a nexus of communities with other subjects engaged in similar practices, I am always more than those perspectives, bodies, and histories, and furthermore those perspectives, bodies, and histories are also always layered with ambiguous and even conflicting moments of meaning. Ultimately, in pushing meaning beyond the static confines of a given history, for example, *I am changing* the very meaning and significance of that history, and thus the nature of its impact on my subjectivity. And of course, since my subjectivity is inextricably linked to a larger intersubjective *milieu*, the *I* here is real and meaningful, but not completely (purely) distinct, ontologically or causally, from that *milieu*. There is a causal reciprocity here that simply cannot be captured by hard distinctions between self and other.

This does not mean that we should necessarily consider the self to be fragmented or multiple. To be sure, the unitary Cartesian ego needs to be rejected, but in its place we are not necessarily left with multiple and fragmented selves. María Lugones's discussion of purity in her book *Pilgrimages/Peregrinajes*, for example, though similar to the one I am articulating here, offers such an ultimate appeal to multiplicity and fragmentation (2003, 121–148). She links purity to a unitary conception of the subject, to "Reason, including its normative aspect," and to "the urge for control" (Lugones 2003, 129). She understands purity as an act of separation, and posits the metaphor of "curdling" as a corrective to separation, linking curdling in turn to *mestizaje*. I am deeply indebted to Lugones's work, and her discussion of purity in particular, though brief, is very stimulating. I take issue, however, with her treatment of agency and subjectivity, especially her appeal to fragmentation.[5]

The thematization throughout her book of traveling and pilgrimage is meant, as I read her, to capture the fragmentation of subjectivity that occurs within "the spatiality of oppressions" (Lugones 2003, 11). Against the unitary, fixed, atomistic conception of agency that Lugones identifies with late modernity, she posits an "active subjectivity" that "does not presuppose the individual subject" and "does not presuppose collective intentionality of collectivities of the same" (6). She abandons "the claim that the subject is unified," stating that the practical decisions of oppressed people "in one reality are not possible for them in the other, given that they are such different people in the two realities" (57). Difficulties arise, she goes on, when one tries to "remember" the intentions of one of one's selves in a different world, such that, ultimately, "the task of remembering one's many selves is a difficult liberatory task" (59). Lugones's treatment of fragmentation and remembering here implies that the various realities, and selves "attached" to those realities, are to a significant degree distinct. But that would seem to maintain the purity, in my sense, of the realities and selves. If the active subject is not unitary but is rather a fragmented collection of discrete selves that must struggle to remember each other between their particular (discrete) realities, then the logic of purity still seems to hold sway here, and to that extent Lugones and I part company. Elsewhere, however, she admonishes the reader "to see ambiguity, see that the split-separated are also and simultaneously curdled-separated" (126), and so there is an ambiguity in her work on the nature of the self that in part illustrates the kind of unsettled, *migratory* project she is advancing. This ambiguity, if I am identifying it correctly, would then be a virtue, and not a failing. In any event, my appeal to Lugones's discussion of purity here is offered not so much as a critique, but as an opportunity both to acknowledge her work, and to bring to the foreground this possible response to the politics of purity that emphasizes fragmentation and multiplicity, which, on its face, fails to challenge the politics of purity in a radical way.

Creolizing subjectivity, as I am describing it, is thus not a result of multiple distinct selves jostling for dominance over time. In maintaining the notion of discrete selves that may or may not "remember" other selves, I am concerned that Lugones's view maintains, at least implicitly, vestiges of the politics of purity. The creolizing subject, as I am offering it, is rather an always emerging unity of the experiences of meaning-constituting within the life-world of that subject. Such experiences are diverse, ambiguous, and even sometimes contradictory, but they are also brought together within, by, and through the same subject that shapes the meaning and significance of those experiences. The Hegelian insight that the self is an achievement, and not a substance, is crucial here (Pippin 2008, 3–11; Hegel 1991, 44–45). The creolizing subject is a *subject* insofar as she is interpreting, reinterpreting, ordering, and reordering her experiences of herself, of the world around her, the interplay between the two, and the often blurry and contentious distinction between them. She is *creolizing* only insofar as this process maintains a clear-eyed view of itself *as a process* that is ongoing and saturated with ambiguity from start to finish.

Thus, the boundary between the self and other is not some fixed locus but rather an ongoing site of contestation and negotiation, and the creolizing subject recognizes this reality and affirms the responsibilities that this recognition engenders. The creolizing subject approaches racial reality in the same way. Race, as I argue in chapter 4, functions as a kind of location from which one enters into the ongoing contestation of the meaning and significance of that location. It is a location that is particularly, but not exclusively, signified in and through bodies. Furthermore, no racial location is pure in the sense of being completely discrete and different from all other such locations, and no particular agent is purely of any particular such location in the sense of being fixed and determined by that location. Finally, race, as the ground from which we engage in these ongoing practices of contestation and negotiation, is always shifting. Creolizing subjectivity is not, therefore, something one achieves, nor is it a status into which one is born. As I argue above, there is a way of being creole that is perfectly consistent with the politics of purity, as a manifestation of being.[6] Creolizing subjectivity rejects the false sense of security offered by the politics of purity, and turns instead to the recognition of the ambiguity and indeterminacy of racial ontology, and the affirmation of the challenges, threats, opportunities, and responsibilities this entails.

The creolizing subject may thus be black *and* white *and* Asian *and* mixed rather than one and only one of these. A creolizing religious practice, like *Santeria*, for example, is European and African and a unique mixture of these elements. To say of it that it is *not* European but rather creole misses two important points. First, it obscures the ways in which the practice is recognizably European by imposing a false dichotomy or distinction between the European and the creole (which distinction is often motivated by a normative privileging of European purity). Second, it presumes the purity of the constitutive elements themselves. European religious practices are already a mixture of Jewish practices with roots in the Middle East, Ancient Pagan practices (which themselves varied dramatically from place to place throughout what would come to be known as the European continent), shamanistic and druidic practices, and of course African practices. The African component of *Santeria*, meanwhile, is a mixture of the practices of the various peoples of West Africa brought to the Americas, who had been in their turn influenced by Middle Eastern (Jewish and Islamic), East African, and Indian practices. In the same way, for any given individual agent, he or she will be constituted by different elements, each of which in turn cannot be properly understood as pure and discrete. The salience and significance of the different elements may vary from place to place and time to time, such that one's blackness may be most significant at time A, and one's whiteness at time B, and one's status as mixed at time C. It does not mean that one ceases being those other elements at the different times, it only means that the terms of the ongoing contestation and negotiation of one's subjectivity have shifted.

For the creolizing subject, this ambiguity and variation do not demonstrate the illusory status of race, nor the fragmentary nature of the subject, but rather provide the means and opportunity for articulating, contesting, and negotiating one's subjectivity *from* a position that is always already located, but ambiguously and dynamically so. Creolization, in this sense, is the on-going process of pushing the boundaries of the self into increasingly varied domains.

It is crucial to recognize here the way in which this upsets the traditional understanding of the relation between self and other. As I argue in chapter 4, the liberal tradition allows for only two ways in which a given element of subjectivity can be properly considered internal: either it is in some strong sense intrinsic to the agent (biological or essential), or it is explicitly voluntarily taken up by the agent. Since the biological account of race as essential and intrinsic to the agent has been rejected, and the normative content of racial terminology and identifications can (it is argued) only ever be harmful to the agent, then racial identities must be understood as in some significant sense *externally imposed*, and therefore as essentially coercive. There have been recent efforts to articulate a positive racial identity within this understanding of the ontology of race (Shelby 2005; and Appiah 2007), but this can only ever be understood as an exclusively political and pragmatic (in the mundane sense of *practical*, not in the philosophical sense) commitment aimed ultimately at the dissolution of race altogether and the realization of a colorblind ideal. The underlying view consistent throughout the liberal treatment of race is that racial categories are pernicious impositions placed upon individuals by others in ways that ultimately undermine human freedom. The meanings generated by others, such as *race*, thus stand as fundamentally external categories that may be accepted or rejected by a given individual. For the creolizing subject, however, the self is constitutively social in that the process of the negotiation of the meaning of the self is a fundamentally communicative act, and meaning is itself inescapably social. Thus, the meanings and categories generated by others are not something "out there" or external to the agent which may be simply taken up or rejected, but are always already part of the self. One's racial being, therefore, inescapably shapes one's subjectivity, not as a result of some intrinsic set of properties independent of human consciousness (such as a positivistic biological essence) or as some externally imposed set of norms, but precisely because it is part of the meaning-constituting activity of others, and the self, as an achievement, is only possible as a process of interaction with such others. To reject race outright, therefore, is to place myself (falsely) outside of my communicative community in a radical way.

At the same time, these meanings are not fixed, given, or pure. They are constitutive of individual subjectivity in that they inescapably condition that subjectivity, but they do not determine it in any fixed way. One's racial being, therefore, is part of one's subjectivity, but as a subject the meaning and significance of racial being is itself conditioned and influenced by that subjectivity. This is what I mean by asserting that the creolizing subject undermines the traditional distinction between self and other. The distinction between self and other, when pursued rigorously, falls apart. The self is the other and the other is the self, but never purely and discretely. And far from making these terms meaningless or illusory, it is what makes them essentially human. Race, as an undeniably significant part of this interaction between self and other, is thus an unavoidably significant part of any given subject. What distinguishes the creolizing subject, therefore, is that he or she appreciates and affirms both the way in which race has shaped his or her consciousness and the way in which he or she is able to shape the meaning and significance of race. Thus, even an individual who is not typically identified (by others or by herself) as racially "mixed" is still never purely of her particular race. This is not to say that such an individual is *the same* as someone who is identified typically as mixed. Such a view would both commit the error of conflating the similar with the same, and elide the significance of embodiment in a particularly pernicious way.

In other words, my claim isn't simply that we are all ultimately "mixed," as if Young Tiger (the calypso singer from Trinidad mentioned above), Tony Blair, and Kofi Annan are all the same. My claim is only that no racial category is really pure insofar as there are indistinct borders and contesting meanings and elements, and no individual is purely of a given category insofar as he or she is an active participant in the ongoing contestation and negotiation of the meaning and significance of that category. There is plenty of conceptual room between this statement, and the idea that we are all the same. Indeed, this is precisely my point about the reification of identity and difference. Young Tiger's assertion that he is a creole can distinguish him from Blair and Annan in a way that is both meaningful, and consistent with the account of creolizing subjectivity I am attempting to capture here. It positions him within the ongoing negotiation and contestation of racial reality, but in a way that is dynamic, ambiguous, and indeterminate (both like the position of everyone else and in its particularities different).

Creolizing subjectivity, in other words, calls upon an agent to recognize the ways in which the person *is* raced in particular ways on the one hand, and the ways in which the person is both more and less his or her race on the other. It is in this way that creolizing subjectivity can be understood as a call to assume responsibility for our (raced) selves. We are more than our race or races in the sense that we are always subjects who participate in the ongoing process of meaning constitution, and thus are never properly determined by or reduced to our racial ascriptions. At the same time, we are less than our race or races insofar as our racialized consciousness does inescapably condition our subjectivity in ways that are constitutive of our identity—race is a significant part of the context from and through which we exercise our agency, and thus constitutive of that agency itself. Within a context deeply informed by the politics of purity, we are also less than our race or races because racial categories themselves are never pure and discrete, and thus we are importantly less than any one of them or the sum of their combination. Within the politics of purity, they posit a superhuman (which is a form of *in*humanity) norm of purity to which we can never fully measure up. The creolizing subject, in understanding and affirming this complicated relationship to the ongoing process of *living* race is thus both affirming herself as an active participant in this process, and avoiding the traps of either pretending that she is somehow outside of or beyond it, or completely fixed and determined by it.

It is in this way that creolizing subjectivity can be understood as inviting or even demanding a sense of responsibility on the part of the agent. One is responsible *to* racial reality insofar as it conditions one's subjectivity, and one is responsible *for* it to the extent that one is an agent actively engaging in the ongoing contestation and negotiation (becoming) of that reality.

As a result, the claim either that race is a completely distinct reality that imposes itself on agents from the outside, or that it is entirely up to the individual what race means and how it functions, must both be understood as evasions of that responsibility. For the creolizing subject, racism as well is not to be bemoaned as an inevitable part of the human condition or treated as a purely subjective and discrete state of mind, but rather must be confronted as a call to be responsible to and for racism as the ongoing practice of purity. One is thus responsible *to* racism insofar as one rises to the challenge of uncovering and confronting it within oneself, within others, and in those habitual and attenuated meanings and practices that constitute our interpretive horizon or orientation. One is at the same time responsible *for* racism to the extent that one takes ownership for one's own contributions to those ongoing practices within and around oneself. Taking responsibility in this sense, therefore, does not mean wallowing in guilt (though the recognition of guilt or culpability can be necessary), or pointing fingers (though it can sometimes be quite responsible to call attention to the practices of others)—at least, never as ends in themselves. The creolizing subject rather takes responsibility as part of the very process of entering into the ongoing contestation of racial reality in a way that will genuinely affect positive change. If one seeks to work for antiracism as a creolizing subject, one cannot assume a ready-made solution, and a *defined* and *fixed* vision of success as an end-state, but must instead be responsible for and to the unfolding processes of racial reality and the practice of purity (racism) within and around oneself, with special attention paid to the way in which that very distinction must be viewed with suspicion.

Lastly, the extremely important function of the politics of purity as an effort to reify difference and identity should be noted. The aim of the drawing of rigid boundaries and distinctions is to make clear that which is the same essentially from that which is different essentially, where difference and identity are understood as mutually exclusive and discrete categories of being. Racial categories make this quite clear, especially when understood analytically as the demand for necessary and sufficient conditions for exclusive membership. My whiteness, within the politics of purity, locates me within an ontology in which I am importantly identical to all other whites and only other whites. So far as our whiteness is concerned, we are interchangeable— we are *identical*. Any individual with mixture or ambiguity is thus *different* from all whites and must by definition belong to some other category, which again must be analytically understood to pick out all and only members of that particular category. That mixture or ambiguity is understood as a threat is therefore a direct result of this reification of identity and difference. So, too, is the tendency of racial thinking within the politics of purity to generate monolithic categories and accounts of group identity. This is a clear problem not only for discussions of race but also of gender, where the worry over the content of the category *woman* has been a recurring theme of feminist thought (at least in the West).[7] That which is ambiguous or mixed, that which fails to be pure, threatens the boundary between identity and difference. That which is the same, that which is identical, cannot also be different and vice versa. This aspect of the politics of purity lurks throughout my discussion thus far. The boundary between the internal and the external, for example, is a demarcation of that which is *identical* to me (self) from that which is *different* from me (other). This is why the politics of purity is in no way limited to race but informs our thinking about gender, about sexuality, and all of the other myriad ways in which we try to identify that which is the same as me, or more often that which is identical with *the human* from that which *is* (as a form of being) different.

For the creolizing subject, the same does not exclude the different, nor is difference devoid of identity. Hegelian logic attempts to capture this approach to relations of difference and identity (Hegel 1969, 409–43; Hahn 2007, 70–78). Hegel states in the *Science of Logic*:

> From this is it evident that the law of identity itself, and still more the law of contradiction, is not merely of analytic but of synthetic nature. For the latter contains in its expression not merely empty, simple equality-with-self, and not merely the other of this in general, but, what is more, absolute inequality, contradiction per se. But as has been shown, the law of identity itself contains the movement of reflection, identity as a vanishing of otherness. (1969, 416)

The fundamental insight of Hegel's logic, which is in turn an organizing theme for the whole of his system, is that true unity does not absorb or eliminate difference but rather preserves difference within unity, which is thus not the same thing as simple (in Hegelian terms, "abstract") identity. For Hegel, the absolute truth of *Geist* is not that everything is one but rather that the ultimate truth of *Geist* is a higher unity that emerges *only* out of the interrelation of different elements or moments. The Logical truth $a=a$ only makes sense, if there is also some sense in which $a \neq a$. If this were not so, if a were truly *the same* as itself, then the only way to express that fact would be a, not $a=a$. Identity, as a *relation*, in other words, *requires* some difference between the relata in order to be coherent, just as difference, as a relation, requires some similarity however abstract, in order to begin the comparison. What places the creolizing subject in opposition to the politics of purity is the effort to make explicit this resistance to the reification of identity and difference both within her own subjectivity, and in her interactions with others (which, of course, cannot themselves be understood as completely different and distinct). This in turn shifts the focus away from identity and difference as fixed states of being and emphasizes the way in which identity and difference can only be understood as ongoing, plastic, and ambiguous *relations* (becoming) between relata that are always *both* different *and* the same.

What all of this amounts to for the individual creolizing subject is, I submit, an ongoing practice of liberation. This is not the traditional liberal vision of liberation that I have characterized as the purification of the subject (the removal of external influence on the exercise of the purely internal will), nor is it the simple negation of this vision as the absorption of the individual into some disciplinary or discursive system. In this dominant view, liberation most often takes the form of asserting mastery and control over those external elements that are seen to stand in the way of the unfettered exercise of the individual (understood in an atomistic way) will. This is why my account of the politics of purity in chapter 5 describes the ongoing practice of asserting domination and mastery as in effect the continuous effort to purify subjectivity and reason. My liberty, in other words, demands that I purify my subjectivity of external elements, and I do this by demonstrating their contingency and inessential nature through their domination and control. Returning to Hegel, this understanding of liberty can be found at the heart of his account of the "moment of Desire" in the *Phenomenology of Spirit*, which is superseded through the reconciliation of the self and the other via "pure recognition" (*reine Anerkennung*).[8] The liberation that is the project of the creolizing subject, however, is not this purification of the subject through the exercise of domination and mastery. Rather, because the creolizing subject understands the way in which the boundary between the self and the other is ambiguous and permeable, liberation is understood not as control over the other nor as simple freedom from external interference, but rather as the maintenance of a *relation* that affirms and builds upon human agency, understood as constitutively social. My liberation, in other works, is a matter of my being in a relation with others such that the social context in which my agency is developing fosters my own sense of agency and value. Of course, since my agency is constituted by the agency of others, when my sense of worth comes at the expense of another (through domination), it is deeply impoverished and no true liberation at all.

RACE AND THE CREOLIZING SUBJECT

Thus, the creolizing subject isn't a matter of being any particular race or set of races, or really about *being* anything at all. Rather, the creolizing subject is a matter of how one relates to and interacts with the ongoing practices of racial reality (becoming). The impurity, ambiguity, and plasticity of racial categories and individual racial membership can in this way be understood as evidence of their fundamental humanity. They, like us, are works in progress, shaped by and shaping human subjectivity in ever-changing and developing ways. One is a creolizing subject, therefore, not by virtue of possessing a particular ancestry or appearance or even a particular attitude, for as a kind of becoming, it cannot be about *possessing* anything at all. Instead, one is a creolizing subject by virtue of manifesting a kind of subjectivity that is working toward an ever-increasing awareness of and responsibility for the way in which one's subjectivity is made manifest to oneself and others within a shared communicative field that is inescapably conditioned by race. In this sense, it demands a constant and active confrontation with both the way in which one's race conditions one's subjectivity, and the way in which one is able in turn to contest, negotiate, and otherwise influence the meaning of race. One is a creolizing subject, in other words, to the extent that one shed a critical light onto racial reality by making explicit for oneself and others the ways in which race has always been and will continue to be a site of contestation and negotiation, and thus always ambiguous and indeterminate rather than a fixed state of being.

To be sure, racial categories, as fixed and discrete modes of being that serve to maintain and legitimate racialized oppression and domination must be subjected to rigorous critique. But part of my argument so far has been that this critique has not often achieved the level of rigor required in order to truly challenge racial oppression. The failure has been to take this dominant understanding of racial reality as definitive and complete—this is all that race has ever been and can ever be. My argument has been that this view maintains the basic structure of the politics of purity, in that it treats racial reality, and ultimately human identity, as fixed and given collections of properties, which are either possessed or lacked by particular individuals or groups (themselves understood as static bearers of such properties). By mounting a more rigorous critical inquiry and thus emphasizing a more dynamic understanding of human subjectivity as participant in an ongoing and fundamentally social process of meaning-constituting, we can come to see that the vast bulk of our thinking about race has to be radically reconfigured. Race is something that we *do*, not something that we *are*, and it is, importantly, something that we always do in concert with others, whose ways of doing race inevitably shape the ways in which we are able to do (or *not* do) race.[9]

Racial purity is, to be sure, a myth of sorts. No individual is purely of a given race, since we are often racially ambiguous in ways we may not even realize, and since races themselves are never strictly pure to begin with, insofar as they have never and can never function as discrete categories of being. This realization is not entirely new, but my point is that it is often offered in a manner consistent with the politics of purity, especially as it relates to whiteness. The claim that individual whites are never *purely* white can be a valuable point to make, not simply insofar as white people often have elements of nonwhite ancestry, but more fundamentally because whiteness has always been a kind of amalgam fraught with ambiguity, conflict, and contention. The problem emerges, in a way that reveals the underlying positivism of the politics of purity, when the further rhetorical move is made from this observation of white impurity to the claim that whiteness is therefore nonexistent or irrelevant, because it is in effect concluding from this observation that no individual is ever purely white that all individuals must be purely *nonwhite*. The creolizing subject, in contrast, confronts the recognition of the way in which whiteness fails to live up to the standards of purity that are its implicit and explicit aims, yet is nevertheless a real and potent force. Race may be something that we *do* more than it is something that we *are*, but it does not follow from this that it is simply something that we can stop doing altogether. One's racial being, in other words, is not a fixed and given essence—it is neither a property that we simply possess, nor is it a strictly contingent activity that we can choose to abandon. It is, I have argued, more a sort of location or context, and it is in this way, as inevitably conditioning one's subjectivity, that racial reality must be understood. One's whiteness, or blackness, or Asianness, or even *mestiza*-ness therefore, is not something that one can *be* purely in the way the politics of purity would have us believe, but it is also impossible for one to purely *not be* raced, or simply decide by voluntary fiat *how* one is raced.

By way of illustration, consider again some of the contemporary debates regarding mixed-race identity in the United States. Those who identify themselves as mixed race, especially those who are most *visibly* mixed, have different experiences from those who are less ambiguous in their appearance. They may experience conflicting appeals to loyalty—if they identify as strictly black, are they denying their white, or Asian, or Latina/o, or Amerindian ancestry and their sense that their experiences are in a significant way different from those who are more "purely" black? On the other hand, if they identify as mixed, are they undermining efforts toward black liberation and solidarity? Are they ultimately furthering antiblack racism by emphasizing their nonblackness? There is a rich literature taking on these and other issues surrounding mixed race identity,[10] and the point I wish to stress is that this dilemma is a consequence of the politics of purity. The politics of purity insists that individuals who manifest this sort of racial mixture must overcome their ambiguous condition (as it poses a threat to purity) either by identifying with a preexisting pure race (black, Asian, and so on), or by abandoning that race and constituting a new one (mixed race). How ought one respond to this quandary in a manner that manifests a creolizing subjectivity?

For the creolizing subject, this is always a false dilemma. One's blackness, for example, can manifest itself in significant ways having to do with shared sets of experiences, shared relations to other individuals, groups and institutions, and even political commitments to antiracism. At the same time, these manifestations of blackness do not rule out simultaneous manifestations of whiteness, Asianness, Latinicity, or even a unique (though never pure) mixed-race set of experiences and relations. One can be *all* of these while at the same time being (purely) none of them (and never *being* any of them in the more robust and static sense). At the same time, what constitutes the uniqueness of the situation for each individual is the significance each category may hold from time to time and place to place. This significance will vary depending upon a variety of conditions. The significance of blackness will be different for the same individual in Kingston, Jamaica, as opposed to Louisville, Kentucky. Over time, as demographics shift in a given city, for example, different aspects of one's racial situation may become more salient. The ultimate point is that a creolizing subject attends to and actively participates in this ever-shifting and developing contestation of the significance and meaning of the racial reality that both shapes and is shaped by her agency. It is not simply up to her to be or not be a particular race, nor is she strictly determined and fixed by her racial background. Rather, she enters into a field of racial meanings from a position that is already constituted as meaningful in particular, though ambiguous and conflicting, ways that in turn condition the kinds of interventions into that field of meanings that are possible for her. Nevertheless, as an agent, she is able to shape, however subtly, the ongoing development of those meanings, and thus change the way they condition her agency, shifting the geography of what is possible for her. It is in this way that she both is and is not a given race, or set of races, and that she is responsible for their meaning and significance within the community that intersubjectively constitutes racial reality.

It must be stressed that, for the creolizing subject, race as a concept and racism as a practice cannot be separated. Against the eliminativist argument that the abolition of race will lead to the end of racism, which treats race and racism as analytically distinct yet causally related, my account emphasizes the way in which race and racism are deeply and constitutively interwoven. Likewise, against the abolitionist reduction of race to hierarchical position within a white supremacist political structure, my account rejects the conflation of race and racism. In other words, race and racism are mutually interdependent (dialectically coconstituted), but at the same time one cannot simply be reduced to or used to explain away the other. Thus, in order to fully understand how race functions for the creolizing subject, an account of racism must also be provided, which account I offered in chapter 5. The question that clearly emerges here is that of how to manifest antiracism as a creolizing subject.

If, as I have argued, racism is not a status or property that one achieves or possesses but an ongoing practice of and commitment to the purification of a reified and static account of the human and a corresponding reification of (an impoverished account of) reason, then antiracism, likewise, cannot be something that we simply achieve or possess. It, too, must be understood as an ongoing practice and commitment. Racism is thus not something that we simply overcome or end—there is no "postracist" world toward which we are aiming. Positing some end state or terminus in this way would treat the human world as (or at least aiming toward) a static state of being, and is thus a manifestation of the politics of purity. What characterizes the creolizing subject above all else is an orientation toward change and development. In her extraordinary work *Queer Phenomenology*, Sara Ahmed offers an account of "orientation" that emphasizes not only the sense in which one is directed toward somewhere or something but also that one is directed from somewhere or something. Perhaps most importantly, she stresses the way in which this understanding of orientation situates one within a larger context

openness/ closure

and environment such that one's orientation makes certain kinds of perception possible and others impossible (2006, 65–79). The politics of purity offers a rigid orientation in Ahmed's sense directed toward static and fixed conceptions of human being. As such, it situates the subject in such a way that ambiguity and creolization are either missed altogether (one is oriented away from them), or understood as threatening (making it difficult to maintain one's *straight* course). The creolizing subject, on the other hand, is oriented toward a dynamic understanding of human development (becoming) that is working to reveal and affirm ambiguity as it informs and conditions both where we are coming from and where we are going.[11]

Most importantly, while one may describe an orientation toward *development*, this does not mean that the creolizing subject is aiming toward some end state, understood as a fixed and discrete terminus. Nevertheless, there is a clear normativity in the concept of development I am appealing to here. While I am not advocating some "one size fits all" ideal state toward which all human activity should aim, the creolizing subject does not represent a relativistic free-for-all, either. There is a normative force in the concept of *openness* that functions here in powerful ways. Recall that the politics of purity can be understood as placing an emphasis on *closure.* The demarcation of clear and distinct borders, the demand for necessary and sufficient conditions, and the epistemic norm of certainty, all point toward a finality—the erasure of ambiguity and questioning with the closure of lines of inquiry that fix meaning once and for all. The creolizing subject, however, is oriented toward openness. One seeks not the cessation of change and growth through the realization of some terminal (closed) ideal but rather works toward the fostering of ever-greater opportunities and capacities for dynamism. Since the self is understood as an ongoing activity, the emphasis is placed on expanding the scope and power of that activity. However, since the self is also fundamentally social, increasing one's individual power at the expense of others ultimately undermines and constrains the activity of self-formation and self-articulation that is the hallmark of the creolizing subject. De Beauvoir makes a very similar claim in *The Ethics of Ambiguity*, where she argues that it is only with and through others that our freedom is able to express itself, and so "[t]o will oneself free is also to will others free" (1943, 73). Thus, the creolizing subject is not only directed toward change, openness, and dynamism within oneself but also must be politically directed toward the facilitation of this sense of *development* within others.

expanding/enriching

Creolizing, in the sense I am using it, is an ongoing process and practice undertaken by the subject, and one can be property described as a creolizing subject only to the extent that one maintains that process and practice, which is a kind of unraveling of the politics of purity. What is more, I have linked the political phenomenon of racism to the politics of purity, and criticized those portrayals of antiracism that fail to radically challenge the politics of purity. What this means is that the creolizing subject, insofar as he or she is engaged in the effort to challenge the politics of purity, is thus simultaneously engaged in antiracist praxis. If the creolizing subject were not engaged in antiracist praxis, then he would not be truly creolizing, and the ongoing process of creolization in the subject is in its own right a kind of antiracist praxis.

All of this is well and good in the abstract, one might quite reasonably object at this point, but why must the creolizing subject be, at the end of the day, a *racialized* one? That is, insofar as the creolizing subject is really about emphasizing a dynamic understanding of individual agency as a process of meaning constituting within a community of other meaning-constituting subjects that make meaning possible in the first place, one could manifest a creolizing subjectivity, it would seem, without needing to reference race at all. Furthermore, while I may have made a case for the necessity of *some* specificity and particularity to our agency, such that we all must come from somewhere and have some content to our subjectivity, rather than being universal and interchangeable abstractions, there is no obvious reason to assume that this particularity and specificity needs to be *racial*. In short, one might very well ask why I reject the abolitionist view that race is an essentially pernicious way of constituting human difference and distinction that we would, ultimately, be better off without. Even if race remains necessary as a tool for the redress of historical injustice, once that injustice has been rectified, would there be any reason to "conserve" race at all? My argument so far has made appeal to the way in which race has inescapably conditioned the development and expression of our subjectivity, such that it is effectively impossible for us to understand ourselves or the social world around (and importantly, the way in which these are not entirely distinct terms) without appeal to racial reality. But if our efforts at creolization are successful, won't race have less impact on our subjectivity, such that it will cease to be this inescapable influence? Why couldn't we, in other words, preserve racelessness as an ideal toward which we would do well to strive?

Part of the reason why I take the commitment to antiracism in the creolizing subject to in fact demand a continued recognition of the racial conditions of identity is for the very reason that the racial eliminativist point of view rejects race altogether—the horror of the history of colonialism and white supremacy. For the eliminativists, the historical legacy of racism, paired with the ultimate *un*reality of race, necessitates its elimination. Even if, as I have argued, race has more reality than the eliminativists would admit, I still need to demonstrate why even our ideal of a racially just world would conserve race. It is one thing to claim that racial identity is necessary to overcome present and past racial injustice, but it seems to be something else entirely to hold that even our ideal must be racialized. If we imagine a world in which racial injustice is in every significant sense behind us, what possible good could there be in continuing to think of myself (and others) in racial terms? Quite a lot, I submit.

Central to my discussion of the historical treatment of race and racism has been the claim that the meaning and significance of racial concepts has always been ambiguous and highly contested. While it is certainly true that race did generally develop along lines quite accurately described by the abolitionist historians, it is also true that there have been, throughout the history of race, undercurrents and sites of resistance, such that this history cannot be properly understood as a *purely* white supremacist one (also, interestingly, described in detail by abolitionist historians). What is happening through the practice of antiracism on the part of the creolizing subject is the uncovering and reinterpretation of those historical moments in which white supremacy was actively resisted, and the possibility for a different racial reality was made (however briefly) visible (cf. Alcoff 2006, 221–23). This engagement with the historical meaning and significance of race naturally conditions our grasp of the present and our vision of the future. Our orientation as creolizing subjects, therefore, in always coming from a deeply racialized point of origin, will always be conditioned by that origin, even as we strive to mitigate the pernicious effects of that history. We can only perform the work of mitigating the evils of racial injustice in the present, therefore, by attending not only to its history but also to the role this history plays in constituting our own agency. And this is why a racially just future cannot ever be raceless—my relation to that history, and thus a significant aspect of my subjectivity, will always be raced.

Furthermore, my understanding of race as a kind of practice, rather than a property, and racism as the ongoing project of purifying humanity, means that antiracism, likewise, cannot ever be properly understood as a *fait accompli*. Thus, one of the framing assumptions of this argument for racial eliminativism or colorblindness—that we could occupy a *postracist* world—is, in the strictest sense, absurd. Nothing so deeply formative of our subjectivity for so long can be completely put behind us. Since racism is not a state we occupy or a set of conditions that can obtain or fail to obtain, there can be no end state "beyond" racism that we can one day reach. The ontology of race I have described is such that we cannot go beyond race but must rather work to alter the meaning and significance of race. This means that antiracism, as the practice of shaping the meaning and significance of race in liberatory ways, is only ever an ongoing and infinite task, and one that can only ever be taken up from and within a racialized context and a racially meaningful sense of agency. Thus, our antiracist praxis should not aim at a future beyond race or a place where race is no longer meaningful. Rather, that praxis just *is* the ongoing effort to shape race in liberatory ways. The moment we believe we have gotten beyond it, we are implicitly, if not explicitly, positing an ahistorical and static conception of human existence. In other words, in the name of human liberation, this strategy takes up a project of dehumanization.

This means that for any given individual agent, antiracist praxis must be undertaken *as* a racialized individual. Our antiracism, if it is to be undertaken effectively, must be a manifestation of what I have described elsewhere as "racial authenticity" (Monahan 2005a). Not the kind of authenticity associated with racial essentialism, where one's behavior is meant to comport with one's "true" racial being, but rather an understanding of authenticity more in line with existentialist thought. According to this account, one manifests racial authenticity by being true to *oneself* about racial reality, which means taking seriously *both* its status as part of the given situation from and through which my consciousness emerges, and as itself constituted by my consciousness in concert with the consciousness of others. One might, following Lewis Gordon, employ a Sartrean terminology by calling this "critical good faith" rather than "authenticity," but the point is still the same (Gordon 1995, 56, 167). Genuine free human action must confront head on, to take up that Sartrean language, both my facticity and my transcendence, without capitulating to a bad faith flight from freedom by immersing myself wholly in one or the other. To hold that racial categories or racial *being* determines human existence is clearly erroneous, but my point here is that holding human existence to be above or beyond racial reality entirely is equally erroneous, and both options, insofar as they fail to address human (racial) reality, will subvert our antiracist practices, no matter how well intentioned.

By way of example, and as a stark contrast to the abolitionist and eliminativist positions, this means that white people must engage in antiracist praxis *as white people*. Of course, being a white person here means that one's status as white within a given context is still a marker of material, moral, political, and epistemic advantage, but within a creolizing context, whiteness itself is never pure, and individual agents are never purely white. Again, one is always more and less than one's racial membership. Thus it is not the case that creolizing subjectivity serves as a kind of "get out of jail free card" when it comes to racial oppression. To simply claim that one is not *really* or *fully* white and therefore bears no responsibility for racial oppression is to fail to take seriously the way in which one *is* (though never as a fixed or static state of being) still white—it becomes a *de facto* claim that one is *purely nonwhite*. The creolizing subject places an emphasis on his or her own agency in shaping the meaning and significance of race, such that he or she is also always more than white, and that whiteness itself remains in effect underdetermined both by its history and its present practice. The project of the creolizing subject, then, is not the reduction of all racial identities to a formless amalgam, or the erasure of individual racial groups altogether. Rather, there is an acknowledgment of the particularity and specificity (though never as fixed or discreet) of different racial memberships, paired with an awareness of how the meaning and significance of those races is both indeterminate, and subject to change and reinterpretation over time. To resist racial oppression as a white person, in this sense, means that one enters into the ongoing contestation over the meaning and significance of whiteness *as* a person whose subjectivity is inescapably conditioned by the meanings and significances presently at play in racial reality, and deeply informed in turn by racial history. It is a direct engagement both with the legacy of centuries of (ambiguous and plastic) racial meaning, and with one's own opportunities and responsibilities for shaping that meaning, such shaping being itself conditioned by one's racial location (the continued relevance of one's whiteness). To insist that antiracism entails a rejection of whiteness both elides the way in which one is taking up the antiracist project *from* a place that is always already racialized, and it posits an abstracted, ahistorical vision of humanity (and of race itself).

The degree to which racial ontology and racial *praxis* are intimately linked should be clear at this point. Race is a kind of meaning-constituting activity, but it is also the sedimented result of centuries of such activity, which sedimentation conditions and shapes the possibilities of our ongoing activity, and will continue to do so, I have argued, insofar as we continue to have a dynamic relationship to that sedimented history. At the same time, however, it is also historically dynamic, such that the meaning and significance of that sedimentation is itself subject to revision and reinterpretation. How we understand and give meaning to that history is thus contingent on our meaning-constituting activity in the here and now—our present conceptions of race inform our past understanding, and vice versa. There is thus a kind of deep reciprocity conditioning every level of racial reality and our participation in it. This reciprocity, and the ambiguity and dynamism that it generates and is generated by, are the hallmark of the creolizing subject. I *am* white, as a result, not simply in the sense that I have some basic property or set of properties (being), but in the sense that the situation from and through which I enter into the ongoing contestation of the meaning and significance of whiteness is one that has been and continues to be constituted as white (becoming). But importantly, my whiteness is ambiguous and unstable not only because its history and its present reality are likewise ambiguous and dynamic but also as a result of the way in which I, as a subject, am able to actively engage with and alter whiteness itself. This is by no means limited to whiteness, of course, for the same will hold true for every individual of any given racial status or set of statuses.

This means that the practice of liberation here, as the critical engagement with racial reality directed toward antiracism, involves simultaneously what I have referred to elsewhere as "propositional" and "practical" moments (Monahan 2010). One must, if one is to engage effectively with racial reality, understand the ways and means of that reality. This means that one must come to understand the history of race, the way it functions in one's own life and in the larger social context in the present, and even how it will shape our future. Equally important, one must try to understand how these different chronological moments influence each other, as I described earlier. But this is not solely the acquisition of propositional knowledge. As an agent, one is never simply a passive object bound up in (and by) racial reality but also an active participant in that reality. As a nexus of meaning, racial reality is the product of the meaning-constituting actions of human subjects, including oneself. To truly understand race, therefore, demands that one interact with or engage it actively. As an ongoing process or phenomenon, race is undergoing a constant process of development and changes. As a social phenomenon, particular agents are always a part of that development. This means that if I wish to understand racial reality, I need to understand my own role in constituting that reality, which means I need to actively and self-consciously interact with it rather than pretending that I can observe it as a discrete and distinct phenomenon. Thus there must be both propositional moments where one gathers information, paired with practical moments where one interacts actively (and, importantly, self-critically) with the phenomenon with which one is engaged.

Genuine understanding of social phenomena such as racial reality requires these propositional and practical moments, but at the same time it blurs the distinction between them and makes clear their reciprocity. There is, in other words, a dialectical reciprocity between the propositional and practical moments, such that each informs and expands the scope of the other. The more we come to understand the history of race and the institutional structures that condition our present racial reality, the more informed and efficacious our interactions with other individuals and institutions will become. At the same time, as we engage in practices of antiracism with others, new insights and avenues of inquiry will open up as to the historical and present aspects of racial reality that condition those practices. Each moment informs and is informed by the other, such that a full and genuine commitment to one necessitates a commitment to the other—indeed, the boundary between the two terms must itself be understood as ambiguous.

Genuine antiracism, therefore, demands this open-eyed engagement with the reciprocal relation both between these propositional and practical moments as well as between the real roles that race plays in all of our lives and our own ability as subjects to critique and alter those roles. The politics of purity treats these as discrete and all-or-nothing categories, and thus demands that antiracism be antirace. But I am in effect arguing, pace the eliminativists and new abolitionists, that it is possible, even necessary, to manifest antiracism *as a raced person*, including even as a *white* person. I have argued against the abolitionist position at length already, but it is important now to say something about how I understand this imperative to take up antiracist praxis as a raced person. Given the way in which, I have argued, an ethos of colorblindness informs the abolitionist and eliminativist positions, this will ultimately be true for any and all racial identities, but I will be using whiteness as my example both because it is the focus of the abolitionist discussion, and because it is a particularly vexing case. Is it possible to manifest antiracism *whitely*, and if so, what could that mean?

As the abolitionist literature quite rightly recognizes, whiteness is, given its history, always a kind of discursive position of dominance and power. Aesthetic, cultural, political, moral, and epistemic norms are all organized, to a greater or lesser extent and with greater or lesser levels of explicitness, around whiteness. The way in which this positioning conditions the subjectivity of individual whites and influences their interaction with other individuals and larger social institutions and norms is the central truth that must be grasped with the shift away from liberal atomistic individualism and toward an understanding of agency as socially constituted. Our racial membership, therefore, is not simply some external and contingent property or imposed identification, but is an inescapable constitutive element of who we are as individuals and as members of larger groups and institutions. What is most important to my argument is that the story of this influence is one that we can never fully know in any complete sense, and so part of understanding how to work against racial oppression is this ongoing project of understanding the role that my race plays in my life. This is, in short, what I mean by the *reality* of race.

What I have been stressing throughout this book, however, are two different ways in which this reality should not be understood in the same way that the politics of purity would have us understand what it would mean for race to be real. First, while the dominant account of the meaning and significance of whiteness is one of domination, there have always been countercurrents, ambiguities, and even contradictions in that account. Given the relation between racial meaning and embodiment, we must understand these moments of resistance to white supremacy on the part of those with pale skin not as moments in which these individuals failed to be white, but rather as moments in which their embodied actions offered a different constitution of the meaning of whiteness. There is a fundamental ambiguity, in other words, not only in racial categories themselves, and in the individuals who occupy those categories, but also in the historical and present meaning of those categories and individuals. In this way, my race does inevitably condition my own subjectivity and my relations with others, but not in a clear, distinct, and discrete (pure) way. My race, in other words, inevitably situates me in a way that I must confront if I am to enter into an effective contestation of that situation, but never in a settled or complete way.

Secondly, this ambiguity in the meaning of race provides us with the opportunity to take up the project of contesting that dominant meaning of race. As a subject, I am inescapably conditioned by my race, but never strictly determined by it. I can take up the task of contesting and renegotiating what race means and how it functions, but my activity must always come *from* somewhere, and will itself be conditioned and shaped by current and historical moments of the constitution of race. Thus, to manifest antiracism *whitely*, to return to the question at hand, means at once to be engaged in an ongoing struggle to understand the role that race plays in my life (both in the sense of conditioning my agency and playing a significant role in my interactions with others, which in turn plays its own significant role in conditioning my agency, and thus cannot be reduced to solipsistic navel-gazing), to take seriously my own active role in perpetuating, negotiating, critiquing, and contesting the meaning and significance of race, and to recognize and critically engage the way in which my activity in its turn becomes part of the unfolding intersubjective constitution of the meaning of race (including whiteness).

To the extent that one takes up the project of antiracism in this way, one cannot be described as abandoning or abolishing race. This is because the ongoing project of understanding past and present meanings, and articulating and negotiating future meanings is both inevitably historical and inevitably directed toward the future. As I argue in chapter 4, our understanding of the history of race conditions and informs our sense of where race is going culturally, and our sense of where we are heading in turn conditions our understanding of the past. As a perfect example, if we accept that the future of humanity ultimately ought to be one in which race no longer exists, then our understanding of what was going on in the nineteenth-century United States, or the seventeenth-century Caribbean, will be such that people were or were not white, or were becoming white, and in which race was being created alchemically as the illusory tool of those bent on domination and exploitation. If instead we place the ambiguity of racial meaning at the center of our understanding of racial reality, this process of understanding and articulating the meaning of race can never be completed, and thus race will always situate us in relation to this ongoing process and its history, such that *my* race, for any given individual, will always inform, to a greater or lesser extent, who I am in meaningful ways. And just as I have argued against the acceptance of the white supremacist meaning of whiteness as the exclusive arbiter of the meaning of whiteness, it is also the case that any revisionist account of whiteness can never be the sole and exclusive meaning of whiteness. White supremacy will always condition the meaning of whiteness, even in an ideal future, as a historical reality of extraordinary potency, and as a future possibility that is always looming on our horizon and against which we must be ever vigilant (again, this is why the "postracial" is untenable). Taking up antiracist practices *whitely*, therefore, stands as a way to ensure that vigilance by stressing in the same action both that one's whiteness is real, but in taking up the antiracist project, the *meaning* of that whiteness is being made a point of open contention.

CREOLIZING REASON—PHILOSOPHY AS A SUBJECT

I have already discussed the sense in which the politics of purity is in part an epistemic project presenting a norm of closure and completeness in our understanding of knowledge that cannot tolerate ambiguity and indeterminacy. In the context of race, this means that races must be understood as discrete categories offering necessary and sufficient conditions that one can *know* as a complete and closed set of properties or conditions. Should this knowledge prove untenable, one can then *know* in the same complete and closed way that race is illusory. All of this in turn is linked to a conception of reason as instrumental, such that rationality has to do with the mastery and organization of discrete units of knowledge that can then be exchanged in a free market of ideas. Instead we must understand knowledge as an ongoing process of questioning and critique, such that our knowing is never a finished, complete, and closed state. Likewise, our understanding of reason must be posited as a manifestation of openness to and active pursuit of revision and critique, such that rationality is understood not as a state to be achieved, but as the ongoing activity of rational questioning not only of the world around us, but of reason itself. This is, I have argued, at the heart of the phenomenological method, and is the motivating ethos of the creolizing subject as a contestation of the conceptions of humanity and reason offered by the politics of purity.

In this section, I want to stress the way in which the creolizing subject is not a rejection of the link between humanity and reason so much as it is a critique of the notion of reason bound up in the politics of purity. What the creolizing subject calls for is in part a creolization of reason itself. Thus the creolizing subject is not meant to refer strictly to subjectivity in the sense of human consciousness, but extends to the notion of subject as in *subject of study*. In other words, the proper response to the politics of purity is not only the creolization of our own subjectivity as agents but also the creolization of the *subjects* of biology, anthropology, psychology, and philosophy, to offer a far-from-exhaustive sample. By opening these subjects of study up to the radical questioning of their own assumptions and methodology, we are in effect ambiguating their content and their boundaries in ways that are ultimately not only liberatory, but significantly more *rational*. Such creolizing is in effect an effort to return the *human* to the human sciences (and to call into question the very distinction between the human sciences and the natural sciences).

In *Disciplinary Decadence*, Lewis Gordon has described a kind of methodological narcissism, whereby particular disciplines become so infatuated with their own evaluative criteria and foundational assumptions that they come to judge all intellectual efforts according to the norms of their own disciplines. Gordon describes the broader phenomenon as follows:

> *Disciplinary decadence* is the ontologizing or reification of a discipline. In such an attitude, we treat our discipline as though it was never born and has always existed and will never change or, in some cases, die . . . Such a perspective brings with it a special fallacy. Its assertion as absolute eventually leads to no room for other disciplinary perspectives, the result of which is the rejection of them for not being one's own. Thus, if one's discipline has foreclosed the question of its scope, all that is left for it is a form of "applied" work. Such work militates against thinking. (2006b, 4–5)

Philosophy is surely guilty, to a significant extent, of this manifestation of "decadence." This guilt is all the more puzzling, since philosophy purports to in essence transcend disciplinarity insofar as it is concerned with reasoning *as such*. Philosophy is thus a particularly effective example of the relation of the politics of purity to reason, and is therefore a good vehicle to explore as a creolizing subject.

The history and present practice of philosophy is, by and large, an extended exercise in the politics of purity in this regard. The establishment

[handwritten note: Eg - Exercise in politics of purity]

and maintenance of boundaries demarcating what is or is not proper philosophy, and who may or may not be a philosopher, is a practice familiar to anyone who has studied the history of philosophy's relationship to race and gender. Those who have struggled to challenge those boundaries (often simply by their presence in the discourse and discipline) have been intimately familiar with ways and means of policing those borders. The struggle for the delineation of "proper philosophy" is still very much alive in the discipline globally, most often in the form of the division between *analytic* and *continental* philosophical traditions. There has been an effort to describe and maintain the purity of the discipline, both in terms of what the proper or true methodology and content of philosophy might be, and in terms of whose very *presence* in the discipline stands as a form of corruption of that method and content.

The long-standing debates over the existence of distinctively African or Latin American philosophy illustrate this process. If one understands philosophy as the purified exercise of a purified conception of reason, then the idea of African or Latin American philosophy stands as a double threat. First, it would threaten the ongoing maintenance of the conception of Europe and the European as the locus of the most rarified reason (and the purest instantiation of the human). Since philosophy is the purest practice of reason, to admit that what is taking place in Africa is *philosophy* would be to admit that Africans are capable of the highest (and purest) forms of reasoning. Second, philosophy, as purified reason in itself, cannot have any specific location, culture, or tradition—it is reason *simpliciter*. Thus, if there is something peculiarly *Latin American* about some philosophical practices, then the conceptual purity of philosophy itself is threatened. It is, therefore, both the *Africanness* (or *Latinicity*) of the philosophy and the *philosophicality* of the African (or Latin American) practices that threaten the purity of the discipline. At the same time, the practice of philosophy in the Universities of Africa and Latin America has largely identified with the traditions of Europe and North America, such that the vision of genuine or pure philosophy as European is maintained even in the non-European world. Just as racial categories must identify that which corrupts its purity and eliminate it, so too must philosophy identify and eliminate that which corrupts its purity (or at least relegate it to less pure subfields—feminist philosophy or African philosophy as opposed to philosophy proper).

Even setting aside questions of race, gender, and ethnophilosophy, the politics of purity can be observed in the ongoing struggle between so-called analytic and continental philosophical traditions. This struggle, I think both sides readily admit, is being decisively won, at least in terms of numerical dominance in academic philosophy departments, by the analytic school. The problem, I submit, is not in the methodologies of analytic or continental philosophy *as such* but rather in their mutual exclusivity, manifesting frequently in a shared hostility that is utterly indifferent to understanding, truth, or ultimately reason.[12] There is a common tendency shared by representatives on both sides of this divide to be blithely dismissive of the very possibility that the other side could have any worthwhile contribution to make to the pursuit of understanding. What is interesting about this mutual indifference or hostility is that in refusing to really attend to what is going on across their respective borders, the opposing parties are effectively betraying that which they each purport to best represent—the love of wisdom. As Gordon points out, the elimination of opposition, either by marginalizing them as normative voices within the discipline, or by simply refusing to attend to them, means that one's voice, perspective, and methodology is never called into question (2006b, 8). This evasion of questioning, the establishment of an unassailable and *closed* methodology posits a clear, if implicit, impoverished understanding of reason as *closure* and *completion* rather than what I have argued is a more genuine understanding of reason as *openness* and ongoing process (of questioning). The purification of philosophy is thus not the safeguarding of reason but rather the failure of reason, and so we must, if we are to genuinely affirm the avowed aim of philosophical practice, issue a call for its creolization.

At its most basic level, philosophy as a creolizing subject would raise consistently, rigorously, and continuously the question of its own methodology and criteria for success. This would mean questioning its pretensions to a closed and purified sense of itself as pathologically *universal* and *abstract*.[13] Philosophy is, like any subject, always oriented in a way that is from somewhere and toward somewhere else, and is thus also always (though never *purely*) particular, and not simply (though still somewhat) universal. The problem therefore, is not whether there is an African or a Latin American philosophy, but that for too long we have failed to recognize and submit to rational scrutiny the Europeanness (and whiteness) of what we have hitherto called simply *philosophy*. At the same time, while all theorizing involves abstraction, such abstraction must always be connected to and in relation with concrete questions and problems. Thus, while philosophy may purport to deal exclusively with the abstract, understood as the truest form of the universal, insofar as it leaves behind all particularity and concrete connection with the lived world it has abandoned reason as an *engaged* inquiry. Philosophy as a creolizing subject therefore must have these moments of engagement and particularity integrated into its guiding ethos, not as ancillary moments of "application,"[14] but as constitutive elements of the infinite task of reasoning about and in the world.

In this way, clearly, philosophy must avoid the vision of itself as pure and transdisciplinary. Philosophy as a creolizing subject must attend to and engage with inquiry in other disciplines, not simply as grist for our own theorizing mills, but as coparticipants in a shared project of understanding. Furthermore, this crossing of disciplinary boundaries cannot be a simple matter of "philosophy and *X*" (philosophy and history, or philosophy and anthropology), where two discrete methodologies are simply applied to the same problem ("combine and stir"). Rather, to be genuinely creolizing, the shared inquiry must come to mutually inform the disciplinary practices themselves—each participant must be open to the revision of his or her disciplinary proclivities. There must be a genuine *mixture* (Lugones's "curdling") at the most basic level, such that the resulting practice is ultimately more than the sum of its constitutive parts.

Another aspect of the creolization of philosophy must be the pursuit and study of voices that have been marginalized, excluded, or otherwise silenced. This process is, to a greater or lesser extent, already underway with the philosophies of Africa, the Middle East, Asia, (indigenous) North America, Latin America (indigenous and *mestizo*), and women around the globe. Nevertheless, this project remains very much incomplete, both in the sense that there is still much more material to be unearthed and in the sense that the discipline as a whole tends to treat these as less valuable (because less pure) subdisciplines—as "poor relations" of *real* philosophy. Philosophy as a discipline remains white in the sense that it incorporates white assumptions, perspectives, and traditions even while it claims to be universal and beyond such particularities as race. The creolization of philosophy demands an engagement with thinkers and traditions that have traditionally been excluded from the purified notion of philosophy, and an engagement *through* these thinkers and traditions with the perennial questions and problems of philosophy. This does not mean an abandonment of European and North American traditions and thinkers, but does insist that they not be permitted to establish themselves as the exclusive arbiters of a purified (and reified) notion of genuine philosophy. These traditions must be brought together in a cooperative venture. Again, it cannot be a simple matter of conjoining two different thinkers on a particular topic, but must allow each to illuminate and influence the other, such that the unifying focus is the line of inquiry, and not the tradition or methodology itself.[15] This is the way to genuinely commit oneself to reason—by prioritizing the openness to and pursuit of truth rather than the defense of purified disciplinary boundaries.

RACIAL JUSTICE AND THE CREOLIZING SUBJECT

Within the confines of the politics of purity, the term *racial justice* is rendered effectively oxymoronic. Race, insofar as it is understood strictly as a kind of coercive imposition upon individual agents from the outside (an impurity), is antithetical to justice. Justice, likewise, since it is construed in a way that treats morally *arbitrary* particularities like race as beyond its universal and disinterested purview, is relevant to matters of race only insofar as it proscribes the use of race in our moral and political deliberations. While it may be possible for justice within the politics of purity to prescribe a kind of ameliorative appeal to race in our moral and political deliberations, such appeal is justified only to the extent that it is conducive toward an ultimately raceless, or at least race neutral, end. Either way, in a truly just world, common wisdom would have it, race would be utterly irrelevant to justice as such.

Thus, aside from offering a critique of the politics of purity and an alternative theoretical framework in my account of the creolizing subject, I am also gesturing toward a way of thinking about that perennial philosophical concern—justice. We must move beyond the characteristic features of the politics of purity: the reification of difference and similarity; the reduction of human agents to discrete atoms with clear and distinct boundaries between the internal and the external; and the insistence on fixed and given categories, rules, and prescriptions to be applied mechanistically with an eye toward the realization of justice as a kind of fixed *state* to be achieved. In short, our typical thinking about justice, too, has been molded, to our detriment, by the politics of purity, and this is especially clear when we look at the dismal failure that traditional theorizations of justice have been in relation to issues of race and gender.

Justice, too, must therefore assume the position of the creolizing subject. Both in the sense that our thinking about justice, like philosophy, must manifest a creolizing ethos and methodology, and in the sense that those of us who take ourselves to be committed to working for justice must recognize that we are, in being so committed, called to bring about our own creolizing subjectivity. Justice must embrace the ambiguity and complexity of human difference rather than struggle to veil, bracket or otherwise ignore it. In other words, justice must not treat ambiguity and complexity always as problems that must be overcome.

Yet, in abandoning the politics of purity with its appeal to fixed states, abstracted and idealized agents, and rigid application of rules and procedures, we are not left with a toothless relativism. As I have tried to stress, the creolizing subject does not abandon all normativity, but must realize that the very conditions for the possibility (to appeal to a Kantian form of argument) of reason, truth, and justice, as kinds of human activity (and not end-states), are the ongoing openness to the myriad kinds of human becoming that are themselves conducive to further such openness.[16] The strength of creolization in relation to conceptions of justice is that it emphasizes a notion of humanity as a kind of activity directed toward becoming, but that activity can only take place when the conditions—material, political, social, psychological—are conducive to that activity. The problem with racism or other forms of oppression, therefore, is not simply that it violates our discrete individual autonomy, or our ideal social contract, or our commitment to individual liberty, but rather that it stands as a closure and denial of this ongoing process of becoming, and in so doing diminishes us all. Just as an ecosystem requires a diversity of species in order to maintain its health in the face of adversity, humanity, as an ongoing project, demands diversity in its particulars in order to be healthy as a universal. *Racial justice*, then, is about fostering the conditions wherein always already racialized selves can truly make manifest their humanity. Of course, the shared humanity here is not some abstract, featureless, universal property shared by all, but is rather this shared participation in the ongoing activity of articulating and contesting who *we* are. Furthermore, insofar as this activity is always coming from and directed toward somewhere particular, one important aspect of our shared humanity just is our shared *particularity*, and not our abstract universality. In this way, racial justice for the creolizing subject points toward a more fully realized conception of the universally human than will ever be possible for the more traditional conceptions of justice appealing to empty and formal accounts of the human.

Notes

1. I have changed the family name to better protect the identity of my land-lord. The Walkers were indeed plantation owners in colonial Barbados, but their property was on the west coast, while I was living near the south coast. It is worth noting that many of the town names in Barbados come directly from the names of the families that owned the plantations upon which the towns now stand.

2. Andrew Walker, "Richest 2% own 'half the wealth.'" BBC News. December 5, 2006. http://tinyurl.com/walker2006.

3. Of course, this isn't entirely unheard of. Every once in a while Bill Cosby will give a speech about black immorality and indolence, or a white comedian will direct a racist tirade at his audience members, or a "race riot" will occur, and suddenly the news media will ask us questions about race in America. Then something else will grab their attention, and they will go back to ignoring matters of race, until they are "shocked" into taking it up again, as if it had come out of nowhere.

4. My use of the term *white supremacy* here is in the spirit of Charles Mills's use of the term both in *Blackness Visible* (1998) and in *The Racial Contract* (1997).

5. Indeed, the recent law prohibiting the teaching of ethnic studies in Arizona seems predicated upon precisely this view. See *Los Angeles Times*, May 12, 2010. http://tinyurl.com/nsantacruz2010.

6. I am much indebted to feminist philosophy for making this point, and especially to bell hooks and Patricia Williams.

7. This phenomenon is clearly related to the expectation that female philosophers will "do feminism," and that nonwhite philosophers will be interested in race theory.

8. I am purposefully using the masculine pronoun here, since women logicians are probably as rare, if not more rare, than white race theorists (see Haslanger 2008). Indeed, I would not be surprised if women studying the "hard" varieties of philosophy such as logic, philosophy of science, and epistemology were asked very similar questions.

9. This discussion is inspired and informed by Lewis Gordon's account of this same phenomenon in his *Disciplinary Decadence* (2006).

10. Of course, if one takes seriously the basic insight of this Husserlian method, then one cannot simply take for granted that the phenomenological method is the best or only way to proceed. I will defend the view that phenomenology is a particularly fruitful way to take up the central questions of this text, but I do not want to suggest or argue that it is the only, or even the best, way to proceed.

I. CONTINGENCY, HISTORY, AND ONTOLOGY: ON ABOLISHING WHITENESS

1. This is at least true of Roediger's earlier works. In *Colored White: Transcending the Racial Past* (2002), Roediger reinterprets his project as an effort to "create the conditions for a non-white society," though he does not reject the characterization of this as abolition outright. By the time of *Working Toward Whiteness: How America's Immigrants Became White* (2005), Roediger seems to be, despite the subtitle of the book, calling into question the presumption that racism, and thus a central component of racial whiteness, was learned after arrival in the United States, and he makes no clear references to his earlier "abolitionist" project.

2. My own use of the term *nonwhite* is not intended to support this particular view, as I have tried to make clear in my introductory remarks.

3. Though he does not ultimately endorse the ontology of the abolitionists, Charles Mills echoes their understanding of whiteness in part when he claims that one need not have light skin to be white, it is simply a matter of political or social positioning within a given context. Thus, the Japanese could be "honorary whites" within the racial hierarchy they had imposed on East Asia in the first half of the twentieth century and during their participation in the Axis alliance, though they certainly were not white from the perspective of U.S. advocates of Japanese-American internment during the World War II (Mills 1997, 80).

4. Indeed, aspects of this story have ultimately come to s
for the Horatio Alger mythos of American meritocracy. These g
with nothing, and were objects of "racism", and yet they now p
implication goes, why haven't blacks, who have been here longer,
succeed in the same way as the Irish (or Italians, or Hungarians)?

5. I once heard it argued, by a prominent philosopher of race, that claims
that the Irish were oppressed in the United States must be false, or at least
greatly exaggerated, because the "Irish" Andrew Jackson had been elected president. While this is a dubious argument on its face, relying as it does on a broad
inductive conclusion from a single exceptional case (I hardly think Colin
Powell's high position of office, or even the election of Barack Obama as
President, thus demonstrates the nonexistence of antiblack racism in the United
States), it is rendered even more suspect when one understands that Jackson's
family were in fact Scotch-Irish descendents of Presbyterians "settled" in Ireland
by the British Crown in an effort to facilitate the control and pacification of the
notoriously "unruly" Irish Catholic populace. They had thus enjoyed full
political and economic liberty in Ireland, and were not subject to the same racial
stigma as "native" Irish Catholics either in Ireland or upon later immigration to
North America.

6. Including especially volunteer fire companies, which were themselves
often aligned with street gangs (including one in Philadelphia quite interestingly
named the "Dock Street Philosophers"), and were important actors in the
drama of civil strife that figures so prominently in Ignatiev's account (Ignatiev
1995, 144).

7. The use of the terms *Native* and *nativism* by groups (themselves descended
from immigrants) and individuals who questioned the fitness of these immigrant
groups for citizenship is, given the continued though all-too-often disavowed
presence of Amerindian peoples, particularly and tragically ironic, not to mention disturbingly familiar to those who follow present political discussions of
the threat posed by immigration (especially of the "illegal" kind) to the United
States.

8. See Falguni Sheth's recent book *Toward a Political Philosophy of Race*
(2009) for an extended and illuminating discussion of the role juridical processes
played (and continue to play) in the shaping of racial reality in the United States.

9. Appiah's distinction between racialism and racism can be instructive here
(Appiah 1992, 13–15).

10. I do not mean to imply that twentieth-century scientists working on race
were properly employing Darwinian genetic science, nor do I wish to suggest
that eugenics is properly Darwinian. I mean only to capture this broad shift in

our understanding of heredity that took place from the middle of the eighteenth to the middle of the twentieth centuries.

11. This can be seen in current lamentations over illegal immigration. The problem is often couched in cultural terms, where the culture is implicitly or even explicitly identified as Hispanic, and understood as a clear threat to the "health" of the American polity. There is, in other words, a racial construal of culture at work in many of the debates about immigration in North America. Anecdotally, I can also say that I have yet to teach a course on race and racism in the last decade in which *culture* has not been offered as the "real meaning" of race by my students.

12. For an illuminating conceptual analysis of race and ethnicity, see Jorge Gracia's *Surviving Race, Ethnicity, and Nationality* (2005).

13. For further elaboration of this point and its implications, see Monahan (2010).

14. Let me stress that I take my appeal to correspondence theory to be incidental to the rough definition I am offering here. Presumably, other theories of truth could apply to propositions about social constructions, and probably could better capture the epistemic practices in question than correspondence theory. But since I ultimately think that the fact of race's "social construction" is not what is most important here, what theory of truth works best is irrelevant.

15. Of course, one could argue, and it has indeed been argued in the past, that a thorough and rigorous program of miscegenation would make race obsolete, since the end result would be one global race. But this would not eliminate the reality of race as an essential category; it would simply eliminate all of the existing representatives of those categories. I understand both the eliminativists and the new abolitionists to be calling for this latter sense of elimination, and they certainly do not advocate the former.

16. A more detailed discussion of the status of premodern *race* will be advanced in chapter 2.

2. TURBULENT AND DANGEROUS SPIRITS:
IRISH SERVITUDE IN BARBADOS

1. With the exception, perhaps, of the so-called Redlegs, who are a relatively discrete, impoverished community of whites living primarily in the Parishes of St. John and St. Andrew to this day. For more details on the Redlegs see Sheppard (1977).

2. In the course of conducting my own research in Barbados, I learned of the work of Jenny Shaw, whose dissertation in Atlantic Studies at NYU breaks important new ground on this historical period in the British West Indies.

3. The Irish soldiery in these countries often ended up making their presence known in the Americas. Witness the presence of an O'Donnell Street in old San Juan, named after a famous colonial general, and the perhaps even more famous Mexican general Obregon, which was an Hispanicized version of O'Brien.

4. The exact meaning and significance of this difference is, of course, the ultimate subject of this book.

5. Again, the use of the term *white* here is problematic, and will be discussed in more detail later in this chapter.

6. This tendency on the part of much contemporary discourse on race to oversimplify the relations between the similar and the different, reducing them to the identical and the radically distinct, is a central aspect of the politics of purity that I will be discussing in greater detail subsequent chapters.

7. One can see this as analogous in a way to the status of the Irish in the United States as free white persons for purposes of immigration, but nonwhite, or less than fully white, or "inbetween" for purposes of employment and housing.

3. RACE AND BIOLOGY: SCIENTIFIC REASON
AND THE POLITICS OF PURITY

1. See, for example, Zack (1993), Gracia (2005), Taylor (2004), and Harris (1999).

2. Art Massara offers an excellent discussion of race as a "stain" upon an otherwise "pure" subjectivity in his "Stain Removal: On Race and Ethics" (2007).

3. This is made explicit in the title of the documentary "Biracial, Not Black Damn It" by Carolyn Battle Cochrane (2010). http://tinyurl.com/cochrane2010.

4. On the most mundane level, this can range from the popular elision of the blackness of figures like Alexandre Dumas to the continued use of Native American "noble savages" as sports mascots. Of course, there are far more overt and even violent manifestations of this phenomenon as well.

5. I do not mean to imply that Aristotle's account fits neatly into this characterization of the politics of purity. My reference to Aristotle here is meant only to acknowledge his appeal to the notion of internal and external sources of action. His view of freedom is, of course, quite complex.

6. I have struggled throughout the writing of this book with the way in which I should address the applicability of my thinking here to gender and sexuality. I do not mean to give the impression that I do not think them important, or even that they are somehow secondary to questions of race, but at the same time, to discuss them with the thoroughness and sophistication that they deserve

would require another book (if not more). I have decided to attempt, as best as I can, to make clear both the importance that I attribute to questions of gender and sexuality, and the way in which I believe that some of the work I am doing here would be applicable to our critical theorizing of these categories. My focus on race in this book is in this way contingent, and not a statement that I take it to be the primary or most fundamental or important manifestation of oppression and the focus of our theorization of liberation. It is my sincere hope that the ways in which the politics of purity inform both gender and sexuality can be explored in the detail they deserve in subsequent work.

7. I assume this is what Zack means by "members of the public," since scientists are clearly also members of the public who would not, one hopes, assume an essentialist typology.

8. It is rather difficult to tell just how far this argument might take us. If no trait exists that is identical across all individuals of *homo sapiens*, this would seem to threaten the reality not just of race as a subspecies but also of speciation itself. What is more, since we are all different from each other, our dis-identity can be placed on a continuum with other species. In short, this argument would seem to threaten not just races, but the very category of the human itself.

9. The appeal to the distinction between sex as biological and gender as cultural within the feminist tradition is another excellent example of this presumed distinction between the biological and the cultural.

10. Again, these peculiarities will not appear universally within that population, nor will they necessarily be strictly limited to the population, there will just be a statistically significant preponderance of that trait within that population.

11. The point here is that individuals do not choose that they are members of a particular racial group, though they clearly may choose whether they affirm or celebrate that membership.

12. I would certainly not go so far as to say that phenomenology is uniquely well suited to this philosophical task. Other philosophical approaches (American Pragmatism springs to mind) and traditions can, I have no doubt, shed welcome light on these questions.

4. "BECOMING" WHITE: RACE, REALITY, AND AGENCY

1. Again, I allow that there are other ways to make these sorts of general points (as I mentioned in relation to feminist epistemology and philosophy of science). I mean here that phenomenology is particularly well suited to this task, not that it is exclusively well suited.

2. This point echoes, and is deeply indebted to, a similar argument made within feminist epistemology (cf. Longino 1987; Fricker 2000).

3. This example comes from a good friend who spent a summer doing ecology work in the area. It is a particularly fruitful example in that it is both incredibly common within a large variety of folk communities around the world, yet despite this fact utterly foreign to most philosophical explorations of practical epistemology.

4. Similar analogies can be made to athletic and other forms of artistic endeavor. One may know how to be a goalie, for example, but there is also always room for improvement on that knowledge. Elsewhere, I have explored this question in the context of the practice of martial arts (Monahan 2007).

5. For example: Butler 1990, 22–46; Butler 2004, 17–39; Alcoff 2006, 71–83; and Gordon 2008, 145–51.

6. The masculinist imagery here is quite intentional, since I take much of the feminist critique of science to be consistent with the phenomenological critique of naturalistic science.

7. Natanson is particularly illuminating on this point: "Philosophy gives coherence to experience; phenomenology elucidates the idea of philosophy; transcendental phenomenology traces out the constitution of the world; the becoming of the world is the theme of history; history is rooted in the life-world. Brought together, these strands establish the focus of Husserl's concern with history as an intentional product" (1973, 175).

8. The use of *privilege* here is meant only to indicate the ways in which whites are beneficiaries of racist oppression. The scope and meaning of white privilege is a rather complicated question that I will not be exploring at this time.

9. Importantly, it is never *won* either, which is why even the *ideal* of racelessness must ultimately be abandoned, as I argue in chapter 5.

5. THE POLITICS OF PURITY: COLONIALISM, REASON, AND MODERNITY

1. Interestingly, there is some textual evidence to support the notion that Husserl would have no objection to this initial oversimplification: "it belongs to the essence of reason that the philosophers at first understand and labor at their task in an absolutely necessary one sided way" (1970, 291). Of course, it further belongs to the essence of reason to recognize the limitations of this one-sidedness, and engage in critical (phenomenological) reflection.

2. There is also a difference in the political and discursive power that they wield, but again, I am focusing for now exclusively, if artificially, on their individual status.

3. The recent recreation of the famous *Brown vs. Board of Education* "doll experiments" commissioned by CNN are an excellent example of this. See http://tinyurl.com/cnn0310.

4. This latter point is particularly ironic, given the extent to which in many parts of the globe, and especially in Africa, the matriarchal family structure is quite traditional indeed.

5. For stimulating critical engagements with this aspect of Appiah's argument, see Goodin (2002) and Gracia (2005, 68–71).

6. To be sure, none of this means that all and only nonwhites have been harmed, or that all and only whites have benefited, and seeing this as in some way undermining this understanding of racism demonstrates a clear commitment to the politics of purity. Just as racial membership cannot be understood as an all-or-nothing set of fixed and distinct categories, neither can the ways and means of racism be neatly and discretely allocated. Just as population-based biology deals with generalities and probabilities within ambiguously defined populations, any assessment of the benefits and costs of global white supremacy must be understood to describe probabilities and generalities across ambiguously defined populations. Generality and ambiguity are only understood as threats to intelligibility within the politics of purity.

7. I cannot do justice to the diversity and complexity of the broad categories of rationalism and empiricism in this chapter, and so I must freely admit that the all-too brief characterization that follows must be taken with a healthy grain of proverbial salt. That being said, insofar as I am not attempting to mount a philosophical critique of either early-modern rationalists or empiricists, but rather merely sketching some of the larger conceptual developments in European thought at that time, I trust that what follows is adequate to my relatively modest purpose, galling as it may be to a historian of that philosophical era.

8. I am grateful to the Caribbean Philosophical Association for the exploration of the concept of the geography of reason and its theme of "shifting" that geography. See Lewis Gordon's discussion of this notion in his essay "African-American Philosophy, Race, and the Geography of Reason" (2006a, 39–47).

9. This is a point that Locke, especially, made clear (1960, 299).

10. I am not ruling out the possibility that there could be times and places where Lithuanian does have the sort of socially generated force and meaning that I am describing here. Indeed, in a café in Berlin in 1909, my anti-Lithuanian sentiments could be interpreted as a particular (if peculiarly specific) manifestation of anti-Slavic or even anti-Semitic sentiment. However, that certainly isn't the case here and now, and that it can be the case at other times and places serves as a further example of the importance of social context in the generation of "individual" meaning.

11. Another example of this is the way in which words can have different meanings depending upon the race of the interlocutors. Growing up in rural southern Indiana, it was quite common to use the word "boy" when we address

our peers. "Boy, you better get your homework done." "Did you see Kevin driving in the demolition derby? That boy is crazy." In the segregated world in which I grew up, this was simply a normal way of interacting with my white peers. But when my family moved to Southern California when I was 11, suddenly my use of the term took on entirely new and unintended meanings when I continued to employ it in a much more racially diverse setting. The *meaning* of the term changed not because I intended it or employed it differently, but because the race of the interlocutors changed. For a white person to refer to a non-white person as "boy" carries a whole set of connotations that are largely absent when both the one addressing and the one addressed are white. Of course, it may very well be the case that the history of the term in Southern Indiana is inextricably linked to its racist uses. That is, since the one using the term "boy" was often chiding or chastising the one addressed, there was a kind of superiority implied, which may very well have to do with the way it was (and is) used against blacks. Nevertheless, the meaning and significance of the term is malleable depending upon the race of the one using the term, and the one to whom the term is applied, independent of one's explicit intentions.

12. Or rather, one has no *racial* impediments to these virtues. Other "pollutants," such as gender or sexuality, may be relevant in a given time and place. That is, being white may be necessary, but not sufficient, for being rational, independent, and so on.

13. This is, to be sure, not *always* the case. When no black people are present, some other group often comes to be the paradigmatic representation of the subhuman, and there have been moments when blacks have stood a rung or two above the very bottom of the racial hierarchy. In Hegel's anthropology, for example, it was the Amerindian who stood at the farthest point from full humanity (1971, 45). That being said, the general norm is one in which blackness stands at the opposite end of the value spectrum from whiteness.

14. This notion goes back at least to Jose Vasconcelos (1948), but a more recent account of this view can be found in Sundstrom (2008, 93–107).

15. I *do not* consider Gordon's critique to be an example of this. While Sundstrom goes so far as to characterize Gordon's argument as "cruel" (2008, 110), I believe this is a misreading of Gordon's essay, and that ultimately their positions are closer than they might at first appear.

16. So, too, are a great many whites.

17. It is worth noting that Gordon's critique of mixed-race identity is *political* in precisely this way, and not moral or existential (1997, 66).

18. I take Sundstrom's use of "phenomenology" here to be more in keeping with the way in which the term has commonly come to be used within analytic philosophy, where it means something like "subjective experience," and not the

more robust Husserlian sense that I have been employing in this text. Though, to be sure, his ultimate point about the interplay between genealogy and social forces is quite in keeping with the Husserlian understanding of phenomenology.

19. My use of the term *fanaticism* is deliberate here. I do not mean to imply that all religious belief functions like this.

20. In the second appendix to his *Notebooks for an Ethics*, Sartre gives a more nuanced account of racial slavery in the United States, though one that remains problematic nonetheless (1992, 561–74).

21. It is worth noting that Hegel made a very similar claim in the *Philosophy of Right*, and for very similar reasons (1991, 86–88).

22. Though certainly none of this is to deny that such dehumanizing practices cause incalculable harm both to those that suffer them in the immediate present and for generations to come. Being subjected to dehumanizing projects is undeniably a terrible harm and injustice. From the horrors of chattel slavery, to Jim Crow segregation, to the ongoing marginalization and exploitation of indigenous peoples throughout the New World, the psychological, physical, and spiritual damage is tremendous and passed on for generations. My point is that the project of dehumanization is both fundamentally ironic, and ultimately impossible to fulfill, which in no way entails the further claim that it is not a grievous harm and injustice.

23. My thanks to Trevor Smith for this felicitous expression of an impoverished understanding of antiracism.

6. CREOLIZING SUBJECTS: ANTIRACISM AND THE FUTURE OF PHILOSOPHY

1. My use of "nation or race" is not meant to imply that these terms are interchangeable. They are both collective entities that one can readily observe engaging in the sorts of practices I am describing as the practice of purification, and, I would argue, they are conceptually related, but the exact nature of their similarity and difference is not within the purview of this book. For an engaging and helpful discussion of this relationship, see Gracia (2005) and Marx (1998).

2. Each of these individual subgroups is of course both part and not part of the larger group. That is, if we take whiteness as an example, white women may seek to dominate poor men and women, poor men may seek to dominate women generally, and so on. Insofar as they are in a position to dominate some other internal group, they make a case for their purity, but insofar as they are in a position to be dominated, their purity is always suspect.

3. Indeed, as Jane Anna Gordon has pointed out, the discourse of creolization was an important component of independence movements in the Caribbean, and

"suggested that there was no singular primordial nation to which the emergent state could refer, no original purity that would be endangered by public recognition of the pluralistic culture that had already grown up there" (2009, 22).

4. For further elaboration of atomistic social ontology see Young (1990, 17–38) and Monahan (2003; 2005b).

5. The discussion of Lugones that follows emerged out of and is indebted to extended discussions with Desiree Valentine as she worked on a summer research project involving the work of Lugones and Judith Butler.

6. Again, there is also a way of meaningfully *being* creole that is consistent with my sense of the creolizing subject.

7. This also informs most discussions of intersectionality—the way in which race, gender, class, sexuality, ability, and so on intersect in a given individual's life or in ongoing liberatory practices. The language of intersection still treats the various categories as discrete lines that remain themselves distinct and fundamentally unaltered by the encounter, though they may intersect at a given point (which interestingly, in a Euclidean framework, would literally have no content, being a mathematical *point*). Creolization can thus be understood in part as an alternative to the discourse of intersectionality.

8. I realize there is a certain irony in the use of Hegel's terminology of "pure" recognition here. However, in a forthcoming work, I will argue that in fact what Hegel calls "pure recognition" can be understood as a manifestation of creolizing subjectivity.

9. There is a clear affinity between my discussion here of race as something one *does* and Judith Butler's account of gender that I wish to acknowledge (Butler 2004, especially 1–16). However, it should also be clear that the genealogy of our approaches is quite different. A more thorough critical investigation of the similarities and differences of our approaches to this question of ontology, identity, and the "doing" of race or gender would be most welcome, and I hope to be able to take it up in the future. However, I have omitted such a discussion at this point for the sake of brevity and focus. A beginning of this exploration, in the form of an examination of the relation between Butler's account of gender and phenomenology, can be found in the work of David Fryer (2003; 2006).

10. In addition to Sundstrom (2008) and Gordon (1997), see also Zack (1993) and Velazco y Trianosky (2003).

11. The creolizing subject can very well be understood as *queer* in Ahmed's sense of the term.

12. By way of an anecdote that I think clearly illustrates this phenomenon, I had a colleague in grad school who would occasionally appear in an office shared by a preponderance of "continental" graduate students, quote a randomly selected passage from Hegel's *Phenomenology of Spirit*, and thereby prove the absurdity

and worthlessness of continental thought (which could never be properly called "philosophy").

13. My use of pathological here is important, since I mean to criticize the reification of universalization and abstraction, but not the universal or the abstract as such. All theorization involves some abstraction and universalization, and I do not wish to be read as suggesting otherwise.

14. It is not at all uncommon, for example, to hear academic philosophers complain about the way students seem to prefer courses in applied philosophy to so-called real philosophy. As if there is a clear distinction, and the applied is at best a country cousin to proper philosophy.

15. As an example of this, see both the "Introduction" by Jane Anna Gordon and Neil Roberts (2009), and the essay "Of Legitimation and the General Will: Creolizing Rousseau through Frantz Fanon" by Jane Anna Gordon (2009).

16. Again, this approach is very much in keeping with de Beauvoir's articulation of an existentialist ethics, wherein she argues that the traditional ethical approach calling for a closed system of universally applicable rules and prescriptions is ultimately a manifestation of childishness (1948, 47).

Works Cited

Ahmed, Sara. 2006. *Queer Phenomenology: Orientations, Objects, Others.* Durham, N.C.: Duke University Press.

Alcoff, Linda Martín. 2006. *Visible Identities: Race, Gender, and the Self.* New York: Oxford University Press.

Allen, Theodore W. 1994. *Racial Oppression and Social Control.* Vol. 1 of *The Invention of the White Race.* New York: Verso.

————. 1997. *The Origin of Racial Oppression in Anglo-America.* Vol. 2 of *The Invention of the White Race.* New York: Verso.

Alleyne, Mervyn C. 2002. *The Construction and Representation of Race and Ethnicity in the Caribbean and the World.* Kingston: University of the West Indies Press.

American Anthropological Association (AAA). 1998. "AAA Statement on 'Race.'" *Anthropology Newsletter* 39 (9): 3.

Andreasen, Robin O. 2000. "Race: Biological Reality or Social Construct?" *Philosophy of Science* 67 (proceedings): S653–S666.

————. 2004. "The Cladistic Race Concept: A Defense." *Biology and Philosophy* 19:425–42.

Anzaldúa, Gloria. 2007. *Borderlands/La Frontera: The New Mestiza.* San Francisco: Aunt Lute Books.

Appiah, Kwame Anthony. 1992. *In My Father's House: Africa in the Philosophy of Culture.* New York: Oxford University Press.

————. 2007. "Does Truth Matter to Identity?" In *Race or Ethnicity: On Black and Latino Identity,* edited by Jorge J. E. Gracia, 19–44. Ithaca, N.Y.: Cornell University Press.

Aristotle. 1987. *A New Aristotle Reader.* Edited by J. L. Ackrill. Princeton, N.J.: Princeton University Press.

Barton, G. T. 1979. *The Prehistory of Barbados.* Halifax, Nova Scotia: Layne Co.

Beauvoir, Simone de. 1948. *The Ethics of Ambiguity.* Translated by Bernard Frechtman. New York: Citadel.

———. 1952. *The Second Sex.* Translated by H. M. Parshley. New York: Knopf.

Beckles, Hilary McDonald. 1989. *White Servitude and Black Slavery in Barbados, 1627–1715.* Knoxville: University of Tennessee Press.

———. 1990. *A History of Barbados: From Amerindian Settlement to Nation-State.* Cambridge: Cambridge University Press.

———. 2000. "A 'Riotous and Unruly Lot': Irish Indentured Servants and Freemen in the English West Indies, 1644–1713." In *Caribbean Slavery in the Atlantic World: A Student Reader,* edited by Verene Shepherd and Hilary Beckles, 226–38. Kingston, Jamaica: Ian Randle Publishers.

Bloom, Alan. 1987. *The Closing of the American Mind.* New York: Simon and Schuster.

Butler, Judith. 1990. *Gender Trouble.* New York: Routledge.

———. 2004. *Undoing Gender.* New York: Routledge.

Canny, Nicholas. 1987. "Identity Formation in Ireland: The Emergence of the Anglo-Irish." In *Colonial Identity in the Atlantic World: 1500–1800,* edited by Nicholas Canny and Anthony Pagden, 159–212. Princeton, N.J.: Princeton University Press.

Carter, J. Kameron. 2008. *Race: A Theological Account.* New York: Oxford University Press.

Caws, Peter. 1988. *Structuralism: The Art of the Intelligible.* Atlantic Highlands, N.J.: Humanities Press International.

———. 1992. "Sartrean Structuralism?" In *The Cambridge Companion to Sartre,* edited by Christina Howells, 293–317. New York: Cambridge University Press.

Code, Lorraine. 1991. *What Can She Know: Feminist Theory and the Construction of Knowledge.* Ithaca, N.Y.: Cornell University Press.

Cohen, Shaye J. D. 1999. *The Beginnings of Jewishness: Boundaries, Varieties, Uncertainties.* Berkeley and Los Angeles: University of California Press.

Du Bois, W. E. B. 1994. *The Souls of Black Folk.* New York: Gramercy Books.

———. 2007. *Black Reconstruction in America.* New York: Oxford University Press.

Dussel, Enrique. 1995. "Eurocentrism and Modernity." In *The Postmodernism Debate in Latin America,* edited by John Beverley, Michael Aronna, and José Oviedo, 65–76. Durham, N.C.: Duke University Press.

Dyer, Richard. 1997. *White.* New York: Routledge.

Ellison, Ralph. 1994. *Invisible Man.* New York: The Modern Library.

Eze, Emmanuel Chukwudi. 1997. "The Color of Reason: The Idea of 'Race' in Kant's Anthropology." In *Postcolonial African Philosophy: A Critical*

Reader, edited by Emmanuel Chukwudi Eze, 103–40. Cambridge, Mass.: Blackwell.

Fanon, Frantz. 1963. *The Wretched of the Earth*. Translated by Constance Farrington. New York: Grove.

———. 2008. *Black Skin, White Masks*. Translated by Richard Philcox. New York: Grove.

Fricker, Miranda. 2000. "Feminism in Epistemology: Pluralism without Postmodernism." In *The Cambridge Companion to Feminism in Philosophy*, edited by Miranda Fricker and Jennifer Hornsby, 146–165. New York: Cambridge University Press.

Fryer, David Ross. 2003. "Toward a Phenomenology of Gender: On Butler, Positivism, and the Question of Experience." *Listening: Journal of Religion and Culture* 38 (2): 136–62.

———. 2006. "On the Possibilities of Posthumanism, or How to Think Queerly in an Antiblack World." In *Not Only the Master's Tools: African-American Studies in Theory and Practice,* edited by Lewis R. Gordon and Jane Anna Gordon, 227–42. Boulder, Colo.: Paradigm.

Garcia, Jorge L. A. 1997. "Current Conceptions of Racism: A Critical Examination of Some Recent Social Philosophy." *Journal of Social Philosophy* 28 (2): 5–42.

Goodin, Patrick. 2002. "Du Bois and Appiah: the Politics of Race and Racial Identity." In *The Quest for Community and Identity: Critical Essays in Africana Social Philosophy*, edited by Robert E. Birt, 73–83. Lanham, Md.: Rowman & Littlefield.

Gordon, Jane Anna. 2009. "Of Legitimation and the General Will: Creolizing Rousseau Through Frantz Fanon." *The CLR James Journal* 15 (1): 17–53.

Gordon, Jane Anna, and Neil Roberts. 2009. "Introduction." *The CLR James Journal* 15 (1): 3–16.

Gordon, Lewis R. 1993. *Bad Faith and Antiblack Racism*. Atlantic Highlands, N.J.: Humanities Press International.

———. 1997. *Her Majesty's Other Children: Sketches of Racism from a Neocolonial Age*. Lanham, Md.: Rowman & Littlefield.

———. 2004. "Critical Reflections on Three Popular Tropes in the Study of Whiteness." In *What White Looks Like: African-American Philosophers on the Whiteness Question*, edited by George Yancy, 173–93. New York: Routledge.

———. 2006a. "African-American Philosophy, Race, and the Geography of Reason." In *Not Only the Master's Tools: African-American Studies in Theory and Practice*, edited by Lewis R. Gordon and Jane Anna Gordon, 3–50. Boulder, Colo.: Paradigm.

———. 2006b. *Disciplinary Decadence: Living Thought in Trying Times*. Boulder, Colo.: Paradigm.

———. 2008. *An Introduction to Africana Philosophy*. Cambridge: Cambridge University Press.

Gracia, Jorge J. E. 2005. *Surviving Race, Ethnicity, and Nationality: A Challenge for the Twenty-first Century*. Lanham, Md.: Rowman & Littlefield.

Gragg, Larry. 2003. *Englishmen Transplanted: The English Colonization of Barbados, 1627–1660*. New York: Oxford University Press.

Greene, Jack P. 1987. "Changing Identity in the British Caribbean: Barbados as a Case Study." In *Colonial Identity in the Atlantic World: 1500–1800*, edited by Nicholas Canny and Anthony Pagden, 213–66. Princeton, N.J.: Princeton University Press.

Greer, Margaret R., Walter D. Mignolo, and Maureen Quilligan. 2007. *Rereading the Black Legend: The Discourses of Religious and Racial Difference in the Renaissance Empires*. Chicago: University of Chicago Press.

Grimshaw, Jean. 1988. "Autonomy and Identity in Feminist Thinking." In *Feminist Perspectives in Philosophy*, edited by Morwenna Griffiths and Margaret Whitford, 90–108. Indianapolis, Ind.: Indiana University Press.

Hahn, Songsuk Susan. 2008. *Contradiction in Motion: Hegel's Organic Concept of Life and Value*. Ithaca, N.Y.: Cornell University Press.

Harlow, Vincent T. 1969. *A History of Barbados: 1625–1685*. New York: Negro Universities Press.

Harris, Leonard. 1999. *Racism*. Amherst, N.Y.: Humanity Books.

Haslanger, Sally. 2008. "Changing the Ideology and Culture of Philosophy: Not by Reason (Alone)." *Hypatia* 23 (2): 210–23.

Headley, Clevis. 2004. "Delegitimizing the Normativity of 'Whiteness': A Critical Africana Philosophical Study of the Metaphoricity of 'Whiteness.'" In *What White Looks Like: African-American Philosophers on the Whiteness Question*, edited by George Yancy, 87–106. New York: Routledge.

Hegel, Georg Wilhelm Friedrich. 1956. *The Philosophy of History*. Translated by J. Sibree. New York: Dover.

———. 1969. *Science of Logic*. Translated by A. V. Miller. London: George Allen & Unwin Ltd.

———. 1971. *Philosophy of Mind*. Translated by A. V. Miller. Oxford: Clarendon.

———. 1991. *Elements of the Philosophy of Right*. Translated by H. B. Nisbet. New York: Cambridge University Press.

Husserl, Edmund. 1965. *Phenomenology and the Crisis of Philosophy*. Translated by Quentin Lauer. New York: Harper Torchbooks.

———. 1970. *The Crisis of European Sciences and Transcendental Phenomenology*. Evanston, Ill.: Northwestern University Press.

Ignatiev, Noel. 1995. *How the Irish Became White*. New York: Routledge.

Ignatiev, Noel, and John Garvey, eds. 1996. *Race Traitor*. New York: Routledge.

Jacobson, Matthew Frye. 1998. *Whiteness of a Different Color: European Immigrants and the Alchemy of Race*. Cambridge, Mass.: Harvard University Press.

Kee, Robert. 1972. *The Green Flag: A History of Irish Nationalism*. London: Weidenfeld and Nicolson.

Kitcher, Philip. 2007. "Does 'Race' Have a Future?" *Philosophy and Public Affairs* 35 (4): 293–317.

Lewis, Hanke. 1959. *Aristotle and the American Indians*. Chicago: H. Regnery.

Lewontin, Richard, Steven Rose, and Leon Kamin. 1984. *Not in Our Genes*. New York: Pantheon.

Ligon, Richard. 2000. *The True and Exact History of the Island of Barbadoes, 1657*. Edited by J. Edward Hutson. St. Michael, Barbados: The Barbados National Trust.

Lloyd, Genevieve. 1984. *The Man of Reason: 'Male' and 'Female' in Western Philosophy*. London: Methuen.

Locke, John. 1960. *Two Treatises of Government*. New York: Cambridge University Press.

Longino, Helen. 1987. "Can There Be a Feminist Science?" *Hypatia* 2 (3): 51–64.

————2001. *The Fate of Knowledge*. Princeton, N.J.: Princeton University Press.

Lugones, María. 2003. *Pilgrimages/Peregrinajes; Theorizing Coalition Against Multiple Oppressions*. Lanham, Md.: Rowman & Littlefield.

Machery, Edouard and Luc Faucher. 2005. "Social Construction and the Concept of Race." *Philosophy of Science* 72:1208–19.

Makalani, Minkah. 2003. "Rejecting Blackness and Claiming Whiteness." In *White Out: The Continuing Significance of Racism*, edited by Ashley "Woody" Doane and Eduardo Bonilla-Silva, 81–94. New York: Routledge.

Maldonado-Torres, Nelson. 2008. *Against War: Views from the Underside of Modernity*. Durham, N.C.: Duke University Press.

Marx, Anthony W. 1998. *Making Race and Nation: A Comparison of South Africa, The United States, and Brazil*. New York: Cambridge University Press.

Massara, Art. 2007. "Stain Removal: On Race and Ethics." *Philosophy and Social Criticism* 33 (4): 498–528.

Mayr, Ernst. 1982. *The Growth of Biological Thought*. Cambridge, Mass.: The Belknap Press of Harvard University Press.

McWhorter, Ladelle. 2009. *Racism and Sexual Oppression in Anglo-America*. Bloomington: Indiana University Press.

Mead, George H. 1934. *Mind, Self & Society: From the Standpoint of a Social Behaviorist*. Chicago: University of Chicago Press.

Mills, Charles. 1997. *The Racial Contract*. Ithaca, N.Y.: Cornell University Press.

————. 1998. *Blackness Visible*. Ithaca, N.Y.: Cornell University Press.

Monahan, Michael J. 2003. "The Person as Signatory: Contractarian Social Ontology at Work in Suburbia." *Listening* 37 (2): 116–35.

———. 2005a. "The Conservation of Authenticity: Political Commitment and Racial Reality." *Philosophia Africana* 8 (1): 37–50.

———. 2005b. "Private Property and Public Interest." *Philosophy in the Contemporary World* 12 (2): 17–21.

———. 2007. "The Practice of Self Overcoming: Nietzschean Reflections on the Martial Arts." *The Journal of the Philosophy of Sport* 34:39–51.

———. 2010. "The Education of Racial Perception." *Philosophy and Social Criticism* 36 (2): 209–29.

Moran, Dermot. 2000. "Husserl and the Crisis of the European Sciences." In *The Proper Ambition of Science*, edited by M. W. F. Stone and Jonathan Wolff, 122–50. New York: Routledge.

———. 2005. *Edmund Husserl: Founder of Phenomenology*. Malden, Mass.: Polity Press.

Moynihan, Daniel Patrick. 1965. "The Negro Family: The Case for National Action." Office of Policy Planning and Research, United States Department of Labor. Washington, D.C. http://tinyurl.com/moynihan1965.

Mulderink, Earl F. 1996. "Book Review of *How the Irish Became White*." *The Journal of American History* 83 (2): 614–15.

Natanson, Maurice. 1973. *Edmund Husserl: Philosopher of Infinite Tasks*. Evanston, Ill.: Northwestern University Press.

Nei, Masatoshi and Arun Roychoudhury. 1993. "Evolutionary Relationships of Human Populations on a Global Scale." *Molecular Biology and Evolution* 10 (5): 927–43.

Nietzsche, F. W. 1966a. *Beyond Good and Evil*. Translated by Walter Kaufmann. New York: Random House.

———. 1966b. *Thus Spoke Zarathustra*. Translated by Walter Kaufmann. New York: Viking Penguin.

———. 1967a. *The Will to Power*. Translated by Walter Kaufmann and R. J. Hollingdale. New York: Vintage Books.

———. 1967b. *On the Genealogy of Morals*. Translated by Walter Kaufmann and R. J. Hollingdale. New York: Random House.

———. 1968. *Twilight of the Idols*. Translated by R. J. Hollingdale. New York: Penguin Putnam.

———. 2001. *The Gay Science*. Translated by Josefine Nauckhoff. New York: Cambridge University Press.

Nirenberg, David. 2007. "Race and the Middle Ages: The Case of Spain and Its Jews." In *Rereading the Black Legend: The Discourses of Religious and Racial Difference in the Renaissance Empires*, edited by Margaret R. Greer,

Walter D. Mignolo, and Maureen Quilligan, 71–87. Chicago: University of Chicago Press.

O'Callaghan, Sean. 2000. *To Hell or Barbados: The Ethnic Cleansing of Ireland.* Dingle, Co. Kerry, Ireland: Brandon.

O'Flaherty, Brendan, and Jill S. Shapiro. 2007. "Apes, Essences, and Races: What Natural Scientists Believed About Human Variation, 1700–1900." In *Race, Liberalism, and Economics,* edited by David Colander, Robert E. Prasch, and Falguni A. Sheth, 21–55. Ann Arbor: The University of Michigan Press.

Outlaw, Lucius T. Jr. 2004. "Rehabilitate Racial *Whiteness?*" In *What White Looks Like: African-American Philosophers on the Whiteness Question,* edited by George Yancy, 159–71. New York: Routledge.

Pigliucci, Massimo, and Jonathan Kaplan. 2003. "On the Concept of Biological Race and Its Applicability to Humans." *Philosophy of Science* 70:1161–72.

Pippin, Robert B. 2008. *Hegel's Practical Philosophy: Rational Agency as Ethical Life.* New York: Cambridge University Press.

Rawls, John. 1971. *A Theory of Justice: Revised Edition.* Cambridge, Mass.: The Belknap Press of Harvard University Press.

Richerson, Peter J., and Robert Boyd. 2005. *Not by Genes Alone: How Culture Transformed Human Evolution.* Chicago: University of Chicago Press.

Roediger, David R. 1991. *The Wages of Whiteness: Race and the Making of the American Working Class.* New York: Verso.

———. 2002. *Colored White: Transcending the Racial Past.* Berkeley: University of California Press.

———. 2005. *Working Toward Whiteness: How America's Immigrants Became White.* New York: Basic Books.

Sandel, Michael J. 1998. *Liberalism and the Limits of Justice.* New York: Cambridge University Press.

Sartre, Jean Paul. 1956. *Being and Nothingness.* Translated by Hazel E. Barnes. New York: Gramercy Books.

———. 1992. *Notebooks for an Ethics.* Translated by David Pellauer. Chicago: University of Chicago Press.

Schacht, Richard. 1983. *Nietzsche.* New York: Routledge.

Shaw, Jenny. 2009. *Island Purgatory: Irish Catholics and the Reconfiguring of the English Caribbean, 1650–1700.* PhD diss. New York University.

Shelby, Tommie. 2005. *We Who Are Dark: The Philosophical Foundations of Black Solidarity.* Cambridge, Mass.: The Belknap Press of Harvard University Press.

Sheppard, Jill. 1977. *The "Redlegs" of Barbados: Their Origins and History.* Millwood, N.Y.: KTO Press.

Spickard, Paul. 2003. "Does Multiraciality Lighten? Me-Too Ethnicity and the Whiteness Trap." In *New Faces in a Changing America: Multiracial Identity in the 21st Century*, edited by Loretta I. Winters and Herman L. DeBose, 289–300. Thousand Oaks, Calif.: Sage.

Stokes, Mason. 2001. *The Color of Sex: Whiteness, Heterosexuality, and the Fictions of White Supremacy*. Durham, N.C.: Duke University Press.

Sullivan, Shannon. 2006. *Revealing Whiteness: The Unconscious Habits of Racial Privilege*. Bloomington: Indiana University Press.

Sullivan, Shannon, and Nancy Tuana, eds. 2007. *Race and Epistemologies of Ignorance*. Albany: SUNY Press.

Sundstrom, Ronald R. 2008. *The Browning of America and the Evasion of Social Justice*. Albany: SUNY Press.

Taylor, Paul. 2004. *Race: A Philosophical Introduction*. Malden, Mass.: Polity Press.

Templeton, Alan R. 1999. "Human Races: A Genetic and Evolutionary Perspective." *American Anthropologist* 100:632–650.

Tuana, Nancy. 1992. *Woman and the History of Philosophy*. New York: Paragon House.

Vasconcelos, José. 1948. *La Raza Cosmica: Misión de la Raza Iberoamericana, Argentina, y Brasil*. Mexico: Espasa-Calpe Mexicana.

Velazco y Trianosky, Gregory. 2003. "Beyond *Mestizaje*: The Future of Race in America." In *New Faces in a Changing America: Multiracial Identity in the 21st Century*, edited by Loretta I. Winters and Herman L. DeBose, 176–93. Thousand Oaks, Calif.: Sage.

Will, George F. 2008. "Making Race Irrelevant." *Pittsburg Tribune Review*. January 1.

Wittgenstein, Ludwig. 1958. *Philosophical Investigations*. Translated by G. E. M. Anscombe. Englewood Cliffs, N.J.: Prentice-Hall.

Yacovone, Donald. 1996. "Book Review of *How the Irish Became White*." *The New England Quarterly* 69 (4): 667.

Young, Iris Marion. 1990. *Justice and the Politics of Difference*. Princeton, N.J.: Princeton University Press.

Zack, Naomi. 1993. *Race and Mixed Race*. Philadelphia: Temple University Press.

———. 1997. "Race, Life, Death, Identity, Tragedy, and Good Faith." In *Existence in Black: An Anthology of Black Existential Philosophy*, edited by Lewis R. Gordon, 99–109. New York: Routledge.

———. 2001. "Philosophical Aspects of the 1998 AAA [American Anthropological Association] Statement on Race." *Anthropological Theory* 1 (4): 445–65.

Index